Chef Pol Martin's
FAVOURITE RECIPES

The Chef's
FAVOURITE
RECIPES

BRIMAR PUBLISHING INC.

Foreword

'Favourite Recipes' is a collection that has developed through out my years as a chef. They include the fundamentals, the techniques, and the finished results. This particular group was chosen because of their adaptation, variation, and versatility in every day cooking.

I'm sure you will find the process of creating these dishes simple and rewarding. Use the techniques and photographs as they are designed to aid you in your venture.

Remember that imagination is difficult to convey in a recipe outline, therefore I urge you to experiment with garnish ideas and overall presentation. Spontaneous creation usually results in success and adds to pleasurable cooking experiences. Do as I do;

Enjoy

Legal deposit: 4th quarter 1985
Bibliothèque nationale du Québec
National Library of Canada

ISBN: 2-920845-00-4

Contents

Chapter I : Batters *6*
Butters *12*
Stuffings *18*
Marinades *26*

Chapter II: Stocks *32*
Sauces *38*
Soups *54*

Chapter III: Hors d'Oeuvre and Small Entrées. *78*
Pasta *98*
Fondues and Eggs *104*

Chapter IV: Salad Dressings *118*
Salads *124*
Vegetables *140*
Rice *164*

Chapter V: Fish and Crustaceans *170*

Chapter VI: Fowl and Game *212*
Meat and Variety Meats *240*

Chapter VII: Desserts *320*

Index *350*

Chapter 1
Butter • Batter
Stuffing • Marinades

Batter for Vegetables

250 g	(8 oz) flour, sifted
2 ml	(1/2 tsp) salt
30 ml	(2 tbs) corn oil
2	eggs
425 ml	(1¾ cups) lukewarm water

Place flour in a mixing bowl and stir in salt.
Add oil and mix well with a wooden spoon.
Blend in eggs and water.

This batter must stand for 2 hours covered with wax paper before using.

Sweet Batter for Fruits

250 g	(8 oz) flour, sifted
	pinch of salt
30 ml	(2 tbs) sugar
500 ml	(2 cups) lukewarm water
2	eggs
2 ml	(1/2 tsp) baking powder

Sift flour and baking powder together in a mixing bowl.
Stir in salt and sugar. Pour water into the mixture and mix well.
Beat in eggs and blend thoroughly.

Beer Batter for Fish

250 g	(8 oz) flour, sifted
2 ml	(1/2 tsp) salt
30 ml	(2 tbs) corn oil
2	egg whites, lightly beaten
500 ml	(16 oz) beer
90 ml	(3 oz) lukewarm water

Place flour in a mixing bowl and stir in salt.
Add oil and mix well with a wooden spoon.
Pour in beer and water. Continue to beat until well blended.
Fold in egg whites just before using.

Dessert Crêpe Batter

Batter for Vegetables or Fruit Fritters

250 g	(8 oz) flour, sifted
2 ml	(1/2 tsp) salt
30 ml	(2 tbs) corn oil
500 ml	(2 cups) lukewarm water
2	egg whites, lightly beaten

Place flour in a mixing bowl and stir in salt.
Add oil and mix well with a wooden spoon.
Pour in water and continue to beat with a wooden spoon.
Fold in egg whites just before using.
The batter is now ready for deep-frying.

Basic Crêpe Batter

Yield: 20 crêpes

250 ml	(1 cup) all purpose flour
2 ml	(1/2 tsp) salt
4	large eggs
425 ml	(1¾ cup) liquid, half milk and half water
75 ml	(5 tbs) clarified butter, melted, lukewarm
5 ml	(1 tsp) fresh parsley, finely chopped

Combine flour and salt in a mixing bowl.
In a separate bowl, lightly beat eggs with a whisk and blend in liquid.
Blend flour to the liquid with a whisk. The batter should have the consistency of heavy cream.
Add clarified butter, in a thin stream, whisking constantly.
Strain the batter through a sieve and add parsley.

Technique: Basic Crêpe Batter

1 Combine flour and salt in a mixing bowl.

2 In a separate bowl, lightly beat eggs with a whisk.

3 Blend in liquid.

4 Blend flour to the liquid with a whisk.

5 Add clarified butter in a thin stream.

6 Strain the batter through a sieve.

Technique: How to Make Crêpes

Use a 20 cm (8 in) steel crêpe pan.

1 Melt 15 ml (1 tbs) butter in the pan over high heat.

2 Remove the pan from the heat. Wipe off excess butter with paper towel.

3 Barely cover the bottom of the pan with batter.

4 Return to the heat and cook over high heat.

The crêpes should be paper thin. Repeat steps 1-3 if the crepes begin to stick.

The crêpes will keep for 3 months if wrapped in wax paper and frozen.

Dessert Crêpe Batter

Yield: 20 crêpes

250 ml	(1 cup) all purpose flour, sifted
1 ml	(1/4 tsp) salt
30 ml	(2 tbs) sugar
4	large eggs
425 ml	(1¾ cup) liquid, half milk and half water
75 ml	(5 tbs) clarified butter, melted and lukewarm

Combine flour, salt, and sugar together in a mixing bowl.

Lightly beat eggs with a whisk in a separate bowl, then blend in liquid.

Add flour to the liquid; continue to blend well with a whisk.

The batter should have the consistency of heavy cream.

Add clarified butter, in a thin stream, whisking constantly.

Strain batter through a sieve.

Clarified Butter, see page 13.

Basic Batter for Deep Frying

This batter is ideal for:
small squares of zucchini
celery hearts
small whole carrots
water chestnuts
asparagus tips
shrimps, etc.

250 ml	(1 cup) all purpose flour
1 ml	(1/4 tsp) salt
30 ml	(2 tbs) vegetable oil
375 ml	(1½ cups), less (3 tbs), cold water
2	egg whites

Combine flour and salt in a mixing bowl.

Add vegetable oil and cold water. Blend well.

Refrigerate, uncovered, for 30 minutes.

Beat egg whites until very stiff.

Remove batter from the refrigerator and gently but thoroughly fold egg white into batter.

Basic Batter for Deep Frying

Clarified Butter

Clarified butter is used to prepare a "roux" and to sauté meat or vegetables. Clarified butter does not burn as quickly as butter which has not been clarified.

Place 250 g (1/2 lb) butter in a stainless steel bowl or in top portion of a double boiler. Set on top of a saucepan half filled with almost boiling water, over very gentle heat.
The butter should not be touched and allowed to melt. Once melted, remove the impurities by:
a) straining butter through a cheese cloth, or
b) cooling the butter. The whitish deposit will sink to the bottom and the clarified butter can easily be skimmed.

This butter will keep refrigerated for approximately 2 weeks.

Bercy Butter

This butter is used on cooked veal chops or fish. (broil until melted)

250 g	(1/2 lb) butter
45 ml	(3 tbs) chopped dry shallots
30-45 ml	(2-3 tbs) dry white wine
	salt and freshly ground pepper
15 ml	(1 tbs) finely chopped fresh parsley
	juice of 1/4 lemon

Place shallots, wine, and pepper in a small saucepan. Cook over high heat and reduce wine by 1/3 of its original volume. Empty contents of saucepan in a bowl. Mix in remaining ingredients.
To store butter, roll in aluminum foil.

This butter will keep frozen for 3 months.

Garlic Butter (p. 17) and Anchovy Butter (p. 14)

Salmon Butter

This butter is used for canapés and with grilled or broiled dover sole. In French cookery, the great chefs use this butter to enhance the flavor of fish sauces.

125 g	(1/4 lb) "scant" smoked or fresh uncooked salmon
250 g	(1/2 lb) unsalted butter, room temperature
5 ml	(1 tsp) chervil
	juice of 1/4 lemon
	small pinch of cayenne pepper
	salt
	freshly ground pepper

In a mortar, grind salmon to a fine paste. Strain through a fine sieve. If a mortar is unavailable, mince salmon at least twice with a meat grinder, then strain.
Blend all ingredients together thoroughly in a mixing bowl.
Correct seasoning, if necessary.
To store, roll in aluminum foil.

This butter will keep frozen for 3 months.

Shrimp Butter

This butter is used to enchance the flavor of smoked salmon, shrimp, and lobster.

125 g	(4 oz) cooked shrimp, shelled and deveined
227 g	(8 oz) butter
	salt and pepper
	juice of 1/4 lemon
15 ml	(1 tbs) finely chopped dry shallot
15 ml	(1 tbs) finely chopped fresh parsley

Purée shrimp in a mixing bowl. Blend in all remaining ingredients.
To store, roll in aluminum foil.

This butter will keep frozen for 3 months.

Chive Butter

125 g	(1/4 lb) butter or margarine, softened
20 ml	(1½ tbs) chives
	juice of 1/4 lemon
	salt and pepper to taste
	a few drops of Worcestershire sauce
15 ml	(1 tbs) fresh chopped parsley

Mix all ingredients together.
Place mixture in the middle of a sheet of foil.
Roll the foil over butter and twist ends shut.

This butter will keep frozen for 3 months.

Tarragon Butter

125 g	(1/4 lb) butter or margarine, softened
30 ml	(2 tbs) fresh tarragon, chopped OR 5 ml (1 tsp) powdered tarragon
	juice of 1/4 lemon
	salt and pepper to taste
15 ml	(1 tbs) fresh parsley

Mix all ingredients together. Place butter mixture in the middle of a sheet of foil. Roll foil over butter and twist ends shut.

This butter will keep frozen for 3 months.

Kneaded Butter (Manié Butter)

This butter is used to thicken sauces.

30 ml	(2 tbs) butter, room temperature
15 ml	(1 tbs) flour, all purpose

Blend butter and flour into a smooth paste.

Anchovy Butter

This butter is used for canapés and for broiled, grilled, or sautéed salmon steak.

71 g	(2½ oz) anchovy fillets
250 g	(1/2 lb) unsalted butter, room temperature
5 ml	(1 tsp) chervil
	juice of 1/4 lemon
	small pinch of cayenne pepper
	salt
	freshly ground pepper
	Tabasco sauce

In a mortar, grind anchovy fillets to a fine paste. Strain through a fine sieve. If a mortar is unavailable, mince fillets at least twice with a meat grinder, then strain.
Blend all ingredients together thoroughly in a mixing bowl.
Correct seasoning, if necessary.
To store, roll in aluminum foil.

This butter will keep frozen for 3 months.

Maître d'Hôtel Butter

250 g	(1/2 lb) butter, soft
30 ml	(2 tbs) freshly chopped parsley
5 ml	(1 tsp) chives, finely chopped
	juice of 1/2 lemon
	salt and pepper
	a few drops of Worcestershire sauce
	a few drops of Tabasco sauce

Mix all ingredients together in a mixing bowl.
Spoon mixture in the middle of a sheet of foil.
Roll the foil over butter and twist ends shut.

This butter will keep frozen for 3 months.

Technique: Anchovy Butter

1 In a mortar, grind anchovy fillets to a fine paste.

2 Strain through a fine sieve.

3 Add butter.

4 Blend well and correct seasoning.

Butter

Garlic Butter

This butter is used on steaks, for barbecues, scampi, garlic bread, and to prepare snails.

250 g	(1/2 lb) unsalted butter, room temperature
30 ml	(2 tbs) finely chopped fresh parsley
5 ml	(1 tsp) chervil
4-5	garlic cloves, crushed and finely chopped salt freshly ground pepper
15 ml	(1 tbs) finely chopped dry shallot juice of 1/4 lemon

Blend all ingredients together in a mixing bowl.
Correct seasoning, if necessary.
To store, roll in aluminum foil.

This butter will keep frozen for 3 months.

Bordelaise Butter

This butter is used for steaks and chops.

250 g	(1/2 lb) butter
45 ml	(3 tbs) chopped dry shallots
30-45 ml	(2-3 tbs) dry red wine salt and freshly ground pepper
15 ml	(1 tbs) finely chopped fresh parsley juice of 1/4 lemon

Place shallots, wine, and pepper in a small saucepan. Cook over high heat and reduce wine to 1/3 of its original volume.
Empty contents of saucepan in a bowl.
Mix in remaining ingredients.
To store, roll in aluminum foil.

This butter will keep frozen for 3 months.

Technique: Garlic Butter

1 Place butter, parsley and spices in a bowl.

3 Add lemon juice. Mix well.

2 Add garlic and shallots.

4 To store, roll in aluminum foil.

Stuffing

Meat Stuffing

125 ml	(1/2 cup) minced lean veal
125 ml	(1/2 cup) ground fresh pork fat
45 ml	(3 tbs) fresh chopped chive
45 ml	(3 tbs) fresh chopped parsley
2 ml	(1/2 tsp) ground mace
15 ml	(1 tbs) flour
15 ml	(1 tbs) cognac or brandy
1	onion, peeled and finely chopped
15 ml	(1 tbs) butter
1	egg, beaten
	salt and pepper
1 ml	(1/4 tsp) savory, ground

Melt butter in a small saucepan over high heat.

Once butter starts to foam, sauté onions until transparent.

Place onions in a bowl and mix in remaining ingredients. Season well.

This stuffing is ideal for chicken, duck, veal, and pork.

Stuffing for Small Fowl

125 ml	(1/2 cup) seedless raisins
750 ml	(3 cups) diced apples
60 ml	(4 tbs) chopped almonds
1 ml	(1/4 tsp) ground ginger
30 ml	(2 tbs) butter
1	large spanish onion, diced

Melt butter in a medium size saucepan. Add onions and sauté for 4 to 5 minutes. Mix in remaining ingredients and continue to cook for 3 to 4 minutes.

Potato Stuffing

	mashed potatoes*
	turkey giblets and neck
1	small onion
1	small carrot
1	small stalk of celery
2-3	onions, finely chopped
30 ml	(2 tbs) butter
	poultry seasoning to taste

Prepare required amount of mashed potatoes and set aside.

Place turkey giblets and neck in a saucepan. Cover with cold water. Bring water to a boil, skim, and discard water. Cover the meat with cold water again. Add whole onion, carrot, and celery stalk. Season with salt and pepper. Bring liquid to a boil.

Reduce heat to low and simmer until giblets are tender. Strain liquid and reserve for use in soups or sauces. Allow giblets to cool, then pare off skin or nerve. Mince giblets and meat from the neck through the fine blade of a meat grinder; set aside.

Melt butter in a small frying pan. Cook onions over low heat until transparent.

Mix onions, mashed potatoes, giblets, and poultry seasoning together. Season with salt and pepper. Stuff the poultry cavities with mixture, truss, and roast bird according to the directions of your favorite recipe.

* Allow 75 ml-125 ml (1/3 - 1/2 cup) of mashed potatoes per 500 g (1 lb).

Stuffing

Stuffing for Suckling Pig

This stuffing is sufficient for a 6.8 kg (15 lb) pig.

250 ml	*(1 cup) raisins*
125 ml	*(1/2 cup) chopped parsley*
125 ml	*(1/2 cup) chopped dry shallots, or onions*
5 ml	*(1 tsp) sage*
5	*apples, peeled, cored, and chopped coarsely*
2	*garlic cloves, chopped*
750 ml	*(3 cups) cooked rice*
45 ml	*(3 tbs) butter*
	salt and pepper

Melt butter in a large saucepan over high heat. Sauté shallots for 2 minutes. Transfer to a bowl. Place apples in saucepan. Sauté for 5 to 6 minutes.

Return shallots to saucepan; mix in remaining ingredients. Season with salt and pepper; cook for 5 minutes. This stuffing can be prepared ahead of time and kept, refrigerated, for 24 hours. Cover with buttered wax paper.

Stuffing for Duckling

250 g	*(1/2 lb) minced lean veal*
250 g	*(1/2 lb) ground duck flesh*
125 ml	*(1/2 cup) ground, fresh pork fat*
75 ml	*(5 tbs) unsweetened apple sauce*
45 ml	*(3 tbs) fresh chopped parsley*
45 ml	*(3 tbs) fresh chopped scallions*
2	*eggs, beaten*
45 ml	*(3 tbs) 35% cream*
15 ml	*(1 tbs) chervil*
	salt and pepper

Mix all ingredients together and season well.

Stuffing for Goose

500 ml	*(2 cups) coarsely chopped bread*
500 ml	*(2 cups) light chicken stock*
125 ml	*(1/2 cup) grated suet*
2 ml	*(1/2 tsp) saffron*
2 ml	*(1/2 tsp) ginger*
	salt and pepper
2	*onions, finely chopped*
30 ml	*(2 tbs) corn oil*

Soak bread in chicken stock for one-half hour.

Heat oil in a sauté pan. When hot, add chopped onions and sauté over medium heat until transparent.

Drain and discard chicken stock. Squeeze out excess stock from bread.

Mix all ingredients together in a bowl. Season to taste with salt and pepper.

Chicken Stock, see pages 33-34.

Stuffing 1

Yield: 500 ml (2 cups)
for a 1.4 to 1.8 kg (3 to 4 lb) chicken

This stuffing is suitable for poultry, beef, or veal.

45 ml	*(3 tbs) butter*
125 ml	*(1/2 cup) finely chopped celery*
125 ml	*(1/2 cup) finely chopped onions*
3	*apples, peeled, cored, and finely chopped*
2	*dried shallots, finely chopped (optional)*
30 ml	*(2 tbs) finely chopped fresh parsley*
5 ml	*(1 tsp) chervil*
	pinch of thyme
2 ml	*(1/2 tsp) sage*
2 ml	*(1/2 tsp) tarragon*
	salt
	freshly ground pepper
250 ml	*(1 cup) very coarse breadcrumbs*
1	*egg, lightly beaten*

In a heavy, medium size saucepan, melt 30 ml (2 tbs) butter over high heat until it begins to foam.

Reduce heat to medium and add all but the last two ingredients. Cook mixture,

Technique: Stuffing 1

uncovered, for 15 minutes . Stir occasionally. Correct seasoning if necessary. Remove saucepan from heat and add breadcrumbs. Mix well, then add remaining butter and beaten egg.

This stuffing will keep for 2 to 3 days if refrigerated and covered with buttered wax paper.

1 Add celery, onions, and shallots to melted butter.

2 Add apples.

3 Add spices. Cook for 15 minutes.

4 Add breadcrumbs.

5 Add beaten egg.

Stuffing 2

This stuffing is sufficient for a 1 kg (2 lb) dover sole, trout, doré or red snapper, etc.

45 ml	(3 tbs) butter
500 g	(1 lb) mushrooms, washed and finely chopped
1	onion, peeled and finely chopped
30 ml	(2 tbs) finely chopped fresh parsley
15 ml	(1 tbs) chervil
	pinch of thyme
	salt
	freshly ground pepper
1 ml	(1/4 tsp) fennel
50 ml	(1/4 cup) breadcrumbs
30 ml	(2 tbs) heavy cream
	or 1 beaten egg
2	drops Tabasco sauce

In a heavy, medium size saucepan, melt butter over high heat until it begins to foam.

Reduce heat to medium and add all ingredients except for the last three. Cook mixture, uncovered, for 15 minutes. Stir frequently.

Correct seasoning if necessary.

Remove saucepan from heat. Mix in breadcrumbs, cream, and Tabasco sauce.

This stuffing can be prepared ahead of time and will keep for 24 hours. Stuffing must be refrigerated and covered with buttered wax paper.

Stuffing 2

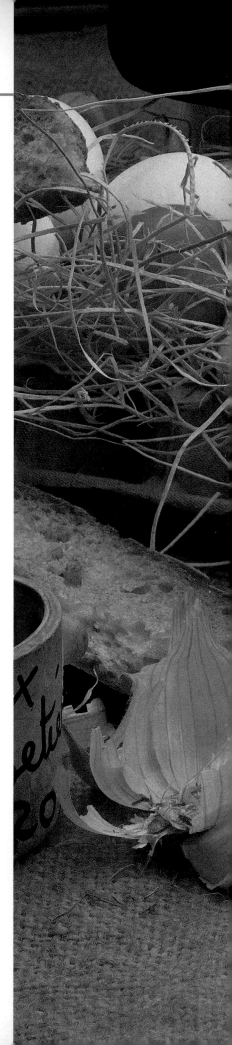

Technique: Stuffing for Capon

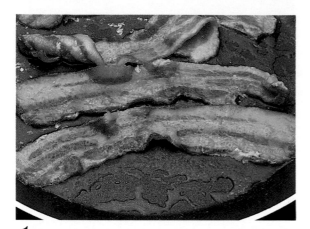

1 Cook bacon until crisp.

2 Chop bacon and set aside in a bowl.

3 Cook onions until transparent.

4 Mix onions and bacon.

5 Force eggs through a fine sieve.

6 Finished product.

Stuffing for Capon

5 or 6	slices of bacon
125 ml	(1/2 cup) finely chopped fresh parsley
3	hard boiled eggs, peeled
2 ml	(1/2 tsp) saffron
1 ml	(1/4 tsp) ground cloves
125 ml	(1/2 cup) raisins
125 ml	(1/2 cup) finely chopped onions
15 ml	(1 tbs) butter
	salt and pepper

Place bacon on a hot grill and cook until crisp. Turn over frequently during cooking process.

Chop bacon and set aside in a bowl.

Melt butter in a small sauté pan. Once butter starts to foam, add onions and cook until transparent.

Transfer onions to the bowl.

Mash eggs, then force through a fine sieve.

Add eggs and remaining ingredients to contents in the bowl. Season generously.

Chestnut and Sausage Stuffing

Yield: for a 4.5 to 6.8 kg (10 to 15 lb) turkey

750 g	(1½ lb) fresh chestnuts
250 ml	(1 cup) breadcrumbs
50 ml	(1/4 cup) milk
45 ml	(3 tbs) butter
2	onions, finely chopped
500 g	(1 lb) sausage meat
15 ml	(1 tbs) fresh chopped parsley
50 ml	(1/4 cup) cognac
	salt and pepper
2	eggs, beaten
1 ml	(1/4 tsp) thyme
1 ml	(1/4 tsp) basil

Slot chestnuts on the domed surface. Place chestnuts in a baking dish with a little water. Roast in the oven for 8 minutes. Peel chestnuts while hot and coarsely chop. Set aside.

Mix breadcrumbs with milk; let stand for 15 minutes.

Melt butter in a small sauté pan. Add onions and cook over medium heat until transparent.

Mix chestnuts, breadcrumbs, milk, onions, and remaining ingredients together.

Stuffing for Fish

This stuffing is excellent for dover sole and red snapper.

125 g	(1/4 lb) cooked halibut, puréed
125 g	(1/4 lb) cooked shrimp, puréed
5 or 6	anchovies, rinsed and puréed
2 ml	(1/2 tsp) pepper
	salt
1 ml	(1/4 tsp) ground nutmeg
1 ml	(1/4 tsp) chervil
125 ml	(1/2 cup) bread
250 ml	(1 cup) milk
30 ml	(2 tbs) butter
5 ml	(1 tsp) cream
2	eggs
3	dry shallots, finely chopped

Place bread and milk in a bowl; let stand for 30 minutes. Drain and discard milk. Squeeze out excess milk from bread.

Melt butter in a small saucepan. Sauté shallots until transparent. Transfer shallots to a bowl.

Separate eggs. Place yolks in the bowl; set egg whites aside.

Mix all remaining ingredients in the bowl; season generously.

Beat egg whites until very stiff, then gently fold into mixture.

Marinades

Beer Marinade

This marinade is for beef.

300 ml	(10 oz) beer
30 ml	(2 tbs) corn oil
1	onion, cut into quarters
1	carrot, cut into quarters
1	celery stalk, cut into quarters
1 ml	(1/4 tsp) basil
1 ml	(1/4 tsp) thyme
2 ml	(1/2 tsp) chervil
5 ml	(1 tsp) fresh parsley
1	garlic clove, crushed (optional)
	salt and pepper

Mix all ingredients together in a bowl. Pour the marinade over the chosen meat and cover with a sheet of wax paper. Press the paper flat on the surface of the meat. Place in the refrigerator for 12 hours. If possible, turn the meat occasionally.

Oil and Lemon Marinade

This marinade is ideal for meat or fish.

125 ml	(1/2 cup) corn oil
	juice of 1 lemon
2	dry shallots, finely chopped
1 ml	(1/4 tsp) thyme
1 ml	(1/4 tsp) basil

Mix all ingredients together in a bowl. Arrange the meat or fish in a bowl and cover with the marinade. Cover with a sheet of wax paper. Press the paper flat on the meat or fish.
Refrigerate and let stand for 12 hours. If possible, turn the meat or fish occasionally.

Marinade for Fish

125 ml	(1/2 cup) corn oil
	juice of 1/2 lemon
15 ml	(1 tbs) chopped fresh parsley
2	dry shallots, finely chopped
1 ml	(1/4 tsp) fennel
1 ml	(1/4 tsp) thyme

Mix all ingredients together in a bowl. Place the chosen fish in a stainless steel roasting pan. Season with salt and pepper.

Pour the marinade over the fish and cover with a sheet of wax paper. Refrigerate for 3 hours, turning the fish occasionally. In the case of rounded fish such as trout or mackerel, slash the flesh before marinating. This will allow the marinade to penetrate the flesh and speed up the cooking time.

Marinade for Game

2	large carrots, sliced
2	medium onions, sliced
2	shallots, sliced
2	garlic cloves, peeled and chopped
90 ml	(6 tbs) corn oil
50 ml	(1/4 cup) red wine vinegar or cider vinegar
1	bottle red or white dry wine
20	peppercorns
	salt and pepper
	water if necessary
	bouquet garni consisting of:
2 ml	(1/2 tsp) thyme
2 ml	(1/2 tsp) rosemary
3	bay leaves
20	sprigs of parsley

Place the game in a large casserole.
Add all dry ingredients, then, pour in liquids.
The game must be completely covered with the liquids. If not, add water.
Refrigerate and let stand for 12 hours.

Marinade 1

This marinade is ideal for beef, veal or chicken. Its purpose is to enhance the flavor of the meat and make it more tender; therefore, I suggest that you use economical cuts of meat.
You can cook the meat in this marinade, especially for such dishes as «boeuf bourguignon» or «coq au vin».
The marinade can also be used in the preparation of sauces and for basting barbecued brochettes of beef.

	beef, veal, or chicken*
	dry red or white wine

1 ml	(1/4 tsp) thyme
2	bay leaves
2	whole cloves
20	whole peppercorns
1 ml	(1/4 tsp) chervil (optional)
2	garlic cloves, crushed (optional)
	freshly ground pepper
1	carrot, peeled and thinly sliced
1	onion, peeled and thinly sliced
45 ml	(3 tbs) vegetable oil

Place the meat in a bowl and add wine to cover. Add the remaining ingredients. Cover with wax paper and refrigerate for a minimum of 12 hours.

This marinade will keep refrigerated for 48 hours.

* Average portions: beef or veal: 250 g (1/2 lb) per person. Chicken: 1/2 chicken per person

Marinade 2

This marinade is used when preparing lamb shish-kebabs.

1 kg	(2 lb) lamb from the loin or shoulder*, cut into 2.5 cm (1 in) cubes
250 ml	(1 cup) vegetable or olive oil
	juice of 1½ lemons
125 ml	(1/2 cup) dry white wine
1	garlic clove, crushed
16	whole peppercorns
1 ml	(1/4 tsp) thyme
2	bay leaves
5 ml	(1 tsp) chervil
1 ml	(1/4 tsp) paprika
5 ml	(1 tsp) tarragon
1	carrot, peeled and thinly sliced
1	onion, peeled and thinly sliced
	salt

Combine all ingredients. Cover with wax paper and refrigerate for a minimum of 12 hours.

This marinade will keep refrigerated for 48 hours.

* Average portion: 250 g (1/2 lb) per person.

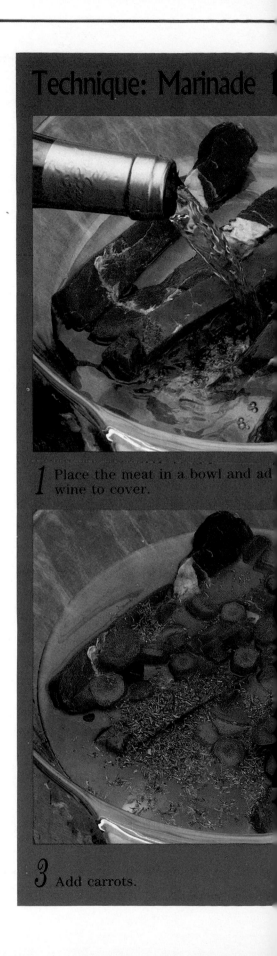

Technique: Marinade 1

1 Place the meat in a bowl and add wine to cover.

3 Add carrots.

2 Add garlic and spices.

4 Add vegetable oil and remaining ingredients.

Marinade 3

This marinade is used for Barbecue chicken. When you barbecue, you should baste the chicken with the marinade.

1 kg	(2 lb) chicken, cut in two*
	paprika
2	garlic cloves, crushed and finely chopped
	juice of 1 lemon
125 ml	(1/2 cup) vegetable oil
1 ml	(1/4 tsp) thyme
2	bay leaves
5 ml	(1 tsp) tarragon
	salt
	freshly ground pepper

Place chicken in a stainless steel tray or platter. Season with salt and pepper. Sprinkle the chicken with paprika and cover with remaining ingredients.
Cover with wax paper, refrigerate, and marinate for a minimum of two hours.

This marinade will keep refrigerated for 12 hours.
* Average portion: 1/2 chicken per person.

Marinade for Small Cuts

This marinade is used for small cuts of fowl, wild game, and meat.

2	large carrots, thinly sliced
2	medium onions, thinly sliced
250 ml	(1 cup) corn oil
375 ml	(1½ cups) wine vinegar
3	garlic cloves*
	salt and pepper
	water if necessary
	bouquet garni, consisting of:
2 ml	(1/2 tsp) thyme
2 ml	(1/2 tsp) rosemary
3	bay leaves
20	parsley stems

Arrange the small cuts in a shallow pan and cover with the vegetables. Season to taste.
Place the bouquet garni and garlic in the middle of the pan.
Pour the liquids over the meat. The marinade should cover the meat, if not, add water.
Cover with wax paper. Press paper flat to seal contents.
Refrigerate for 8 hours. If possible, turn the small cuts occasionally.
* For lamb, use 6 garlic cloves.

Technique: Marinade for Small Cuts

1 Arrange the small cuts in a shallow pan.

2 Cover with the vegetables.

3 Add spices.

4 Add olive oil.

5 Add wine vinegar.

Chapter II

Stocks • Sauces • Soups

Basic Fish Stock (Court Bouillon)

This sauce is mainly used to prepare fish sauces, chowders, and casseroles. It can also be used to poach fish and crustaceans.

15 ml	*(1 tbs) butter*
1 kg	*(2 lb) fish bones from white, lean fish*
2	*medium size carrots, thinly sliced*
1	*leek, thinly sliced*
2	*medium size onions, thinly sliced*
1	*celery stalk, thinly sliced*
20	*mushrooms, sliced (optional)*
2 ml	*(1/2 tsp) thyme*
2-3	*bay leaves*
18	*whole peppercorns*
2	*whole cloves*
5 ml	*(1 tsp) chervil*
	few sprigs fresh parsley
2 ml	*(1/2 tsp) tarragon*
1 ml	*(1/4 tsp) fennel seeds*
375 ml	*(1½ cups) dry white wine OR juice of 1 lemon OR 45 ml (3 tbs) white vinegar*
2.5 l	*(2½ quarts) cold water salt freshly ground pepper*

In a large saucepan, melt butter over high heat until it begins to foam. Reduce heat to low and add fish bones, vegetables, and spices. Cover and cook for 15 to 18 minutes.

Add white wine (or substitute) and water. Season with salt and pepper. Bring liquid to a boil, then simmer uncovered for 35 minutes.

Strain through cheesecloth or fine sieve.

This stock will keep refrigerated (uncovered) for 3 to 4 days. It will keep frozen for 3 months.

Celery and Chestnut Velouté Soup (p. 68)

Basic Fish Stock with Vinegar (Court Bouillon)

60 ml	*(4 tbs) wine vinegar*
750 ml	*(3 cups) water*
2	*carrots, thinly sliced*
1	*onion, thinly sliced*
	bouquet garni, consisting of:
1 ml	*(1/4 tsp) fennel seeds*
2 ml	*(1/2 tsp) thyme*
2	*bay leaves*
2	*cloves*
2 ml	*(1/2 tsp) tarragon*
	fresh parsley
1	*celery stalk, cut in two*
10	*peppercorns*
	salt and pepper juice of 1/4 lemon

Place all dry and liquid ingredients in a stockpot over high heat. Bring to a boil, then simmer for approximately 15 minutes.

Strain through a cheesecloth or fine sieve. This stock will keep refrigerated for 3 to 4 days. It will keep frozen for 1 month.

NOTE: Although this stock is prepared without fish, it should only be used when cooking fish.

Basic Chicken Stock I

This stock can be used to prepare cream soups, white sauces, vegetable soups, etc.

1.8 kg	*(4 lb) capon, thoroughly washed*
2	*medium size carrots, coarsely diced*
2	*celery stalks, coarsely diced*
2	*large onions, coarsely diced*
	bouquet garni, consisting of:
2 ml	*(1/2 tsp) thyme*
2	*bay leaves*
5 ml	*(1 tsp) chervil*
2 ml	*(1/2 tsp) rosemary*
1	*whole clove*
	fresh parsley
	celery
	salt
	freshly ground pepper
2.5 - 3 l	*(2 1/2 - 3 quarts) water*

Place all ingredients in a stockpot. Bring to a boil over high heat. Skim, and season to taste.

Reduce heat to medium, and simmer uncovered for 2-1/2 hours. To test if capon is cooked, pierce thigh. If no trace of blood is apparent, the capon is done.

Remove capon and discard vegetables. Strain stock through cheesecloth or fine sieve. Cool the broth and remove fat.

This stock will keep refrigerated (uncovered) for 7 to 10 days. It will keep frozen for 3 months.

Basic Chicken Stock II

This stock is used for cream soups, white sauces, vegetable soups, etc.

1	*chicken bouillon cube*
1 l	*(4 cups) boiling water*
	salt
	freshly ground pepper
	bouquet garni, consisting of:
1 ml	*(1/4 tsp) thyme*
1	*bay leaf*
2 ml	*(1/2 tsp) chervil*
1 ml	*(1/4 tsp) rosemary*
1	*whole clove*
	fresh parsley
	celery

In a medium size saucepan, whisk chicken cube into boiling water until well blended. Season, if necessary.

Add bouquet garni and simmer uncovered for 30 to 40 minutes.

Strain broth through cheesecloth or fine sieve.

This stock will keep refrigerated (uncovered) for 7 to 10 days. It will keep frozen for 3 months.

Basic Brown Beef Stock

This stock can be used for brown sauces, French onion soup, braised beef, etc.

1	*beef bouillon cube*
1 l	*(4 cups) boiling water*
	salt
	freshly ground pepper

	bouquet garni, consisting of:
1 ml	*(1/4 tsp) thyme*
2 ml	*(1/2 tsp) chervil*
1	*bay leaf*
1 ml	*(1/4 tsp) basil*
1	*whole clove*
	fresh parsley
	celery

In a medium size saucepan, whisk the beef cube into boiling water until well blended. Season, if necessary.

Add bouquet garni and simmer uncovered for 30 to 40 minutes.

Remove bouquet garni from stock and strain liquid through a cheesecloth or fine sieve.

This stock will keep refrigerated (uncovered) for 7 to 10 days. It will keep frozen for 3 months.

Basic Vegetable Stock

This stock is used to prepare cream soups and vegetable soups.

15 ml	*(1 tbs) butter*
2	*medium size onions, thinly sliced*
2	*medium size carrots, thinly sliced*
2	*celery stalks, thinly sliced*
1	*leek, thinly sliced*
2.5 l	*(2½ quarts) water*
	salt
	freshly ground pepper
	bouquet garni, consisting of:
2 ml	*(1/2 tsp) thyme*
2	*bay leaves*
2 ml	*(1/2 tsp) basil*
	fresh parsley
	celery

In a large saucepan, melt butter over high heat until it begins to foam. Add all vegetables, reduce heat to low, cover and cook for 10 minutes. Stir occasionally.

Add water and bouquet garni. Season to taste with salt and pepper. Bring to a boil over high heat. Reduce heat to medium and simmer uncovered for 35 to 40 minutes.

Strain through cheesecloth or fine sieve.

Stocks

This stock will keep refrigerated (uncovered) for 7 to 10 days. It will keep frozen for 3 months.

Turkey Stock

	leftover turkey, carcass, wings, skin
2	onions
2	carrots
1	leek
2	celery stalks
4	tomatoes
2 ml	(1/2 tsp) thyme
1	bay leaf
2 ml	(1/2 tsp) chervil
3 l	(3 quarts) cold water
	salt and pepper

Cut onions, leek, and celery into 5 cm (2 in) pieces. Cut tomatoes in four.
Place leftover turkey and vegetables into a large stockpot.
Add herbs, cover with cold water, and bring to a boil.
Season with salt and pepper. Simmer for 2 hours; skim occasionally.
Strain through a fine sieve.

This stock will keep refrigerated for 7 days. It also freezes well.

Stock Ménagère

250 g	(1/2 lb) beef chuck
250 g	(1/2 lb) veal shoulder
2-3	veal bones
1	onion, diced
2	carrots, diced
1	celery stalk, diced
45 ml	(3 tbs) corn oil
	salt and pepper
30 ml	(2 tbs) flour
	enough water to cover ingredients
	bouquet garni, consisting of:
2 ml	(1/2 tsp) thyme
5 ml	(1 tsp) chervil
2	bay leaves
2 ml	(1/2 tsp) rosemary
1	whole clove
	fresh parsley
1	celery stalk, cut in two

Set a roasting pan over two burners on the stove. Heat oil and when hot add meat. Sear on all sides for 2 minutes. Sprinkle meat with flour; continue to brown for 15 minutes. Season to taste with salt and pepper.
Transfer meat to a large stockpot; add bones.
Brown vegetables in the roasting pan, then transfer to stockpot.
Cover ingredients with water, add bouquet garni, and season with salt and pepper. Bring to a boil, then simmer for 2 hours.
Strain stock through a sieve.

This stock will keep frozen for 2 to 3 months.

Veal Stock

1 kg	(2 lb) veal (bones or shoulder*)
3	carrots, cut in two
2	onions, cut in two
1	leek, wash well and cut in two
	salt and pepper
	enough water to cover all ingredients
	bouquet garni, consisting of:
2 ml	(1/2 tsp) thyme
2	bay leaves
5 ml	(1 tsp) chervil
2 ml	(1/2 tsp) basil
1	whole clove
2	sprigs fresh parsley
1	celery stalk, cut in two

Place veal in a stockpot, cover with water. Bring to a boil over high heat. Drain and rinse meat under cold water.
Return veal to stockpot and add vegetables. Include bouquet garni and season with salt and pepper. Cover with water; bring to a boil.
Reduce heat and simmer for 1 hour 30 minutes.
Strain through a sieve.

This stock will keep frozen for 2 months.
* Chicken necks or backs could be added or replace part of the required amount of veal.

Sauces

Roux

A roux is a mixture of butter or another fatty substance, and flour. It is used to thicken sauces and cream soups.

AMOUNT OF FLOUR	AMOUNT OF FAT*	AMOUNT OF LIQUID	YIELD**
15 ml (1 tbs)	*15 ml (1 tbs)*	*250 ml (1 cup)*	*150 ml (2/3 cup) thin sauce*
20 ml (1½ tbs)	*20 ml (1½ tbs)*	*250 ml (1 cup)*	*150 ml (2/3 cup) thick sauce*

Once a roux has been cooked, it will keep, refrigerated and covered for 2 to 3 weeks.

* Butter, margarine, fat, roast meat drippings, etc.

** These proportions are based on a cooking time of 15 to 20 minutes.

White Roux

Melt the fat* in a small, heavy saucepan. Add an equal amount of flour and cook over low heat, for 4 minutes. Stir constantly with a wooden spoon.

The roux is cooked when it bubbles considerably.

* Butter, margarine, or roast chicken drippings.

Brown Roux

Preheat oven to 120°C (250°F).

Melt the fat* in a small, ovenproof casserole.

Mix in an equal amount of flour. Cook on top of the stove over low heat for 4 minutes. Stir constantly with a wooden spoon. Place casserole in the oven and cook, uncovered, stirring often.

The roux is cooked when it becomes a light brown color. Do not let the flour burn.

* Butter, margarine, or roast chicken drippings.

Devilled Sauce

Yield: 425 ml (1¾ cups)

Serve this sauce with pork chops, *barbecued steaks, shish-kebabs, and pork tenderloin.*

175 ml	*(6 oz) dry white wine*
45 ml	*(3 tbs) wine vinegar*
30 ml	*(2 tbs) dried shallot, finely chopped*
2 ml	*(1/2 tsp) freshly ground pepper*
500 ml	*(2 cups) basic brown sauce thin, hot*
	salt
	dash of cayenne pepper
15 ml	*(1 tbs) fresh parsley, finely chopped*
5 ml	*(1 tsp) fresh chives, finely chopped*
5 ml	*(1 tsp) english powdered mustard*
	the juice of 1/4 lemon

In a medium size saucepan, bring wine, vinegar, shallot, and pepper to a boil over high heat. Reduce by 2/3.

Add brown sauce and season with salt, pepper, and cayenne pepper.

Bring to a boil over high heat. Reduce heat to low, and simmer for 30 minutes, uncovered. Stir occasionally.

Mix in parsley, chives, mustard, and lemon juice.

This sauce will keep for 2 to 3 days, if covered with buttered wax paper and refrigerated. Note that the wax paper must touch the surface of the sauce.

Basic Brown Sauce Thin, see page 42.

Basic White Sauce

Yield: 750 ml (3 cups). Made with chicken stock, medium thick.

This sauce is used with chicken, for casserole dishes, vol-au-vent, and to prepare other sauces.

60 ml	*(4 tbs) butter*
60 ml	*(4 tbs) flour*
875 ml	*(3½ cups) hot basic chicken stock*
125 ml	*(1/2 cup) light cream*
	salt
	freshly ground white pepper
	small pinch cayenne pepper
2	*egg yolks*
15 ml	*(1 tbs) light cream*

Melt butter in a saucepan over high heat until it begins to foam. Reduce heat to medium, add flour and cook "roux", uncovered, for 5 minutes. Stir constantly with a wooden spoon.

Remove from heat and add 250 ml (1 cup) chicken stock. Stir with a wooden spoon until well blended.

Return saucepan to stove over low heat. Add remaining chicken stock 250 ml (1 cup) at a time, stirring constantly.

Add 125 ml (1/2 cup) cream; season with salt, pepper, and cayenne pepper.

Technique: Basic White Sauce

1 Melt butter in a saucepan. Add flour, mix and cook, uncovered, for 5 minutes.

2 Incorporate chicken stock.

3 Incorporate cream.

4 Before serving, combine egg yolks with remaining cream. Blend mixture into the sauce.

Bring to a boil over high heat. Reduce heat to low, then simmer, uncovered, for 30 minutes. Stir occasionally. Remove from the stove.

Before serving, combine egg yolks with remaining cream. Blend mixture into the sauce with a whisk and serve immediately. This sauce, without egg yolk and cream mixture, will keep for 2 days, if covered with buttered wax paper and refrigerated. Be sure that the paper touches the surface of the sauce.

Basic Chicken Stock, see pages 33-34.

White Sauce (Béchamel Sauce) Thick

Yield: 875 ml (3½ cups). Made with milk.

This sauce is used in casserole dishes, fish dishes, pasta, and macaroni and cheese.

90 ml	*(6 tbs) butter*
90 ml	*(6 tbs) flour*
1.1 l	*(4½ cups) hot milk*
1	*onion, studded with a whole clove*
	salt
	freshly ground white pepper
	dash of nutmeg

Follow the procedure outlined in Basic White Sauce Thin.

Basic White Sauce Thin, see page 41.

Dill and Caper Sauce

Serves 4

30 ml	*(2 tbs) butter*
30 ml	*(2 tbs) flour*
300 ml	*(1¼ cups) hot chicken stock*
1	*egg yolk*
30 ml	*(2 tbs) 35% cream*
45 ml	*(3 tbs) capers*
30 ml	*(2 tbs) dills, chopped*
1 ml	*(1/4 tsp) lemon pepper*
4 ml	*(1/4 tbs) lemon juice*
	pinch of cayenne
	salt and pepper

Pour chicken stock into a small saucepan and bring to a boil. Reduce heat and let stand.

Melt butter in a heavy saucepan. When it begins to foam, mix in flour with a wooden spoon. Cook the ''roux'' for 2 minutes over low heat.

Gradually whisk in the chicken stock. Season with salt, pepper, lemon pepper, cayenne, and lemon juice.

Remove from the stove and mix in capers, dills, and cream. Return to the stove and simmer for 5 minutes.

Remove from the stove and stir in egg yolk. Serve.

NOTE: If you intend on using the sauce only the next day, let it cool before refrigerating. Next day, reheat the sauce without boiling.

Chicken Stock, see pages 33-34.

Sauce Ravigote

Yield: 125 ml (1/2 cup)

45 ml	*(3 tbs) capers*
15 ml	*(1 tbs) chopped parsley*
15 ml	*(1 tbs) tarragon*
5 ml	*(1 tsp) Dijon mustard*
1	*small onion, finely chopped*
45 ml	*(3 tbs) wine vinegar*
105 ml	*(7 tbs) olive oil*
	salt and pepper
	few drops of lemon juice

Combine the salt, capers, parsley, tarragon, mustard, and pepper in a small bowl. Mix well.

Add vinegar mixing with a whisk. Mix in onion.

Gradually whisk in the oil, then stir in lemon juice. Serve.

Basic White Sauce (Béchamel Sauce) Thin

Yield: 875 ml (3 1/2 cups). Made with milk.

This sauce is used in casserole dishes, fish dishes, pasta, and macaroni and cheese.

60 ml	*(4 tbs) butter or margarine*
60 ml	*(4 tbs) flour*
1 l	*(4 cups) hot milk*
1	*onion, studded with a whole clove*
	salt
	freshly ground white pepper
	dash of nutmeg

In a heavy, medium size saucepan melt butter over high heat until it begins to foam. Reduce to medium, then add flour and cook "roux" uncovered, for 5 minutes. Stir constantly.

Remove saucepan from heat and add 250 ml (1 cup) milk. Stir with a wooden spoon until well blended.

Return saucepan to stove over low heat. Add remaining milk, 250 ml (1 cup) at a time, stirring constantly.

Drop in onion and season with salt, pepper, and nutmeg. Simmer over low heat, uncovered, for 30 minutes. Stir occasionally. Remove onion before serving.

This sauce will keep for 2 days if covered with buttered wax paper and refrigerated. Be sure that the paper touches the surface of the sauce.

Basic Thin Brown Sauce

Yield: 875 ml (3 1/2 cups)

65 ml	*(4½ tbs) butter, margarine, or beef drippings*
1	*small carrot, diced*
1/2	*celery stalk, diced*
1	*small onion, diced*
1	*bay leaf*
	pinch of thyme
1 ml	*(1/4 tsp) chervil*
65 ml	*(4 1/2 tbs) flour*
1.1 l	*(4 1/2 cups) beef stock, warm*
	salt and pepper

Technique: Basic Thin Brown Sauce

1 Melt fat in a casserole. Add vegetables and cook uncovered for 7 minutes.

2 Add spices. Continue to cook for 2 minutes.

3 Stir in flour. Cook in the oven until flour is golden brown. Remove from the oven. Let cool.

4 Add beef stock; mix throughly with a spoon. Continue to cook.
Pass sauce through a sieve.

Preheat oven to 120°C (250°F).
Melt chosen fat in a small ovenproof casserole, placed over high heat.
Add vegetables, reduce heat to medium and cook uncovered for 7 minutes. Stir frequently.
Drop in bay leaf and other spices. Continue to cook for 2 minutes.
Stir in flour and transfer casserole to oven. Cook until flour is golden brown. Remove from oven and let cool for several minutes. Add 250 ml (1 cup) beef stock; mix thoroughly with a spoon. Add remaining stock 250 ml (1 cup) at a time. Place over medium heat and stir constantly for several minutes.
Bring to a boil over high heat, then simmer uncovered for 30 minutes.
Strain sauce before using.

Madeira Sauce

Yield: 625 ml (2½ cups)

Ideal for kidneys, chicken, veal, etc.

15 ml	**(1 tbs) chopped dry shallot**
5 ml	**(1 tsp) butter**
500 ml	**(2 cups) medium brown sauce, hot**
50 ml	**(1/4 cup) Madeira wine**
15 ml	**(1 tbs) parsley**
	salt and pepper

Melt butter in a saucepan over very low heat. Add shallot and cook for 2 minutes. Add parsley and brown sauce; continue to simmer for about 8 minutes.
Season to taste, add wine, and cook for 6 minutes.
This sauce will keep refrigerated for 2 to 3 days.

Medium Brown Sauce, see page 43.

Basic Fish Sauce

Yield: 875 ml (3½ cups)

This sauce is served with white fish and used to prepare fish casseroles, coquilles St-Jacques, Lobster Thermidor, and Lobster Newburg.

65 ml	**(4½ tbs) butter**
15 ml	**(1 tbs) finely chopped dry shallot**

250 ml	**(1 cup) dry white wine**
60 ml	**(4 tbs) flour**
60 ml	**(4 tbs) hot basic fish stock**
	salt
	freshly ground white pepper
30 ml	**(2 tbs) heavy cream (optional)**

Melt 5 ml (1/2 tbs) butter in a heavy, medium size saucepan over high heat. When butter begins to foam, reduce heat to low. Add shallot and simmer, uncovered, for 2 minutes. Stir occasionally.
Add wine and bring to a boil over high heat. Reduce wine to one-third of its original volume.
At the same time, in a separate saucepan, melt remaining butter over high heat. When butter begins to foam, reduce heat to medium. Add flour and cook the "roux" uncovered, for 3 minutes. Stir constantly with a wooden spoon.
Remove the saucepan containing the "roux" from the stove and mix in 250 ml (1 cup) fish stock. Mix with a wooden spoon until well blended. Return to the stove over low heat. Add remaining fish stock, 250 ml (1 cup) at a time, stirring constantly. Transfer reduced wine to the sauce; season with salt and pepper. Bring to a boil over high heat, then reduce to low and simmer, uncovered, for 35 minutes. Stir occasionally.
Strain sauce.
Before serving, add 30 ml (2 tbs) heavy cream.
This sauce will keep for 2 days, if covered with buttered wax paper and refrigerated. Be sure that the paper touches the surface of the sauce.

Basic Fish Stock, see page 33.

Basic Medium-Thick Brown Sauce

Yield: 875 ml (3½ cups)

The basic ingredients are identical to those used in the Basic Thin Brown Sauce. However, the quantity of fat and flour should be increased to 90 ml (6 tbs)

To prepare, follow the procedure outlined in the Basic Thin Brown Sauce.

Basic Brown Sauce Thin, see page 42.

43

Brown Mushroom Sauce

Yield: 625 ml (2 1/2 cups)

This sauce can be served with veal, steaks, fillet, fondue bourguignon.

30 ml	*(2 tbs) butter*
250 g	*(1/2 lb) mushroom, washed and sliced*
2	*dried shallots, finely chopped salt freshly ground pepper*
250 ml	*(1 cup) dry white wine*
625 ml	*(2½ cups) basic brown sauce thin, hot*
2 ml	*(1/2 tsp) tomato paste*

	pinch of tarragon
	pinch of thyme
	pinch of chervil
45 ml	*(3 tbs) heavy cream (optional)*
15 ml	*(1 tbs) fresh parsley, finely chopped*

Melt butter in a heavy medium size saucepan, over high heat. Reduce heat when butter begins to foam. Set at medium high, add mushrooms, shallots, and sauté, uncovered for 5 minutes. Stir frequently. Season with salt and pepper. Add wine and bring to a boil. Reduce by 2/3.

Add brown sauce, tomato paste, and spices. Correct seasoning, if necessary.

Technique: Brown Mushroom Sauce

1 Melt butter in a saucepan. Add mushrooms and shallots; sauté, uncovered for 5 minutes.

2 Season with salt and pepper. Add white wine and bring to boil. Reduce by 2/3.

3 Add brown sauce.

4 Add tomato paste and spices. Continue to cook.

Bring to a boil over high heat, then reduce to low. Simmer, uncovered for 30 minutes. Stir occasionally.

Mix in cream just before serving and garnish with chopped parsley.

Basic Brown Sauce Thin, see page 42.

Sauce Charcutière

1	*small onion, diced*
30 ml	*(2 tbs) butter*
125 ml	*(4 ounces) dry white wine*
500 ml	*(2 cups) brown sauce, hot*
30 ml	*(2 tbs) Dijon mustard*
15 ml	*(1 tbs) parsley*
3	*gherkins, finely chopped*
	salt and pepper

Melt butter in a saucepan. Add onion, cover and cook over low heat for 3 to 4 minutes.

Remove cover, and add parsley and white wine. Continue to cook until wine has reduced by 2/3.

Add brown sauce; continue to cook for 15 minutes, uncovered. Season to taste.

Mix in mustard and gherkins. Serve.

Basic Brown Sauce, see page 42.

Sauce Parisienne

Yield: 750 ml (3 cups)

This is a white sauce.

30 ml	*(2 tbs) butter*
30 ml	*(2 tbs) chopped onion*
250 ml	*(1 cup) dry white wine*
625 ml	*(2½ cups) basic medium-thick white sauce*
45 ml	*(3 tbs) sour cream the juice of 1/4 lemon salt and pepper*
5 ml	*(1 tsp) chopped fresh parsley*

Melt butter in a saucepan over medium heat. When butter begins to foam, add onions and cook for 3 to 4 minutes. Do not brown the onions.

Add wine and reduce by 2/3.

Add white sauce and season to taste. Cook for 5 minutes over medium-low heat.

Remove saucepan from heat and stir in sour cream and lemon juice.

Sprinkle with the parsley before serving.

Basic Medium-Thick White Sauce, see page 41.

Technique: Sauce Charcutière

1 Melt butter in a saucepan. Add onions and cook. Add parsley and white wine. Continue to cook.

2 Add brown sauce. Continue to cook.

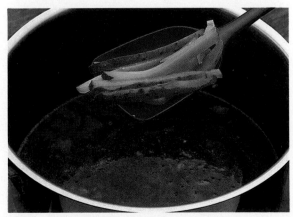

3 Mix in mustard and gherkins.

Technique: Bourguignon Sauce

Bourguignon Sauce

Yield: 625 ml (2½ cups)

Serve this sauce with fondue bourguignon, steak, pork and veal chops, sweetbreads, stuffed mushroom crêpes, etc.

5 ml	*(1 tsp) butter*
15 ml	*(1 tbs) finely chopped dry shallot*
	freshly ground pepper OR
5 ml	*(1 tsp) finely chopped fresh chives*
500 ml	*(2 cups) dry red wine*
1	*bay leaf*
500 ml	*(2 cups) hot basic brown sauce thick*
15 ml	*(1 tbs) finely chopped fresh parsley*

1 Melt butter in a saucepan. Add shallots; cook, uncovered, for 2 minutes.

2 Add spices.

3 Add red wine.

4 Reduce wine over high heat to one-third of its original volume.

5 Add brown sauce and bring to boil. Simmer over very low heat.

Melt butter in a heavy, medium size saucepan over high heat. When butter begins to foam, reduce heat to medium. Add shallot and cook, uncovered, for 2 minutes. Stir occasionally.

Add wine, pepper or chives, and bay leaf. Reduce wine over high heat, to one-third of its original volume.

Add brown sauce and bring to a boil. Simmer over very low heat, uncovered, for 20 minutes. Stir occasionally.

Remove bay leaf and serve with chopped parsley.

This sauce will keep for 2 to 3 days, if covered with buttered wax paper and refrigerated. Be sure that the paper touches the surface of the sauce.

Basic Brown Sauce, see page 42.

Mousseline Sauce

Serve with asparagus, broccoli, and use to glaze fish.

175 ml	**(3/4 cup) Hollandaise sauce**
60 ml	**(4 tbs) heavy cream, whipped very stiff**

Gently fold cream into the Hollandaise sauce.

Hollandaise Sauce, see page 50.

Portuguese Sauce

Yield: 375 ml (1½ cups)

This sauce is ideal with fish, cold vegetables, and also can be used for fondue dishes.

1	**red onion, finely chopped**
2	**scallions, finely chopped**
60 ml	**(4 tbs) olive oil**
5 ml	**(1 tsp) corn oil**
375 ml	**(1½ cups) canned tomatoes, drained and finely chopped**
1	**clove of garlic, smashed and chopped**
30 ml	**(2 tbs) wine vinegar juice of 1/2 lemon salt and pepper**
15 ml	**(1 tbs) chopped parsley**

Heat corn oil in a sauté pan over medium heat. When hot, sauté the onions, garlic

Technique: Portuguese Sauce

1 Sauté onions, garlic and scallions in hot oil for 4 minutes.

2 Add tomatoes. Continue to cook.

3 Add olive oil, lemon juice and vinegar.

and scallions for approximately 4 minutes. Cover.

Remove cover, and add tomatoes. Season to taste and continue to cook for 7 to 8 minutes.

Remove pan from heat, and add olive oil, lemon juice, and vinegar.

Stir and add parsley. Serve.

Horseradish with Walnut Sauce

Yield: 625 ml (2½ cups)

A good idea for trout, salmon, halibut, and turbot.

125 ml	*(1/2 cup) horseradish, grated*
125 ml	*(1/2 cup) walnut, chopped*
30 ml	*(2 tbs) breadcrumbs*
375 ml	*(1½ cups) sour cream*
15 ml	*(1 tbs) wine vinegar OR juice of 1/4 lemon*
	pinch of chopped parsley

Mix all ingredients together in a small bowl.

Spicy Tomato Sauce

Yield: 500 ml (2 cups)

An ideal sauce to use with pork, lamb, veal chops, or as a garnish with steaks.

15 ml	*(1 tbs) corn oil*
1	*small onion, finely chopped*
30 ml	*(2 tbs) chopped shallot (optional)*
796 ml	*(28 oz) can of tomatoes, drained and chopped*
1	*garlic clove, finely chopped*
2 ml	*(1/2 tsp) fresh parsley, finely chopped*
2 ml	*(1/2 tsp) chervil*
1 ml	*(1/4 tsp) oregano*
1	*bay leaf*
1	*small can of tomato paste*
	salt and pepper
	pinch of cayenne pepper

Heat oil in a sauté pan over high heat. When hot, add onion and cook until transparent.

Add shallot; cook for an additional 2 minutes.

Add remaining ingredients and cook over medium high heat. Cook the sauce until it thickens and liquid has evaporated. Stir occasionally.

Discard bay leaf. Correct seasoning.

Purée sauce through a food mill or pass through a sieve.

Herb Sauce for Fish

Serves 4

15 ml	*(1 tbs) finely chopped dry shallot*
	juice of 1/2 lemon
	salt and pepper
5 ml	*(1 tsp) finely chopped fresh parsley*
60 ml	*(4 tbs) butter or margarine*

Place shallot and lemon juice in a small saucepan over high heat. Reduce the liquid by 2/3.

Remove from the stove and add remaining ingredients. Season to taste, then cook over low heat until butter melts.

Pour sauce over fish steaks.

Béarnaise Sauce

Yield: 175 ml (3/4 cup)

This sauce is served with steaks, brochettes, salmon steak, scallops, fondue bourguignon, eggs, chops, etc.

2	*dried shallots, finely chopped*
10	*peppercorns, coarsely smashed*
45 ml	*(3 tbs) dry white wine*
5 ml	*(1 tsp) tarragon*
30 ml	*(2 tbs) wine vinegar*
2	*egg yolks*
15 ml	*(1 tbs) cold water*
175 ml	*(3/4 cup) clarified butter*
	salt
	freshly ground pepper
	dash of cayenne pepper
15 ml	*(1 tbs) fresh parsley, finely chopped*
	lemon juice to taste

In a stainless steel bowl, or in top part of double boiler, combine shallots, peppercorns, white wine, tarragon, and vinegar. Cook over medium heat directly on top of the stove until all liquid has evaporated. Remove from heat and let cool for a few minutes.

Blend in egg yolks and water with a whisk. Place on top of a saucepan half-filled with almost boiling water. Whisk constantly until thick.

When sauce has thickened, add butter in a fine stream. Whisk constantly. Season with salt, pepper and cayenne. Sprinkle with lemon juice and parsley. Cover with buttered wax paper.

Sauce will keep on top of double boiler over very low heat for 2 hours.

Clarified Butter, see page 13.

Technique: Béarnaise Sauce

1 In a stainless steel bowl, combine shallots, peppercorns, white wine, tarragon.

2 Cook until all liquid has evaporated. Let cool for a few minutes.

3 Blend in egg yolks and water with a whisk.

4 Incorporate butter in a fine stream.

5 Finished product.

French Dressing, or Vinaigrette

Serves 4

Serve with salads and cold vegetable hors-d'oeuvre.

1 ml	(1/4 tsp) salt
	freshly ground pepper to taste
5 ml	(1 tsp) Dijon mustard
15 ml	(1 tbs) dried shallot, finely chopped
5 ml	(1 tsp) fresh parsley, finely chopped
45 ml	(3 tbs) wine vinegar
105-135 ml	(7 to 9 tbs) olive oil
	juice of 1/4 lemon

Combine all ingredients, except oil and lemon juice, in a mixing bowl with a whisk.
Add oil in a steady thin stream, whisking constantly.
Add lemon juice; blend well and adjust seasoning.

This dressing will keep for 2 to 3 weeks, if refrigerated and covered.
Shake well before using.

Hollandaise Sauce

Yield: 175 ml (3/4 cup)

2	egg yolks
30 ml	(2 tbs) cold water
175 ml	(3/4 cup) melted clarified butter
	salt
	freshly ground white pepper
	juice of 1/4 lemon

Place egg yolks in a stainless steel bowl or in top part of a double boiler. Blend in the water with a whisk. Place on top of a saucepan half-filled with almost boiling water. Whisk until thick.
When mixture has thickened, add butter in a fine stream. Whisk constantly.
Season with salt and pepper. Blend in lemon juice.
Cover with buttered wax paper.

This sauce will keep on top of double boiler, over very low heat for a maximum of 2 hours.

Clarified Butter, see page 13

Lime Butter Sauce

Yield: 50 ml (1/4 cup)

125 g	(1/4 lb) butter or margarine
	juice of 2 limes
15 ml	(1 tbs) freshly chopped chives
	salt and pepper

Melt butter (margarine) in a double boiler. Skim.
Mix in lime juice, chives, and season to taste.
Pour over fish.

Cold Mustard Sauce

This sauce is ideal with cold pork and pork hocks.

15 ml	(1 tbs) Dijon mustard
30 ml	(2 tbs) Worcestershire sauce
15 ml	(1 tbs) ketchup
1 ml	(1 tsp) sugar
	freshly ground pepper

Mix all ingredients together in a small bowl. Serve.

Clear Vegetable Sauce

Serves 4

30 ml	(2 tbs) butter or margarine
1	small onion, thinly sliced
125 ml	(1/2 cup) reduced cooking liquid*
250 g	(1/2 lb) mushroom, thinly sliced
1	green pepper, seeded and thinly sliced
	salt and pepper
	lemon juice
1 ml	(1/4 tsp) chervil
	pinch of fennel
30 ml	(2 tbs) dry white wine or vermouth (optional)

Melt half of butter or margarine in a small saucepan over high heat. Add onion and cook over medium heat until transparent.

Add reduced cooking liquid, wine or vermouth, and lemon juice. Bring liquid to a gentle simmer. Reduce heat to low, simmer for 8 minutes.

Melt remaining butter or margarine in a sauté pan over high heat. Add green pepper and cook for 1 to 2 minutes, stirring frequently. Add mushroom and herbs; continue to cook for 2 to 3 minutes. Season with salt and pepper.

Transfer vegetables into the saucepan. Serve immediately.

* The cooking liquid can be chicken, fish, or vegetable stock depending on what you are serving.

Rémoulade Sauce

375 ml	*(1½ cups) mayonnaise*
30 ml	*(2 tbs) Dijon mustard*
30 ml	*(2 tbs) gherkins, chopped*
15 ml	*(1 tbs) capers chopped*
15 ml	*(1 tbs) parsley*
5 ml	*(1 tsp) chervil*
15 ml	*(1 tbs) tarragon*
	juice of 1/4 lemon
	salt and pepper

Mix all ingredients together in a small bowl. Serve.

Note that this sauce will keep, refrigerated for 2 days.

Technique: Rémoulade Sauce

1 Place mayonnaise in a mixing bowl.

2 Add Dijon mustard.

3 Add gherkins.

4 Add lemon juice and remaining ingredients.

Tartare Sauce

Yield: 625 ml (2½ cups)

Serve with cold or hot fish.

4	*hard boiled eggs*
	salt and pepper
250 ml	*(1 cup) olive oil*
30 ml	*(2 tbs) wine vinegar*
45 ml	*(3 tbs) prepared mayonnaise*
15 ml	*(1 tbs) chives*
15 ml	*(1 tbs) parsley*
	the juice of 1/4 lemon

Cut eggs in two and force through a sieve. Place in a stainless steel bowl and season with salt and pepper.

Mix in vinegar then gradually blend in oil. Add all remaining ingredients and mix well.
Serve.

Curry Sauce

Yield: approximately 500 ml (2 cups)

1	*large onion, coarsely chopped*
20 ml	*(1½ tbs) corn oil or clarified butter*
30 ml	*(2 tbs) curry powder*
60 ml	*(4 tbs) flour*
1	*garlic clove, smashed and chopped*
1 l	*(4 cups) very light chicken stock*

Technique: Curry Sauce

1 Heat oil in a sauté pan. Add onion and brown until golden. Add curry powder.

2 Stir in flour. Sauté until flour is very brown. Do not burn. Add garlic and continue to cook.

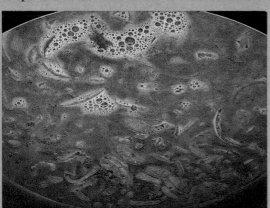

3 Gradually pour in chicken stock.

4 Add grated coconut. Stir well until blended.

*250 ml   (1 cup) grated coconut, fresh if
             available
             ground ginger to taste
             salt*

Heat oil in a sauté pan over high heat.
When oil is hot, add onion. Brown onion
until golden.

Stir in curry powder and flour. Sauté until flour is very brown. Do not burn. Add
garlic and continue to cook for 2 to 3
minutes.

Gradually pour in chicken stock. Add grated coconut and stir well with a wooden
spoon until blended. Add salt and ginger
to taste. Simmer for 20 minutes; stirring
frequently.

Strain sauce before serving.

Clarified Butter, see page 13.
Basic Chicken Stock, see pages 33-34.

Technique: Tartare Sauce

1 Cut eggs in two and force through a
sieve. Place in a bowl and season
with salt and pepper.

2 Mix in vinegar.

3 Gradually blend in oil.

4 Add mayonnaise and remaining
ingredients. Mix well.

5 Finished product.

Potage Breton

Serves 4

15 ml	(1 tbs) butter
2	small leeks OR 1 large leek
2	celery stalks
2	onions
250 g	(1/2 lb) mushrooms
15 ml	(1 tbs) finely chopped parsley
15 ml	(1 tbs) fresh chervil, finely chopped, OR 10 ml (2 tsp) dried chervil
1.5 l	(6 cups) hot chicken stock
	garlic croutons
	salt and pepper

Thinly slice all vegetables.

Melt butter in a medium size saucepan. Add leeks, celery, and onions. Season well, cover, and cook for 9 to 10 minutes over low heat.

Add mushrooms, spices, and cover. Cook for 3 to 4 minutes.

Pour in stock and correct seasoning. Simmer for 3 to 4 minutes.

Place croutons in the bottom on each soup bowl. Cover with soup. Serve.

Chicken Stock, see pages 33-34.

Mushroom and Barley Soup

Serves 6

75 ml	(5 tbs) butter
75 ml	(1/3 cup) chopped onions
2 l	(2 quarts) warm turkey stock
75 ml	(1/3 cup) chopped celery
250 g	(1/2 lb) fresh mushrooms, diced
125 ml	(1/2 cup) pearl barley
	salt and pepper to taste
45 ml	(3 tbs) flour
30 ml	(2 tbs) fresh chopped parsley
	chopped turkey giblets (optional)

Melt 30 ml (2 tbs) butter in a large saucepan. Add onions, celery, cover and cook over low heat for 2 to 3 minutes.

Add mushrooms, cover and cook for 6 to 7 minutes.

Add turkey stock and mix in barley. Season with salt and pepper. Bring to a simmer. Simmer gently, uncovered, for 40 to 45 minutes.

Melt remaining butter in another saucepan. Add flour and cook the "roux" over medium low heat for 3 to 4 minutes. Gradually stir the roux into the first saucepan. Increase heat to high and bring to a simmer.

Add giblets and gently simmer, uncovered, for about 10 minutes.

Sprinkle in chopped parsley to individual servings.

Turkey Stock, see page 36.

Fish Chowder

Serves 4

150 g	(1/3 lb) halibut
150 g	(1/3 lb) haddock fillets
150 g	(1/3 lb) scallops
30 ml	(2 tbs) butter
2	celery stalks, diced
1	carrot, peeled and diced
1	small leek, diced
1 l	(4 cups) warm fish stock
2	dry shallots, finely chopped
	salt and pepper
15 ml	(1 tbs) fresh chopped parsley
500 ml	(2 cups) warm water
250 ml	(1 cup) croutons

Melt butter in a medium size saucepan. Add diced vegetables and shallots. Cook, covered, for 4 to 5 minutes.

Stir in fish stock and bring to a simmer. Gently lower halibut and haddock into saucepan. Poach fish, while stock is barely simmering, for 5 minutes.

Gently lift fish from saucepan and transfer to a bowl.

Drop scallops into saucepan and poach gently for 2 minutes. Transfer scallops to bowl.

Fish Stock, see page 33.

Potato Soup

Soups

Flake fish with a fork and add a bit of cooking liquid to keep it warm.
Add water to saucepan. Simmer for 15 to 20 minutes.

Gently stir in fish and scallops to ingredients in saucepan. Season to taste. Garnish chowder with croutons and parsley. Serve at once.

Fish Chowder

Technique: Fish Chowder

1 Melt butter in a saucepan. Add vegetables and shallots. Cook, covered, for 4 to 5 minutes.

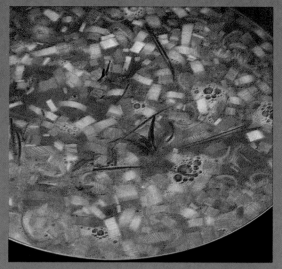

2 Stir in fish stock and bring to a simmer.

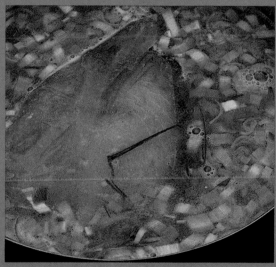

3 Gently lower halibut and haddock into the saucepan. Poach fish, while stock is barely simmering, for 5 minutes.

4 Gently lift fish from saucepan and transfer to a bowl.

Potage of Carrots

Serves 4

5	*medium size carrots, peeled*
3	*small potatoes, peeled*
30 ml	*(2 tbs) butter*
1	*onion, peeled and chopped*
1	*bay leaf*
	pinch of thyme
5 ml	*(1 tsp) herbes de provence*
1.5 l	*(6 cups) light chicken stock*
	salt and pepper

Slice carrots and potatoes.

Melt butter in a medium size saucepan over high heat. When butter becomes hot, add onions. Reduce heat to low and cook, covered, for 3 to 4 minutes.

Add remaining ingredients; season with salt and pepper.

Bring soup to a boil. Reduce heat to low and simmer for about 30 minutes.

Purée soup.

If you wish, add a bit of sour cream just before serving.

Decorate with fresh parsley sprigs.

Chicken Stock, see pages 33-34.

Cream of Turnip Soup

Serves 4

1 l	*(4 cups) sliced turnips*
2	*medium potatoes, sliced*
1	*onion, sliced*
20 ml	*(1½ tbs) butter*
1 ml	*(1/4 tsp) thyme, basil, and tarragon*
2 ml	*(1/2 tsp) chervil and chopped parsley*
1.5 l	*(6 cups) hot light chicken stock*
	salt and pepper
30-45 ml	*(2-3 tbs) 35% cream (optional)*

Melt butter in a medium size saucepan. Add onion and cook over low heat until transparent.

Add sliced vegetables, herbs, and chicken stock. Season with salt and pepper.

Bring to a boil over high heat. Reduce to medium and simmer until vegetables are tender.

Purée soup through the fine blade of a food mill.

Chicken Stock, see pages 33-34.

If mixture is too thick, add a bit of hot stock or water.

To serve, reheat soup then stir in cream.

Onion Soup au Gratin

Serves 4

3	*medium onions, peeled and thinly sliced*
30 ml	*(2 tbs) butter*
50 ml	*(1/4 cup) white wine OR 45 ml (3 tbs) cognac*
30 ml	*(2 tbs) flour*
1.5 l	*(6 cups) hot basic beef stock*
1	*bay leaf*
	salt
	freshly ground pepper
	drop of Tabasco sauce
375 ml	*(1½ cups) gruyère cheese, grated*
4	*slices toasted french bread*
4	*ovenproof earthware onion soup bowls*

In a heavy, medium size saucepan, melt butter over high heat. When butter begins to foam, reduce to low. Simmer onions, uncovered for 20 minutes. Stir occasionally. (Add a bit of butter during cooking process, if necessary.)

Increase heat to high and add wine. Reduce by 2/3.

Reduce heat to medium and sprinkle flour over onions.

Gradually mix in stock, add bay leaf, and season with salt and pepper.

Bring to a boil over high heat. Reduce to low and simmer, uncovered, for 30 minutes. Stir occasionally.

Add a drop of Tabasco sauce to soup and correct seasoning.

Remove bay leaf from soup.

Preheat oven to broil.

Place 15 ml (1 tbs) grated cheese in bottom of each soup bowl. Add soup. Cover with a slice of bread, and top with remaining cheese.

Broil soup in the middle of the oven for 15 to 20 minutes.

This soup will keep for 3 days covered with buttered wax paper and refrigerated. It will keep frozen for 3 months.

Beef Stock, see page 34.

Onion Soup au Gratin

Cream of Asparagus Soup

Serves 4

1	bunch fresh asparagus, cooked OR 1-14 oz can asparagus, drained OR 10 oz frozen asparagus, cooked, AND coarsely chopped*
45 ml	(3 tbs) asparagus tips, reserve for garnish
90 ml	(6 tbs) butter
1	small onion, thinly sliced
75 ml	(5 tbs) flour
1.5 l	(6 cups) hot basic chicken stock OR 1.5 l (6 cups) hot asparagus stock
	salt
	freshly ground pepper
	bouquet garni, consisting of:
1 ml	(1/4 tsp) thyme
1	bay leaf
2 ml	(1/2 tsp) chervil
1 ml	(1/4 tsp) basil
1	whole clove
	fresh parsley
	celery
30 ml	(2 tbs) heavy cream (optional)
15 ml	(1 tbs) fresh parsley, finely chopped OR 15 ml (1 tbs) fresh chives, finely chopped

In a heavy, medium size saucepan, melt 75 ml (5 tbs) butter over high heat. When butter begins to foam, reduce heat to low and add onion. Cover and simmer for several minutes.

Add asparagus, cover and simmer for 15 minutes. Stir occasionally.

Add flour and cook, uncovered, for 3 minutes. Stir constantly.

Remove saucepan from heat. Mix in 250 ml (1 cup) of stock thoroughly with a wooden spoon. Return to heat and add remaining stock 250 ml (1 cup) at a time, until desired consistency is reached. Stir constantly.

Season soup to taste and drop in bouquet garni. Bring to a boil, then reduce heat to low. Simmer, uncovered, for 40 minutes. Stir occasionally.

Correct seasoning and strain.

If soup is too thick, mix in a bit of stock with a wooden spoon.

In a small saucepan, simmer the reserved asparagus tips in 15 ml (1 tbs) butter for 3 minutes.

Before serving, mix in cream and garnish with asparagus tips, parsley, or chives.

This soup, without the cream, will keep for 2 to 3 days, refrigerated and covered with buttered wax paper. If you wish to serve the soup chilled, add 50 ml (1/4 cup) heavy cream, rather than 30 ml (2 tbs) cream.

Chicken Stock, see pages 33-34.

* Drop asparagus into a large saucepan filled with salted, boiling water. Cover and blanch for 8 to 10 minutes. Remove saucepan from heat, and cool asparagus under running water for at least 4 minutes. Drain.

Clam Chowder

Serves 4

36	fresh clams, removed from shells, coarsely chopped OR 2 - 10 oz cans of clams, drained and reserve liquid
15 ml	(1 tbs) butter
1	medium onion, peeled and diced
1	green pepper, seeded and diced
2	small raw potatoes, peeled and diced
625 ml	(2½ cups) hot basic fish stock
	pinch of thyme
1	bay leaf
5 ml	(1 tsp) fresh parsley, finely chopped
1ml	(1/4 tsp) chervil
	pinch of tarragon
	salt
	freshly ground pepper
	paprika to taste
500 ml	(2 cups) light cream

In a heavy, medium size saucepan, melt butter over high heat. When butter begins to foam, reduce to medium. Add onions and green pepper. Cover and simmer for 3 minutes, stirring occasionally.

Add potatoes, stock, reserved liquid from

clams, and the herbs. Season with salt and pepper.

Bring to a boil over high heat.

Reduce to medium, and simmer, uncovered, until potatoes are cooked. Add clams to the chowder and simmer for 3 to 4 minutes.

Correct seasoning; mix in cream, paprika, and serve.

Fish Stock, see page 33.

Technique: Clam Chowder

1 Melt butter in a saucepan.
Add onions and green pepper. Cover and simmer for 3 minutes, stirring occasionally.

2 Add potatoes.

3 Add chicken stock, reserved liquid from clams and herbs. Season with salt and pepper. Bring to boil.

4 Add clams to the chowder and simmer 3 to 4 minutes.

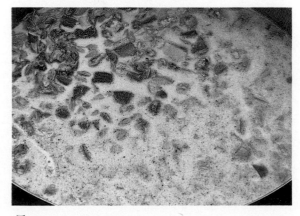

5 Mix in cream and paprika.

Soups

Minestrone Soup

Minestrone Soup

Serves 4

15 ml	(1 tbs) olive oil
1	chopped onion
2	stalks of celery, diced
2	carrots, diced
1	796 ml (28 oz) can of tomatoes, drained and chopped
1.2 l	(5 cups) light chicken stock, hot
1 ml	(1/4 tsp) oregano
1	bay leaf
2	potatoes, peeled and diced
250 ml	(1 cup) medium bow noodles
250 ml	(1 cup) chinese cabbage, thinly sliced
	pinch of thyme
	grated parmesan cheese
	salt and pepper

Heat oil in a large saucepan. Add onions, celery and carrots. Season with salt and pepper; cover and cook 4 minutes.
Add tomatoes, chicken stock and spices. Correct seasoning. Bring to boil and cook 10 to 12 minutes over low heat.
Add potatoes and noodles; continue cooking 10 to 12 minutes.
2 minutes before the end of cooking, add chinese cabbage.
Serve with grated parmesan cheese.

Chicken Stock, see page 33.

Chilled Avocado Soup

Serves 8

3	very ripe avocados*
30 ml	(2 tbs) butter
1	small onion, finely chopped
30 ml	(2 tbs) flour
15 ml	(1 tbs) curry powder
	juice of 1 garlic clove
1 l	(4 cups) light chicken stock
	salt and pepper to taste
250 ml	(1 cup) sour cream

Melt butter in a saucepan. Add onion, cover, and cook over medium heat until transparent. Add curry powder and flour. Cook mixture over medium heat for 3 minutes. Stir constantly.
Gradually stir in chicken stock. Season with garlic juice, salt, and pepper.

Bring liquid to a boil, then simmer for 15 to 20 minutes. Stir occasionally.
To serve, strain soup and chill well in the refrigerator.
Peel avocados, discard pits, and slice flesh. Purée flesh then whisk into soup. Whisk in sour cream.
If necessary, thin soup with a bit of chilled chicken stock. Season with salt and pepper. Serve in chilled bowls.

Chicken Stock, see pages 33-34.

* A ripe avocado yields to the touch. The skin is often spotted with rough textured brown areas.

Cream of Cucumber Soup

Serves 4

I recommend that this soup be served chilled.

3	cucumbers, peeled, seeded, and finely sliced
1/2	cucumber, finely chopped, reserve as garnish
90 ml	(6 tbs) butter
1	small onion, thinly sliced
75 ml	(5 tbs) flour
1.5 l	(6 cups) hot basic chicken stock
	salt
	freshly ground pepper
	bouquet garni, consisting of:
1 ml	(1/4 tsp) thyme
1	bay leaf
2 ml	(1/2 tsp) chervil
1 ml	(1/4 tsp) basil
1	whole clove
	fresh parsley
	celery
30 ml	(2 tbs) heavy cream (optional)
15 ml	(1 tbs) fresh parsley, finely chopped OR 15 ml (1 tbs) fresh chives, finely chopped

In a heavy, medium size saucepan, melt 75 ml (5 tbs) butter. When butter begins to foam, reduce heat to low and add onions. Cover and simmer for several minutes.
Add sliced cucumbers, cover and simmer for 15 minutes. Stir occasionally. Add flour to the saucepan. Cook, uncovered, for 3 minutes. Stir constantly.
Remove saucepan from heat. Add 250 ml

(1 cup) of stock and mix thoroughly with a wooden spoon. Return saucepan to heat. Add remaining stock, 250 ml (1 cup) at a time, until desired consistency is reached. Stir constantly.

Season soup to taste and drop in bouquet garni. Bring to a boil, then reduce to low. Simmer, uncovered for 40 minutes. Stir occasionally.

Correct seasoning and strain.

If soup is too thick, mix in a bit of hot chicken stock with a wooden spoon.

In a small saucepan, melt 15 ml (1 tbs) of butter over high heat. When butter begins to foam, reduce to medium and add reserved cucumbers. Simmer, uncovered for several minutes.

Before serving, mix in cream and garnish with chopped cucumbers and parsley. (chives)

If you wish to serve this soup chilled, add 50 ml (1/4 cup) heavy cream rather than 30 ml (2 tbs).

Chicken Stock, see pages 33-34.

Soupe Normande

Serves 4

4	carrots
3	potatoes
2	leeks, white section only
45 ml	(3 tbs) rice, cooked
2 l	(2 quarts) light hot chicken stock
	salt and pepper
5 ml	(1 tsp) parsley
2	bay leaves
1 ml	(1/4 tsp) thyme
1 ml	(1/4 tsp) basil
2	garlic cloves, unpeeled
30 ml	(2 tbs) butter
	grated gruyère cheese, to taste

Thinly slice all vegetables.

Melt butter in a large saucepan. Add carrots, leeks, and spices. Cover and cook over medium heat for about 20 minutes. Add potatoes and rice. Pour in all of the chicken stock. Cook for another 30 minutes.

Pass soup through a food mill and spoon into a soup terrine.

Sprinkle with grated cheese and serve.

Chicken Stock, see pages 33-34.

Country Beef Soup

Serves 4

1 kg	(2 lb) blade steak, fat trimmed several bones, if available cold water
2	leeks, cut into 2
4	carrots
2	celery stalks, cut into 2
1	small turnip, cut into 8
4	small potatoes, peeled and cut into 2
	bouquet garni, consisting of:
2 ml	(1/2 tsp) chervil
1 ml	(1/4 tsp) thyme
1 ml	(1/4 tsp) basil
1 ml	(1/4 tsp) rosemary
	fresh parsley
	salt and pepper

Place steak and bones in a large saucepan. Cover with cold water and bring to a boil. Reduce heat to low; simmer for 1 hour and 15 minutes. Skim liquid frequently until it becomes clear.

Tie 1/2 leek, 1 carrot, and 1/2 celery stalk together with kitchen string. Repeat until you have 4 bundles of vegetables.

Drop vegetables, along with turnip, potatoes, and bouquet garni in saucepan. Season with salt and pepper. Bring liquid to a simmer and cook until vegetables are done.

Place vegetables in large soup bowls along with a bit of cooking liquid to keep them warm. Discard string.

Continue to simmer beef until tender. Discard bones and bouquet garni.

Slice beef and place over vegetables in bowls.

Strain the broth and pour over the beef and vegetables.

Serve immediately.

Cream of Yellow Pepper

Serves 4

45 ml	(3 tbs) butter
1	onion, finely chopped
2	yellow peppers, thinly sliced
60 ml	(4 tbs) flour

Cream of Yellow Pepper

1.2 l	(5 cups) light chicken stock, hot
50 ml	(1/4 cup) 10% cream
	lemon juice
	chopped parsley
	salt and pepper

Heat butter in a saucepan over medium heat. Add onions and peppers; cover and cook 6 to 7 minutes over low heat.

Add flour; mix well.

Add chicken stock; mix with a whisk. Season to taste. Cook 8 to 10 minutes over low heat.

Incorporate cream; stir. Sprinkle with lemon juice.

Sprinkle with chopped parsley. Serve.

Chicken Stock, see pages 33-34.

Parmentier Cream Soup

Serves 4

30 ml	(2 tbs) butter
2	leeks, white section only, thinly sliced
1	large onion, sliced
750 g	(1½ lb) OR 4 potatoes, large, raw, peeled and thinly sliced
1.5 l	(6 cups) hot chicken stock, basic
	bouquet garni, consisting of:
1 ml	(1/4 tsp) thyme
1	bay leaf
1 ml	(1/4 tsp) basil
2 ml	(1/2 tsp) chervil
	fresh parsley
	celery
	salt
	freshly ground pepper
30 ml	(2 tbs) heavy cream

In a heavy, medium size saucepan, melt butter over high heat. When butter begins to foam, reduce heat to low. Add leeks and onion; cover and simmer for 15 minutes. Stir occasionally.

Add potatoes and enough chicken stock until desired consistency is reached. Drop in bouquet garni; season with salt and pepper.

Bring to a boil over high heat. Reduce to medium, simmer uncovered for 40 minutes. Stir occasionally.

Strain and correct seasoning.

If soup is too thick, mix in a bit of hot stock with a wooden spoon. Before serving, mix in cream. This soup, without cream, will keep for 2 to 3 days, refrigerated and covered with buttered wax paper.

Chicken Stock, see pages 33-34.

Technique:
Parmentier Cream Soup

1 Melt butter in a saucepan. Add leeks and onion; cover and simmer for 15 minutes. Stir occasionally.

2 Add potatoes and enough chicken stock until desired consistency is reached.

Cream of Mushroom Soup

Vichyssoise

Serves 4

1.2 l	(5 cups) parmentier cream soup
125-250 ml	(¹/₂-1 cup) heavy cream
15 ml	(1 tbs) fresh chives, finely chopped

Add cream to the parmentier cream soup and mix well.
Cover soup with buttered wax paper and refrigerate overnight.
Serve chilled, and garnish with chives.

Cream of Mushroom Soup

Serves 4

375 g	(3/4 lb) fresh mushrooms, finely sliced OR 1-14 oz can mushrooms, drained and chopped
60 ml	(4 tbs) mushrooms, finely chopped, reserve for garnish
75 ml	(5 tbs) butter
1	small onion, thinly sliced
75 ml	(5 tbs) flour
1.5 l	(6 cups) hot basic chicken stock
	salt
	freshly ground pepper
	bouquet garni, consisting of:
1 ml	(1/4 tsp) thyme
1	bay leaf
2 ml	(1/2 tsp) chervil
1 ml	(1/4 tsp) basil
1	whole clove
	fresh parsley
	celery
30 ml	(2 tbs) heavy cream (optional)
15 ml	(1 tbs) fresh parsley, finely chopped OR 15 ml (1 tbs) fresh chives, finely chopped

In a heavy medium size saucepan, melt butter over high heat. When butter begins to foam, reduce heat to low. Add onion and simmer, covered for several minutes.
Add mushrooms, cover and simmer for 15 minutes. Stir occasionally.
Add flour to saucepan. Cook, uncovered for 3 minutes. Stir constantly.

Technique: Cream of Mushroom Soup

1 Melt butter in a saucepan.
Add onion; cover and simmer several minutes.

2 Add mushrooms; cover and simmer for 15 minutes.

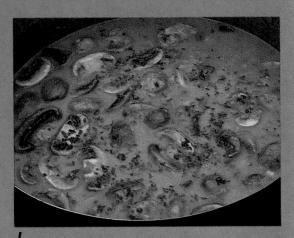

3 Add flour to saucepan. Cook for 3 minutes.

4 Add chicken stock and stir.

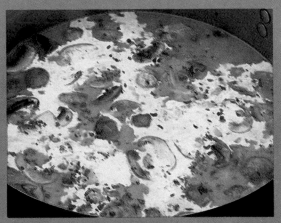

5 In a small saucepan, simmer the reserved mushrooms in 125 ml (1/2 cup) chicken stock.

6 Before serving, mix in cream and garnish with reserved mushrooms.

Remove saucepan from heat. Mix in 250 ml (1 cup) of stock thoroughly with a wooden spoon. Return to heat and add remaining stock, 250 ml (1 cup) at a time, until desired consistency is reached. Stir constantly.

Season soup to taste and drop in bouquet garni. Bring to a boil, then reduce heat to low. Simmer uncovered, for 40 minutes. Stir occasionally. Correct seasoning and strain.

If soup is a bit too thick, mix in a bit of stock with a wooden spoon.

In a small saucepan, simmer the reserved chopped mushrooms in 125 ml (1/2 cup) chicken stock, for several minutes.

Before serving, mix in cream and garnish with reserved mushrooms and parsley or chives.

This soup, without the cream, will keep for 2 to 3 days, covered with buttered wax paper and refrigerated.

Chicken Stock, see pages 33-34.

Manhattan Clam Chowder

Serves 4

500 ml	(2 cups) basic fish stock with vinegar
4	slices of bacon, diced
1	can of clams
1	onion, diced
30 ml	(2 tbs) flour
1 ml	(1/4 tsp) thyme
1	bay leaf
250 ml	(1 cup) clam juice
500 ml	(2 cups) water
	salt and pepper
2	potatoes, diced
5 ml	(1 tsp) corn oil
3	tomatoes, peeled and chopped
	several drops of lemon juice

Drain clams and reserve liquid.

Set bacon in a saucepan over medium heat. Cook until most of the fat has melted.

Add onion to bacon fat: cook until transparent. Add flour, thyme, and bay leaf. Cook for 4 minutes, stirring constantly. Gradually stir in reserved clam liquid, fish stock, and water. Add potatoes and sea-son lightly with salt and pepper. Bring to a boil.

In the meantime, heat corn oil in a small sauté pan. Add tomatoes and cook over high heat for 5 minutes.

Season and transfer to saucepan. Simmer until potatoes are tender.

Stir in clams and lemon juice. Reheat chowder for several minutes and correct seasoning. Garnish with chopped parsley.

Fish Stock, see page 33.

Celery and Chesnut Velouté Soup

Serves 4

30 ml	(2 tbs) butter
30 ml	(2 tbs) finely chopped onions
2	stalks of celery, thinly sliced
45 ml	(3 tablespoons) flour
1 l	(4 cups) hot chicken stock
125 ml	(1/2 cup) chestnut purée
45 ml	(3 tbs) 10% cream
	lemon juice
	chopped parsley
	salt and pepper

Melt butter in a saucepan over medium heat. Add onions and celery; cover and cook 4 to 5 minutes over low heat.

Add flour; mix and cook 1 minute.

Stir in chicken stock and chestnut purée; stir with a whisk. Season to taste. Sprinkle with lemon juice; cook 15 to 16 minutes.

Pass through a food mill. Incorporate cream; stir. Correct seasoning.

Sprinkle with chopped parsley. Serve.

Chicken Stock, see pages 33-34.

Gazpacho

Serves 4

1	cucumber, peeled, seeded, and thinly sliced
5	garlic cloves, crushed and finely chopped
1 ml	(1/4 tsp) cumin seeds
50 ml	(1/4 cup) ground almonds

30 ml	(2 tbs) wine vinegar
50 ml	(1/4 cup) olive oil
3	tomatoes, peeled, seeded, and cut in two
1.6 l	(6½ cups) cold basic brown beef stock
	freshly ground pepper
1/2	green pepper, seeded and thinly sliced
15 ml	(1 tbs) fresh parsley, finely chopped

Place cucumber slices in a mixing bowl. Sprinkle with salt and set aside for 30 minutes.
Drain.
Blend garlic, cumin seeds, and almonds together.
Add vinegar and oil; blend again.
Add cucumbers and tomatoes; blend well.
Thoroughly blend in beef stock. Season to taste.
Cover soup with buttered wax paper and refrigerate for at least 4 to 5 hours.
Pour the gazpacho into a soup tureen and garnish with the green pepper and parsley.

Basic Brown Beef Stock, see page 34.

Cream of Leek Soup

Serves 4

3	leeks, white section only, thinly sliced
30 ml	(2 tbs) leek, thinly sliced, reserve as garnish
40 ml	(2½ tbs) butter
1	large onion, thinly sliced
750 g	(1½ lb) OR 4 large raw potatoes, peeled and thinly sliced
1.5 l	(6 cups) hot basic chicken stock
1	bouquet garni, consisting of:
1 ml	(1/4 tsp) thyme
1	bay leaf
1 ml	(1/4 tsp) basil
2 ml	(1/2 tsp) chervil
	fresh parsley
	celery
30 ml	(2 tbs) heavy cream
	salt and pepper

In a heavy, medium size saucepan melt 30 ml (2 tbs) butter over high heat. Add sliced leeks and onions. Cover and cook over low heat for 15 minutes. Stir occasionally.
Add potatoes and enough stock, until desired consistency is reached. Season to taste. Add bouquet garni. Bring to boil over high heat. Reduce to medium and simmer uncovered for 40 minutes. Stir occasionally.
If soup is too thick, mix a bit of hot stock with a wooden spoon.
In a small sauté pan, melt 5 ml (1 tsp) butter over high heat. Reduce heat to medium, then add reserved leek. Simmer uncovered, for 3 minutes. Stir occasionally. Before serving, mix in cream and garnish with sauteed leeks.

Basic Chicken Stock, see pages 33-34.

Chilled Mexican Soup

Serves 10

4	fresh tomatoes, peeled and seeded, finely chopped
250 ml	(1 cup) celery, finely chopped
2	scallions, finely chopped
2	medium size cucumbers, finely chopped
1	small hot green pepper, seeded and finely chopped*
1 l	(1 quart) chilled tomato juice
2 ml	(1/2 tsp) Tabasco sauce
15 ml	(1 tbs) olive oil
	salt and lemon pepper to taste

Place finely chopped ingredients in a bowl. Thoroughly mix in Tabasco sauce, tomato juice, olive oil, salt, and lemon pepper.
Chill for several hours.
Serve soup in chilled bowls and garnish with a thin slice of lemon.

* Hot peppers have a very strong essence which can irritate your eyes. It is therefore important to wash your hands thoroughly with soap and warm water after handling.

Chilled Mexican Soup

Lentil Soup

Lentil Soup

Serves 4

250 ml	(1 cup) lentils
30 ml	(2 tbs) butter
1	chopped onion
1	stalk of celery, chopped finely
1	bay leaf
3	sprigs of parsley
1	clove of garlic, smashed and chopped
1.5 l	(6 cups) hot chicken stock
1/4	chinese cabbage, washed and thinly sliced
	salt and pepper

Soak lentils in cold water for 3 hours. Drain and set aside.

Melt 15 ml (1 tbs) butter in a large saucepan. Add onions and celery; cook 3 to 4 minutes over medium heat.

Add lentils. Season with salt and pepper. Add spices and garlic; mix well. Cover and cook for 3 minutes.

Stir in chicken stock. Season with salt and pepper. Cook for 1½ hours over low heat.

5 minutes before the end of cooking: melt remaining butter in a sauté pan. Add chinese cabbage; cook 2 minutes.

Incorporate chinese cabbage to lentil soup. Stir and serve.

Cream of Carrot Soup

Serves 4

4	large carrots, peeled and thinly sliced
4	slices of bacon, diced
1	large onion, sliced
4	large raw potatoes, peeled and thinly sliced
1.5 l	(6 cups) hot basic chicken stock
	bouquet garni, consisting of:
1 ml	(1/4 tsp) thyme
1	bay leaf
1 ml	(1/4 tsp) chervil
1 ml	(1/4 tsp) basil
2 ml	(1/2 tsp) chervil
	fresh parsley
	celery
	salt

	freshly ground pepper
30 ml	(2 tbs) heavy cream

In a heavy, medium size saucepan cook bacon over medium heat, uncovered for 5 minutes. Add sliced onion, cover and simmer for several minutes. Stir occasionally. Reduce to low, add carrots, cover, and simmer for 15 minutes. Stir occasionally.

Add potatoes and enough stock until desired consistency is reached. Drop in bouquet garni. Season with salt and pepper. Bring to a boil over high heat. Reduce to medium, and simmer, uncovered for 40 minutes. Stir occasionally. Correct seasoning and strain through a fine sieve. If soup is too thick, add a bit of hot stock. Stir in cream before serving. This soup, without cream, will keep for 2 to 3 days, covered with buttered wax paper and refrigerated.

Basic Chicken Stock, see pages 33-34.

Potato Soup

Serves 4

15 ml	(1 tbs) corn oil
1	leek, thinly sliced
2	onions, thinly sliced
1	celery stalk, thinly sliced
4	small potatoes
1.5 l	(6 cups) hot light chicken stock
	bouquet garni, consisting of:
2 ml	(1/2 tsp) chervil
1 ml	(1/4 tsp) thyme
1 ml	(1/4 tsp) basil
1 ml	(1/4 tsp) rosemary
	fresh parsley
	salt and pepper
30 ml	(2 tbs) 35% cream (optional)

Heat the oil in a medium size saucepan over high heat.

Reduce heat to low, add leek, onions, and celery. Cover and cook for 10 minutes.

Add potatoes, chicken stock, bouquet garni, salt and pepper.

Simmer until potatoes are done. Discard bouquet garni.

Purée soup in a blender or through the fine disc of a food mill.

Correct seasoning and mix in cream before serving.

Chicken Stock, see pages 33-34.

Cream of Pumpkin Soup

Serves 6 to 8

1/2	small pumpkin
1 l	(4 cups) milk
1 l	(4 cups) water
45 ml	(3 tbs) rice flour OR all purpose flour
45 ml	(3 tbs) butter
	salt and pepper
30-45 ml	(2-3 tbs) sugar

Seed pumpkin, then pare off skin. Cut pumpkin flesh into 2.5 cm (1 in) pieces. Place in a saucepan.

Pour enough water to cover; bring to a boil. Simmer until tender and very well done. Strain and purée.

Place puréed pumpkin in a saucepan. Reserve 50 ml (1/4 cup) of milk, then add remaining milk and water to saucepan. Bring to a simmer.

Mix flour with reserved milk. Stir mixture into saucepan.

Continue to simmer over low heat for 15 to 20 minutes. Stir occasionally.

Blend in butter, season with salt and pepper.

To serve, pour soup into bowls and sprinkle a bit of sugar over each serving.

Vegetable Soup

Serves 4

15 ml	(1 tbs) butter
1/2	leek, thinly sliced
1	small onion, diced
	pinch of basil
2 ml	(1/2 tsp) chervil
1	bay leaf
	pinch of thyme
1/2	green pepper, seeded and diced
1/2	celery stalk, diced
1	small carrot, finely chopped
1	medium raw potato, peeled and diced (optional)
1.2 l	(5 cups) hot beef, chicken, or vegetable stock
	salt
	freshly ground pepper
	croutons

15 ml	(1 tbs) fresh parsley, finely chopped

In a heavy, medium size saucepan, melt butter over high heat. Reduce heat to low and add leek, onions, and cover. Simmer for several minutes.

Add the herbs, remaining vegetables, and stock. Season with salt and pepper.

Bring to a boil over high heat.

Reduce to medium, and simmer uncovered until the vegetables are cooked.

Garnish with croutons and parsley.

Herb Soup

Serves 4

4	potatoes, peeled
1	bunch of watercress
15 ml	(1 tbs) chives, finely chopped
30 ml	(2 tbs) fresh parsley, finely chopped
2	bay leaves
1.2 l	(5 cups) hot light chicken stock
	salt and pepper
	35% cream (optional)

Place all ingredients, except cream, in a saucepan. Season to taste.

Bring to a simmer and cook gently for 40 minutes.

Discard bay leaves, then purée soup through a sieve or food mill.

To serve hot, mix in 30 ml (2 tbs) heavy cream just before serving.

To serve cold, mix in 125-250 ml (1/2-1 cup) sour cream just before serving.

Chicken Stock, see pages 33-34.

Cream of Pumpkin Soup

Chapter III

Hors d'Oeuvre and Small Entrées
Pasta • Fondues and Eggs

Cocktail Mushroom Caps

Serves 6 to 10

1 l	*(4 cups) medium size mushroom caps*
125 ml	*(1/2 cup) water*
125 ml	*(1/2 cup) dry white wine*
50 ml	*(1/4 cup) olive oil*
30 ml	*(2 tbs) wine vinegar*
	bouquet garni, consisting of:
1 ml	*(1/4 tsp) thyme*
2	*bay leaves*
1 ml	*(1/4 tsp) fennel seeds*
5 ml	*(1 tsp) chervil*
	fresh parsley
	celery
	salt
	freshly ground pepper

Combine all ingredients in a medium size saucepan.

Cover, bring liquid to a boil, then simmer mushrooms over medium heat for 8 minutes.

Let mushrooms cool and refrigerate in the marinade for at least 12 hours.

The mushrooms will keep refrigerated for 48 hours in the marinade. Drain and discard the bouquet garni.

Serve with toothpicks.

Stuffed Celery Stalks

Serves 4

4	*celery stalks*
5 ml	*(1 tsp) Dijon mustard*
250 g	*(1/2 lb) Philadelphia cream cheese*
125 ml	*(1/2 cup) sweet peppers, cooked and diced*
2 ml	*(1/2 tsp) cumin*
1	*clove of garlic, smashed and chopped*
15 ml	*(1 tbs) sour cream*
	lemon juice
	salt, pepper
	paprika

Cut celery stalks in 5 cm (2 in) pieces and soak for 1 hour in cold water.

Peel celery pieces with a small paring knife. Pat dry and set aside.

Place mustard in a bowl. Add cheese and mix until softened. Add remaining ingredients. Season to taste.

Stuff celery stalks. Serve.

Stuffed Celery Stalks

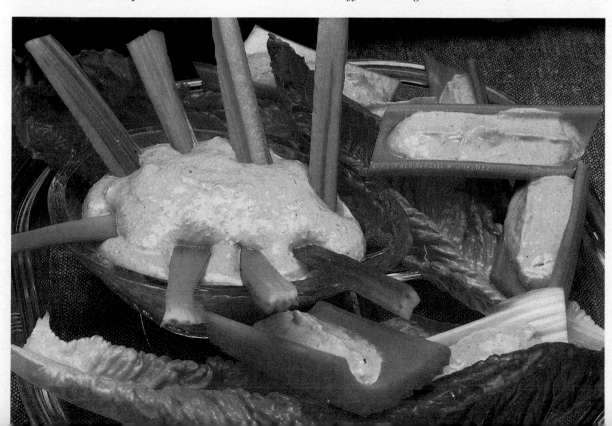

Hors d'Oeuvre
and Small Entrées

Ailloli on Toast
(Garlic Dip)

Serves 6 to 8

This sauce is very popular in the south of France. You can serve this sauce cold with poached fish such as halibut.

4	garlic cloves, crushed and finely chopped
2	egg yolks
175 ml	(3/4 cup) olive oil
	salt
	freshly ground pepper
	lemon juice to taste
	dash of cayenne pepper or drop of Tabasco sauce
	melba toast or toasted French bread

In a mortar or small mixing bowl, thoroughly blend garlic and egg yolks with a whisk, until mixture is thick.

Add oil, drop by drop, whisking constantly.

Add salt, pepper, lemon juice, cayenne pepper (or Tabasco sauce). Correct seasoning, if necessary.

Your guests should spread the ailloli on melba toast or toasted French bread.

You can prepare this recipe ahead of time. Be sure to cover with buttered wax paper and refrigerate.

Mushroom Caps Stuffed with Crab Meat

Serves 6 to 8

24	large mushroom caps, 3.8 cm (1½ in) in diameter
30 ml	(2 tbs) butter
2	dried shallots, finely chopped
250 g	(1/2 lb) crab meat, fresh or canned, drained and coarsely chopped
	salt
	freshly ground pepper
	few drops of Tabasco sauce
125 ml	(1/2 cup) hot white sauce thick

125 ml	(1/2 cup) grated swiss or mozzarella cheese

Preheat oven to 180°C (350°F).

In a medium, heavy saucepan, melt butter over high heat. When butter begins to foam, reduce heat to medium. Add shallots and cook, uncovered, for 3 minutes. Mix in crab meat and season with salt, pepper, and Tabasco sauce.

Cook over low heat, uncovered, for 4 minutes. Stir in white sauce and season well.

Arrange mushroom caps in an oiled baking dish. Season with salt and pepper. Fill caps with crab mixture. Sprinkle with grated cheese.

Bake in the oven for 15 minutes.

Serve immediately on individual plates.

White Sauce Thick, see page 41.

Curried Mushroom Canapés

Serves 4

45 ml	(3 tbs) butter
1	chopped shallot
15 ml	(1 tbs) chopped parsley
15 ml	(1 tbs) curry powder
114 g	(1/4 lb) chopped mushrooms
45 ml	(3 tbs) flour
375 ml	(1½ cups) hot milk
	pinch of nutmeg
	lemon juice
	grated parmesan cheese
	toasted bread
	salt and pepper

Preheat oven to 200°C (400°F).

Melt butter in a sauté pan over medium heat. Add shallot and parsley. Sprinkle with curry powder; cook 2 minutes mixing with a wooden spoon.

Add mushrooms; season with salt and pepper. Sprinkle with lemon juice; cook 4 to 5 minutes.

Incorporate flour; mix well. Add milk; stir. Sprinkle with nutmeg; cook 8 to 10 minutes.

Spread mixture on slices of toasted bread. Sprinkle with grated cheese.

Broil in the oven for 3 minutes. Serve.

Curried Mushroom Canapés

Hearts of Palm Deep Fried in Batter

Serves 4

1	*can hearts of palm*
3	*eggs*
250 ml	*(1 cup) fine breadcrumbs*
	salt and pepper
	chili powder to taste
	thin slices mozzarella cheese
	vegetable oil for the deep fryer

Drain the hearts of palm and slice into lengthwise pieces. Beat eggs and season them with salt, pepper, and a dash of chili powder.
Dip hearts of palm pieces into eggs and roll in breadcrumbs.
Repeat above procedure.
Heat deep fryer to 180°C (350°F).
Deep fry hearts of palm until golden and crisp. Remove and drain on paper towel.
Arrange pieces in an ovenproof dish and top with thin slices of mozzarella cheese.
Bake in a preheated oven at 200°C (400°F) until cheese melts.

Hearts of Palm Salad

Serves 4

1	*can hearts of palm*
1	*small purple onion, sliced*
3	*tomatoes, sliced*
4	*hard boiled eggs, sliced*
	your favorite dressing
	pitted green olives
	green scallions
	fresh parsley sprigs

Drain hearts of palm and cut each piece in 4 to 6 strips, lengthwise.
Arrange eggs, tomatoes, palm strips, and onions in rows, side by side, on a serving dish.
Pour on enough dressing to moisten everything well. Place in the refrigerator and let salad marinate for 2 hours.
At serving time, decorate with the olives, scallions, and parsley.

Cheese Dip

Yield: 500 ml (2 cups)

This dip can be spread on water biscuits, carrot sticks, and/or small pieces of celery.

250 g	*(1/2 lb) cheddar cheese*
50 ml	*(1/4 cup) sour cream*
	cayenne pepper to taste
	lemon pepper to taste
	pinch of nutmeg
125 g	*(1/4 lb) butter, softened*

Blend cheese until smooth.
Incorporate cayenne, lemon pepper, nutmeg, and butter.
Just before serving, mix in sour cream and correct seasoning.

Mushroom Barquettes

Serves 4

45 ml	*(3 tbs) butter*
250 g	*(1/2 lb) sliced mushrooms*
5 ml	*(1 tsp) cumin*
15 ml	*(1 tbs) chopped parsley*
45 ml	*(3 tbs) flour*
625 ml	*(2½ cups) hot milk*
30 ml	*(2 tbs) vermouth*
125 ml	*(1/2 cup) grated cheddar cheese*
4	*small individual breads*
	pinch of nutmeg
	salt and pepper

Preheat oven to 200°C (400°F).
Melt butter in a saucepan. Add mushrooms and cumin. Season with salt and pepper; cook 4 to 5 minutes over medium heat.
Add parsley and flour; mix well.
Stir in hot milk and vermouth. Correct seasoning. Sprinkle with nutmeg; cook 8 to 10 minutes.
Slice breads in two lengthwise and remove the crumb. Broil bread shells in the oven for a few minutes.
Pour mushroom mixture into toasted bread shells. Sprinkle with grated cheese. Cook in the oven for 7 to 8 minutes at 200°C (400°F).
Garnish with slices of hard boiled egg. Serve.

Mushroom Barquettes

Roquefort Canapés

Approximately 20 canapés

250 ml	*(1 cup) roquefort or blue cheese, room temperature*
50 ml	*(1/4 cup) softened butter lemon pepper to taste pinch of cayenne pepper*
5 ml	*(1 tsp) cognac*
1	*small French baguette, thinly sliced OR crackers*
30 ml	*(2 tbs) sour cream*

Trim crust from each slice of bread. Place bread on cookie sheet and bake in a preheated oven at 200°C (400°F) until toasted. Set aside.
Mash cheese and mix in butter, lemon pepper, cayenne pepper, and cognac.
Just before serving, stir in sour cream. Spread on toasted bread or crackers.

Marinated Mushrooms

60 ml	*(4 tbs) wine vinegar*
150 ml	*(2/3 cup) olive or corn oil*
125 ml	*(1/2 cup) water juice of 1 lemon*
4	*garlic cloves, whole and unpeeled*
20	*peppercorns salt and pepper*
2	*bay leaves*
1 ml	*(1/4 tsp) thyme*
2 ml	*(1/2 tsp) tarragon*
500 g	*(1 lb) fresh white whole button mushrooms, sliced*
1	*large pickling jar*

Place oil, vinegar, water, lemon juice, garlic, and peppercorns in a saucepan over high heat. Add all remaining spices. Bring to a boil, cover and reduce to low. Simmer for 15 minutes.
Strain liquid; set aside.
In the same saucepan, sauté mushrooms at high heat for 2 to 3 minutes. Stir constantly. Transfer mushrooms to a bowl containing set aside liquid. Discard liquid in saucepan.

When mushrooms are cool, cover bowl with wax paper and refrigerate or place in pickling jar.*

* This recipe will keep 7 days stored in a pickling jar and refrigerated. To serve mushrooms use a slotted spoon, as it is important that the marinating liquid remain in the jar to act as a preservative.

Halibut Served on Lettuce Hearts

Serves 4

500 g	*(1 lb) halibut salt freshly ground pepper pinch of thyme*
1	*bay leaf*
5 ml	*(1 tsp) chervil*
5	*mushrooms, sliced*
125 ml	*(1/2 cup) white wine OR 30 ml (2 tbs) wine vinegar juice of 1/4 lemon*
12	*green olives, pitted and sliced*
5	*water chestnuts, thinly sliced*
125 ml	*(1/2 cup) french dressing*
4	*lettuce hearts*
1	*hard boiled egg, cut into 4*
4	*lemon wedges fresh parsley*

Wash fish under cold running water. Place in a buttered pan and season with salt and pepper. Add thyme, bay leaf, chervil, mushrooms, wine or wine vinegar, lemon juice, and cold water to cover.
Cover pan with buttered wax paper. The paper must touch the surface of the ingredients. Bring to a boil over high heat. Reduce heat to low and simmer for 15 minutes.
Remove pan from heat and allow halibut to cool in the liquid.
Remove fish from pan; transfer to a mixing bowl. Flake with a fork. Mix in olives, water chestnuts, and french dressing. Season to taste.
Arrange halibut on the lettuce hearts. Decorate with hard boiled egg, lemon wedges, and parsley.

French Dressing, see page 50.

Halibut Served on Lettuce Hearts

Avocado à la Martin

Anchovy Canapés

Yield: 25 canapés

125 ml	*(1/2 cup) cream cheese, room temperature*
5 ml	*(1 tsp) fresh chopped chives*
	lemon pepper to taste
	few drops of lemon juice
2	*small cans of flat anchovy fillets*
16	*thin slices French bread*

Preheat oven to broil.
Trim crust from bread. Place bread slices on a cookie sheet. Toast under broiler on both sides. Set aside.
Mix cheese, chives, lemon pepper, and lemon juice together in a small bowl.

Just before serving, spread mixture on the toasted bread. Arrange 2 anchovy fillets on each canapé.
Decorate with thin slices of lemon.

Avocado à la Martin

Serves 2

1	*avocado*
5-6	*cooked shrimp, peeled and deveined 15 to 20 shrimps per 500 g (1 lb)*
3-4	*walnuts, coarsely chopped*
45 ml	*(3 tbs) mayonnaise*
	salt

freshly ground pepper
few drops of Tabasco sauce
5 ml   (1 tsp) fresh parsley, finely
chopped

Using a spoon, scoop the flesh from the avocado. Cut shrimp in two, on an angle. Mix all ingredients together, including avocado flesh.
Spoon mixture into avocado shell. Serve.

Smoked Salmon Canapés

Serves 6 to 8

Smoked salmon should be rubbed lightly with oil when refrigerated, to prevent drying.

15	thin slices smoked salmon, cut on an angle
15	pieces melba toast OR toasted french bread
250 g	(1/2 lb) cream cheese, room temperature
15	very thin slices dried shallot
15 ml	(1 tbs) capers
	few lemon wedges
	freshly ground pepper

Spread cream cheese on melba toast or french bread.
Cover with a slice of salmon.
Top with slice of shallot and several capers.
Arrange canapés on a platter and decorate with lemon wedges.
Top with freshly ground pepper.

Snails au Gratin

Snails au Gratin

Serves 2

250 g	(1/2 lb) garlic butter, room temperature
12	large canned snails, drained
45 ml	(3 tbs) grated gruyère cheese dash of cayenne pepper
2	ovenproof ceramic snail dishes

Preheat oven to broil.
Spoon 1 ml (1/4 tsp) of garlic butter inside each slot of snail dish. Drop a snail in each slot.
Sprinkle snails with the cheese and season with a dash of cayenne pepper.
Broil in the middle of the oven for 15 minutes.

Garlic Butter, see page 16.

Brochettes of Scampi

Serves 4

24	uncooked scampis in the shell 18 to 24 scampis per 500 g (1 lb)
24	mushroom caps
4-5	bacon slices, cut into 2.5 cm (1 in) squares
60 ml	(4 tbs) garlic butter, room temperature salt freshly ground pepper juice of 1 lemon

Preheat oven to broil.
Remove scampi from the shell.
On a skewer, alternate scampi, mushroom caps, and bacon.
Season the brochettes placed in a baking dish and dab with garlic butter.
Broil 15 cm (6 in) away from top element for 3 minutes on each side.
Before serving, squeeze lemon juice over brochettes.

Garlic Butter, see page 16.

Shrimp on Toast

Serves 6 to 8

250 g	(1/2 lb) cooked shrimp, peeled, deveined, and finely chopped
45 ml	(3 tbs) mayonnaise
15 ml	(1 tbs) fresh parsley, finely chopped
5 ml	(1 tsp) fresh chives, finely chopped salt freshly ground pepper
5 ml	(1 tsp) curry powder OR curry powder to taste juice of 1/4 lemon
2	drops of Tabasco sauce

Blend all ingredients together thoroughly in a mixing bowl.
Correct seasoning, if necessary.
If you wish to prepare shrimp mixture ahead of time, it will keep for 6 to 7 hours, covered with buttered wax paper and refrigerated.
To serve, spread mixture on toasted French bread, cut in various shapes, or on melba toast or crackers.
The canapés will keep for 1 hour.

Butterfly Shrimp

Serves 6 to 8

500 g	(1 lb) raw shrimp, in their shell (15 to 20 shrimps per pound)
2	garlic cloves, crushed and finely chopped juice of 1 lemon salt freshly ground pepper peanut oil basic batter for deep frying

Peel each shrimp down to the last section, leaving it and the tail attached. Devein and wash. Cut each shrimp 3/4 of the way through along its inner curve. Flatten with the palm of your hand.
In a mixing bowl, combine all ingredients, except peanut oil. Cover shrimp with wax paper; set aside.
While shrimp are marinating, prepare batter.
Half fill a deep fryer with peanut oil and heat to 180°C (350°F).
Dip shrimp, one at a time, into batter then drop carefully into hot oil.
Deep fry shrimp for 3 to 4 minutes or until golden brown.
Drain on paper towel and serve with plum sauce.

Basic Batter for Deep frying, see page 10.

Hors d'Oeuvre and Small Entrées

Curried Indian Meatballs

Serves 4

30 ml	(2 tbs) corn oil
1	Spanish onion, finely chopped
750 g	(1½ lb) top round, ground
30 ml	(2 tbs) breadcrumbs
	salt and pepper
2 ml	(1/2 tsp) chili powder
2 ml	(1/2 tsp) tumeric
2	garlic cloves, crushed and finely chopped
1	egg
15 ml	(1 tbs) parsley

Heat 15 ml (1 tbs) oil in a large sauté pan over medium high heat. When oil is very hot, add onion and cook for about 4 minutes.

Remove onion and transfer to a bowl. Add all remaining ingredients to the bowl in the order listed. Blend together then shape into bite size meatballs.

Pour remaining oil into the sauté pan over high heat.

Brown meatballs, reduce heat to medium, and cook until done to taste.

Serve with curry sauce or an onion sauce.

Asparagus Tartlets with Hollandaise Sauce

Serves 4

5 ml	(1 tsp) butter
8	fresh asparagus, cooked and diced
375 ml	(1½ cups) hot white sauce
8	cooked tartlets
	Hollandaise sauce
	pinch of nutmeg
	salt and white pepper

Preheat oven to 200°C (400°F).

Melt butter in a small saucepan. Add asparagus and pepper; cover and simmer for several minutes over low heat.

Incorporate white sauce and nutmeg; stir and simmer 6 to 7 minutes.

Pour mixture into cooked tartlets. Coat with hollandaise sauce.

Broil in the oven for 3 minutes. Serve.

White Sauce, see page 40.
Hollandaise Sauce, see page 50.

Mushrooms à la Crème on Toast

Serves 2

250 g	(1/2 lb) mushrooms
3 ml	(3/4 tsp) butter
	salt
	freshly ground pepper
2	dried shallots, finely chopped
60 ml	(4 tbs) dry vermouth (optional)
250 ml	(1 cup) hot white sauce thick
2	slices toasted french bread
15 ml	(1 tbs) mozzarella cheese, grated
15 ml	(1 tbs) fresh parsley, finely chopped

Preheat oven to broil.

In a sauté pan, melt butter over high heat. When butter begins to foam, reduce to medium. Cook mushrooms for 5 minutes, stirring occasionally. Season with salt and pepper.

Add shallots and vermouth. Increase heat to high, and reduce liquid, uncovered, for 2 minutes.

Mix in white sauce and correct seasoning. Arrange bread in a baking dish. Spoon mushroom mixture over toasted bread. Sprinkle with grated cheese.

Broil 10 cm (4 in) away from top element, for 3 to 4 minutes.

Garnish with parsley and serve at once.

White Sauce Thick, see page 41.

Endives au Gratin

Serves 4

500 g	(1 lb) endives
8	ham slices
250 ml	(1 cup) thin white sauce, hot
125 ml	(1/2 cup) gruyère cheese, grated
1 ml	(1/4 tsp) tarragon
	salt and pepper

Preheat oven to 190°C (375°F).

Poach endives in salted boiling water also containing some lemon juice over medium heat for 10 minutes.

Drain well; season with salt and pepper.

Wrap endives in ham slices.

Place in a buttered gratin dish. Season with tarragon.

Pour white sauce over endives and sprinkle with cheese.

Cook in the oven for 20 minutes.

White Sauce Thin, see page 41.

Baked Oysters au Gratin

Serves 4

24	fresh oysters in the shell
625 ml	(2½ cups) hot white sauce thick
	dash of cayenne pepper
15 ml	(1 tbs) melted butter
125 ml	(1/2 cup) grated parmesan cheese
60 ml	(4 tbs) butter

Preheat oven to broil.

Remove oysters from the shell and reserve liquid. Thoroughly clean oyster shells.

In a mixing bowl, place white sauce, cayenne pepper, melted butter, and reserved oyster liquid. Mix.

Arrange shells in a baking dish.

Spoon 15 ml (1 tbs) white sauce mixture into each shell.

Add oyster to shell. Spoon remaining sauce over shells and sprinkle with grated cheese.

Dot shells with butter.

Broil 10 cm (4 in) away from top element for 3 to 4 minutes.

White Sauce Thick, see page 41.

Snails Provençale

Serves 2

125 g	(1/4 lb) garlic butter, room temperature
12	large canned snails, drained
12	shells

Preheat oven to broil.

Spoon 1 ml (1/4 tsp) of garlic butter inside each shell. Place snails in the shells and seal with remaining garlic butter.

Arrange shells in snail dishes.

Broil, 10 cm (4 in) from top element for 8 to 10 minutes.

The snails are ready when butter turns golden brown.

Garlic Butter, see page 16.

Snails Provençale

Crêpes Stuffed with Salmon Roes

Serves 4

4	*thin crêpes*
50 ml	*(1/4 cup) homemade mayonnaise*
1	*small bottle of salmon roes*

Spread a light coat of mayonnaise on each crêpe.

Cover mayonnaise with a light coat of salmon roes.

Roll each crêpe and cut in two. Serve.

Mayonnaise, see page 119.

Crêpes Stuffed with Shrimp

Serves 4

4	*crêpes*
500 g	*(1 lb) cooked shrimp, peeled and deveined*
30 ml	*(2 tbs) butter*
30 ml	*(2 tbs) dried shallots, finely chopped paprika to taste*
125 ml	*(1/2 cup) port wine*
375 ml	*(1½ cups) hot white sauce thick*
125 ml	*(1/2 cup) grated gruyère or mozzarella cheese*
15 ml	*(1 tbs) chopped parsley salt freshly ground pepper*

Preheat oven to 180°C (350°F).

Slice shrimp diagonally.

In a sauté pan, melt butter over high heat. When butter begins to foam, reduce to medium. Add shallots and shrimp. Cook, uncovered, for 3 minutes. Stir occasionally.

Mix in paprika to taste and add wine. Increase heat to high and cook uncovered, for 2 to 3 minutes. Add white sauce, season, and remove pan from heat.

Separate mixture in half. Reserve half.

Stuff the crêpes with one half of mixture. Roll edges of crêpes over mixture. Arrange

Crêpes Stuffed with Salmon Roes

Coquille of Scallops and Peppers

crêpes in a buttered baking dish, rolled edge down and pour remaining mixture on top.

Sprinkle with cheese.

Broil crêpes in the oven on middle rack for 15 minutes.

Before serving, sprinkle with parsley.

White Sauce Thick, see page 41.

Snails Bourguignon

Serves 2

12	large canned snails, drained
30 ml	(2 tbs) butter
12	mushrooms, quartered
2	dried shallots, finely chopped
20	croutons
	salt
	freshly ground pepper
125 ml	(1/2 cup) hot bourguignon sauce
15 ml	(1 tbs) fresh parsley, finely chopped

In a small sauté pan, melt butter over high heat. When it begins to foam, add mushrooms and sauté for 5 minutes. Stir frequently.

Reduce heat to medium, add shallots, croutons, and snails. Cook, uncovered, for 2 minutes. Stir occasionally.

Add sauce to the pan, and simmer, uncovered, for 2 minutes. Season to taste and top with parsley.

Serve in a Coquille St. Jacques shell.

Bourguignon Sauce, see page 46.

Coquille of Scallops and Peppers

Serves 4

500 g	(1 lb) scallops
1	green pepper, diced
1	red pepper, diced
24	fresh mushrooms, washed
500 ml	(2 cups) cold water
45 ml	(3 tbs) butter
45 ml	(3 tbs) flour
50 ml	(1/4 cup) 10% cream
50 ml	(1/4 cup) grated mozzarella cheese
	lemon juice
	salt and pepper

Preheat oven to 200°C (400°F).

Place scallops, pepper and mushrooms in a large saucepan. Season with pepper and sprinkle with lemon juice.

Add water. Season with salt; bring to boil over low heat.

As soon as the liquid begins to boil, remove scallops from saucepan and set aside.

Continue to cook liquid and vegetables, over low heat, for 7 to 8 minutes. Season to taste.

Melt butter in a small saucepan over medium heat. Add flour; mix and cook 1 minute.

Add cooking liquid and vegetables; mix well.

Incorporate cream; simmer 7 to 8 minutes. Add scallops; stir.

Pour mixture into individual shell-shaped dishes. Sprinkle with grated cheese. Cook in the oven for 3 minutes. Serve.

Mini-Pizza

Mini-Pizza

Serves 4

4	*commercial mini-pizza breads*
5 ml	*(1 tsp) vegetable oil*
1	*chopped onion*
1	*clove of garlic, smashed and chopped*
1	*796 ml (28 oz) can of tomatoes, drained and chopped*
15 ml	*(1 tbs) tomato paste*
1	*green pepper thinly sliced, blanched*
1	*pepperoni, thinly sliced*
250 ml	*(1 cup) grated mozzarella cheese*
	salt and pepper

Preheat oven to 190°C (375°F).
Heat oil in a sauté pan over medium heat.
Add onions and garlic; cook 2 to 3 minutes.
Add tomatoes and tomato paste; mix well.
Season with salt and pepper; cook for 10 to 12 minutes.
Place pizza breads on a cookie sheet. Spread tomato mixture on pizza. Garnish with pepperoni, pepper and grated cheese.
Cook in the oven for 15 minutes. Serve.

Macaroni à la Barbara

Serves 2

250 g	(1/2 lb) macaroni
30 ml	(2 tbs) butter
500 g	(1 lb) mushrooms, washed and sliced
	salt
	freshly ground pepper
375 ml	(1½ cups) hot quick tomato sauce
125 ml	(1/2 cup) mozzarella cheese, grated

Preheat oven to broil.

Cook macaroni in a stock pot half filled with boiling salted water, uncovered, for 10 minutes. Rinse macaroni under running water for 6 minutes, drain and set aside.

In a sauté pan, melt 30 ml (2 tbs) butter over high heat. When butter begins to foam, reduce to medium. Cook mushrooms, uncovered, for 5 minutes. Stir occasionally. Season with salt and pepper.

Rewarm macaroni by placing noodles in a large sieve and immersing sieve in hot water for 4 minutes. Drain.

In a buttered baking dish, alternate layers of macaroni, mushrooms, and tomato sauce. Finish with a layer of macaroni and top with cheese.

Cook, uncovered in the middle of the oven, for 15 minutes.

Macaroni with Olives

Serves 6

750 g	(1½ lb) elbow macaroni
50 ml	(1/4 cup) olive oil
2	garlic cloves
1	small pimento, finely chopped
30	black olives, pitted
45 ml	(3 tbs) capers, drained
15 ml	(1 tbs) parsley, chopped
2	cans of tomatoes, drained 454 g (16 oz)
125 ml	(1/2 cup) parmesan cheese, grated
	salt and pepper

Penne with Tomato Sauce (p. 101)

Heat 45 ml (3 tbs) of oil in a sauté pan, over medium heat.

When hot, add garlic and pimento. Cook for 2 minutes, stirring frequently.

Coarsely chop tomatoes, then add to pan. Season with salt, pepper, and parsley. Cook over medium heat until liquid has evaporated. Stir frequently.

Reduce heat to low and mix in capers and olives.

Fill a large stock pot with salted water and bring to a boil. Add macaroni and cook to taste. Add remaining oil to the water to prevent macaroni from sticking together. When macaroni is done, drain thoroughly, then mix into the sauce.

Top with grated cheese.

Spaghetti, Tomato and Mushroom Sauce

Serves 4

30 ml	(2 tbs) olive oil
1	chopped onion
1	clove of garlic, smashed and chopped
125 g	(1/4 lb) fresh mushrooms, washed and diced
2	796 ml (28 oz) cans of tomatoes, drained and chopped
1	small can of tomato paste
125 ml	(1/2 cup) hot chicken stock
1 ml	(1/4 tsp) oregano
125 ml	(1/2 cup) grated parmesan cheese
4	portions of cooked spaghetti, hot
	several crushed red peppers
	salt and pepper

Heat oil in a sauté pan over medium heat.

Add onions and garlic; cook 2 minutes.

Add mushrooms; season with salt and pepper. Cook 4 to 5 minutes.

Add tomatoes and tomato paste; mix well.

Incorporate chicken stock; stir and bring to boil.

Add spices; cook 1 hour low heat.

Pour sauce over hot spaghetti. Sprinkle with grated cheese. Serve.

Chicken Stock, see pages 33-34.

Spaghetti, Tomato and Mushroom Sauce

Macaroni Casserole au Gratin

Macaroni Casserole au Gratin

Serves 4

500 ml	*(2 cups) cooked macaroni*
500 ml	*(2 cups) thin white sauce, hot*
125 ml	*(1/2 cup) grated cheddar cheese*
125 ml	*(1/2 cup) seasoned breadcrumbs*
	salt and pepper

Preheat oven to 180°C (350°F).
Place cooked macaroni in a saucepan. Add white sauce; stir and cook several minutes over low heat.
Add half of cheese. Season to taste; mix well.
Pour mixture into a baking dish. Sprinkle with breadcrumbs and remaining cheese.
Cook in the oven for 10 to 12 minutes.
Serve.

White Sauce Thin, see page 41.

Penne with Tomato Sauce

Serves 4

250 g	*(1/2 lb) green penne noodles*
30 ml	*(2 tbs) olive oil*
1	*onion finely chopped*
1	*clove of garlic, smashed and chopped*
2	*796 ml (28 oz) cans of tomatoes, drained and chopped.*
1	*small can of tomato paste*
1 ml	*(1/4 tsp) basil*
2 ml	*(1/2 tsp) tarragon*
	pinch of sugar
	grated parmesan cheese
	salt and pepper

Cook penne following direction on the package. Drain and set aside.
Heat oil in a sauté pan. Add onions and garlic; mix, cover, and cook for 2 minutes.

Gnocchi, Tomato Cream Sauce

Add tomatoes; stir well.

Add tomato paste; mix. Add spices and sugar; stir and cover partially. Cook 10 to 12 minutes over low heat.

Add drained penne and cheese; stir and cook for 2 minutes. Serve.

Gnocchi, Tomato Cream Sauce

Serves 4

5 ml	*(1 tsp) olive oil*
1	*chopped onion*
1	*stalk of celery, thinly sliced*
1	*796 ml (28 oz) can of tomatoes,*
	drained and finely chopped
250 ml	*(1 cup) hot white sauce*
250 ml	*(1 cup) grated mozzarella cheese*
4	*portions of cooked gnocchi, hot*
	pinch of nutmeg
	salt and pepper

Preheat oven to 190°C (375°F).

Heat oil in a sauté pan. Add onions and celery; cover and cook for 5 to 6 minutes. Add tomatoes and white sauce; season with salt and pepper. Add nutmeg; cook 10 to 12 minutes over low heat. Pass sauce through a food mill.

Pour sauce into a mixing bowl. Add 1/4 of cheese. Add gnocchi, mix and pour into

Tortellini with Peppers

a baking dish.
Sprinkle with grated cheese. Cook 16 to
18 minutes in the oven. Serve.

White Sauce, see page 40.

Tortellini with Peppers

Serves 4

5 ml	*(1 tsp) olive oil*
2	*onions, finely chopped*
1	*clove of garlic, smashed and chopped*
1	*green pepper, thinly sliced*
1	*pepperoni, thinly sliced*
1	*796 ml (28 oz) can of tomatoes, drained and chopped*
30 ml	*(2 tbs) tomato paste*

125 ml	*(1/2 cup) hot chicken stock*
4	*portions of cooked tortellini, hot*
	salt and pepper
	pinch of sugar

Preheat oven to 190°C (375°F).
Heat oil in a sauté pan. Add onions and
garlic; cook 3 to 4 minutes.
Add tomatoes and tomato paste; stir and
season with salt and pepper. Add sugar;
cook 8 to 10 minutes over low heat.
Add green peppers, pepperoni and
chicken stock; mix well. Add cooked tortellini; mix again.
Pour mixture into a baking dish. Cook in
the oven for 15 minutes. Serve.

Chicken Stock, see pages 33-34.

The Art of Making Omelettes

For best results use an omelette pan, which is an 8 in steel frying pan with rounded edges. You should only use this pan for making omelettes. The pan should never be scrubbed, simply wipe clean after use.

2 or 3	large eggs
15 ml	(1 tbs) light cream or water
15 ml	(1 tbs) butter
	salt
	freshly ground pepper, white

In a mixing bowl, lightly beat eggs and cream (or water), salt and pepper. Use a fork. Melt butter in the pan over very low heat. The butter should coat the bottom of the pan.
As soon as the butter stops foaming, add eggs. Cook over very high heat.
Shake pan often until eggs are almost set.
With a fork or spoon, gently bring the right side of omelette towards the middle.
If you wish to stuff omelette, you should add warm stuffing into middle of omelette at this point.
Carefully slide omelette towards left side of pan until it overhangs by 1.2 cm (1/2 in). Turn omelette upside down on a heated dish and serve immediately.

Eggs Chasseur

Recommended as an intimate brunch for two.

5	slices of bacon, cut into small pieces
12	mushrooms, quartered
	salt
	freshly ground pepper
2 ml	(1/2 tsp) fresh parsley, finely chopped
4	large eggs
30 ml	(2 tbs) butter
30 ml	(2 tbs) light cream

In a sauté pan, cook bacon over high heat for 2 to 3 minutes. Stir frequently.
Add mushrooms, season to taste, and cook for 4 minutes, uncovered. Stir frequently.
Remove pan from heat.

Prepare the scrambled eggs.
Transfer eggs to a heated platter.
Spoon bacon/mushroom mixture over eggs. Garnish with parsley.
Serve at once.

Party Beef Fondue

284 g	(10 oz) fillet (smaller end of the beef tenderloin) cut into, 2.5 cm (1 in) cubes (per person)
50 ml	(1/4 cup) hot béarnaise sauce (per person)
50 ml	(1/4 cup) hot bourguignon sauce (per person)
50 ml	(1/4 cup) ailloli (per person) peanut oil is recommended

Serve fondue with mushroom caps broiled with garlic butter.

Béarnaise Sauce, see page 48.
Bourguignon Sauce, see page 46.
Ailloli, see page 80.
Garlic Butter, see page 16.

Cheese Fondue

Serves 4

500 g	(1 lb) gruyère cheese, diced
250 g	(1/2 lb) emmenthal cheese, diced
1	garlic clove, peeled
90 ml	(3 oz) Kirsch
50 ml	(1/4 cup) white wine
5 ml	(1 tsp) cornstarch
	salt
	freshly ground pepper, white
	pinch of nutmeg
	French bread, cut into 2.5 cm (1 in) cubes

Rub the inside of an earthware dish with the garlic clove. Discard garlic.
Mix Kirsch, white wine, and cornstarch together.
Light burner under fondue dish.
Melt cheese in fondue dish, stirring constantly.
When cheese begins to melt, stir in Kirsch mixture. Season with salt, pepper, and nutmeg.
Stir constantly until mixture becomes thick.
Serve with French bread cubes.

Eggs à la Française

Serves 1

2	large eggs
5 ml	(1 tsp) butter
	salt
	freshly ground pepper, white

Carefully break eggs into a dish.
In a small crêpe pan, melt butter over very low heat. When melted, but barely lukewarm, gently slide eggs into pan.
Cook over low heat, uncovered, until egg whites are the color of milk and completely firm.
Season well with salt and pepper.
Transfer to a heated plate. Serve at once.

Eggs Florentine

Serves 4

8	eggs
375 ml	(1½ cups) cooked spinach
15 ml	(1 tbs) butter
	salt and pepper
125 ml	(1/2 cup) thick white sauce
50 ml	(1/4 cup) cheese
30 ml	(2 tbs) butter or margarine for baking dish

Preheat oven to 200°C (400°F).
Squeeze spinach dry, chop and set aside.
Melt butter in a small saucepan. Add spinach, cover, and cook over low heat for 4 to 5 minutes. Spread spinach in the bottom of buttered baking dish.
Gently break eggs over spinach. Cover each egg with 30 ml (2 tbs) of white sauce. Sprinkle with cheese.
Bake eggs for 7 to 8 minutes. Season and serve immediately.

White Sauce Thick, see page 41.

Eggs Florentine

Eggs with Cream

Eggs with Cream

Serves 1

2	large eggs
30 ml	(2 tbs) heavy or light cream
5 ml	(1 tsp) butter
	salt
	freshly ground pepper, white

Preheat oven to 150°C (350°F).
Slowly melt butter in a custard dish over very low heat.
Carefully break the eggs into the dish. Cover eggs with cream.
Bake in the oven in a bain-marie, for 8 to 10 minutes, or until egg whites are firm.
Season with salt and pepper. Serve immediately.

Scrambled Eggs

Scrambled Eggs

Serves 2

4	*large eggs*
30 ml	*(2 tbs) butter*
30 ml	*(2 tbs) light cream*
	salt
	freshly ground pepper, white

Half fill the bottom of a double boiler with

water. Bring to a boil.

Lightly beat eggs and cream in a mixing bowl.

Melt butter in top part of double boiler. Pour eggs in melted butter and place over bottom part containing water. Cook eggs slowly, whisking constantly, until they become creamy.

Transfer to heated platter; season to taste. Serve at once.

Poached Eggs Forestière

Serves 4

8	eggs
	water
15 ml	(1 tbs) white vinegar
250 g	(1/2 lb) mushrooms, thinly sliced
1	garlic bud, crushed and finely chopped
125 ml	(1/2 cup) of your favorite tomato sauce
50 ml	(1/4 cup) breadcrumbs
15 ml	(1 tbs) corn oil
	salt and pepper
1	buttered gratin dish

Preheat oven to broil.

Heat oil in a sauté pan over high heat. Add mushrooms and sauté for 2 minutes. Add garlic and sauté for 2 minutes; set aside. Season.

Pour enough water into a deep sauté pan to reach the depth of 5 cm (2 in).

Bring to a boil, add vinegar and reduce heat. When water is barely simmering, gently slide in eggs. Poach 2 or 3 at a time, for 3 minutes. While poaching, gently gather the egg white over the yolk, so that yolk is completely covered.

Drain poached eggs on paper towel.

Place mushrooms in bottom of gratin dish. Arrange eggs overtop. Spread the tomato sauce over eggs, sprinkle with breadcrumbs.

Broil in middle of the oven for 1 to 2 minutes. Serve.

Eggs Orientale

Serves 4

4	large eggs
750 ml	(3 cups) water
15 ml	(1 tbs) white vinegar
15 ml	(1 tbs) butter
4	slices of tomato, 3.8 cm (1½ in) thick
	salt
	freshly ground pepper, white
125 ml	(1/2 cup) Hollandaise sauce OR Béarnaise

Preheat oven to broil.

In a saucepan, bring water and vinegar to a boil.

Eggs Orientale

Break eggs into a dish and gently slide into boiling liquid. Poach for 3½ minutes. Remove eggs from liquid with a slotted spoon and set aside on a warm platter. In a saucepan, melt butter over high heat. When butter begins to foam, reduce to

110

medium high, and sauté tomato for 2 minutes on each side.
Arrange tomato in a buttered baking dish. Place an egg on each tomato slice; season well.
Cover with Hollandaise sauçe.

Bake eggs 10 cm (4 in) away from top element for 2 to 3 minutes.
Serve immediately.

Hollandaise Sauce, see page 50.
Béarnaise Sauce, see page 48.

Quiche Maison

Yield: 4-6 slices

22 cm	*(9 in) pie shell*
5	*bacon slices (optional)*
125 ml	*(1/2 cup) grated gruyère cheese*
4	*large eggs OR*
	5 medium size eggs
15 ml	*(1 tbs) fresh parsley, finely chopped*
375 ml	*(1½ cups) heavy cream*
	salt
	freshly ground pepper
	pinch of nutmeg

Bake pastry shell at 200°C (400°F) for 10 minutes.

Remove from oven and cool.

Preheat oven to 190°C (375°F).

Blanch bacon in a saucepan filled with boiling water, for 3 to 4 minutes. Dice and drain on paper towel.

Place bacon in a sauté pan. Cook, uncovered, over high heat for 3 minutes. Drain again on paper towel.

Place bacon in the bottom of pie shell. Cover with grated cheese.

In a mixing bowl, beat eggs, parsley, cream, salt, pepper, and nutmeg together with a whisk.

Pour mixture into pie shell.

If this mixture is not sufficient to fill the pie shell, top with milk or cream.

Bake the quiche for 30 to 35 minutes, or until a knife inserted in the middle comes out clean.

Eggs Gascon

Serves 4

8	*eggs*
	salt and pepper
1	*large eggplant, sliced*
1	*large Spanish onion, sliced*
45 ml	*(3 tbs) corn oil*
3	*tomatoes, peeled and coarsely chopped*
250 ml	*(1 cup) ham, cut into thin strips*
4	*buttered egg dishes or ramequins*

Quiche Maison

Preheat oven to 180°C (350°F).

Heat oil in a large sauté pan over high heat. When hot, add onion and sauté until transparent.

Add eggplant, reduce heat to medium, sauté until nicely browned.

Add tomatoes; season well with salt and pepper. Cook over medium heat until eggplant is well done. Add ham and cook for several more minutes.

Divide mixture into egg dishes and carefully break 2 eggs into each dish.

Cover and bake eggs for 8 to 10 minutes, or until done to your taste.

Season with salt and pepper. Garnish with chopped parsley.

Omelette Mousseline with Cheese

Serves 2

3	egg yolks
2	whole eggs
30 ml	(2 tbs) sour cream
	salt and pepper
3	egg whites, beaten until they hold firm peaks
30 ml	(2 tbs) butter
50 ml	(1/4 cup) parmesan cheese, grated

Place egg yolks and 2 whole eggs in a bowl. Beat until pale yellow. Season generously with salt and pepper.

Mix in cream with a fork. Set aside.

Fold egg whites into egg yolk mixture with a spatula.

Melt butter in a frying pan over high heat. When butter begins to foam, pour mixture into pan and cook over high heat. Shake pan often until eggs are almost set and bring edges toward the center.

When omelette is almost cooked, place cheese in the middle. Carefully slide omelette towards the left side until the

edge of the omelette overhangs by 1.2 cm (1/2 in).

Turn omelette upside down on a warm dish. Sprinkle with parsley and serve at once.

Omelette à la Mireille

Serves 2

1	*basic omelette recipe*
1	*small onion, thinly sliced*
15 ml	*(1 tbs) butter*
50 ml	*(1/4 cup) tomato sauce*
1 ml	*(1/4 tsp) tarragon*

45 ml   (3 tbs) cheddar cheese, grated
*   salt and pepper*

Melt butter in a sauté pan over high heat. When butter begins to foam, add onion and cook for 3 to 4 minutes.

Add tarragon and mix in tomato sauce. Season to taste with salt and pepper. Add cheese and remove from heat.

Prepare omelette. Place filling in middle of omelette, fold, and serve.

NOTE: For variety, reserve 30 ml (2 tbs) of filling and garnish over the omelette before serving.

The Art of Making Omelettes, see page 105.

Baked Eggs with Chicken Liver

Serves 4

500 g	(1 lb) chicken livers, trimmed
15 ml	(1 tbs) corn oil
8	eggs
	salt and pepper
250 ml	(1 cup) your favorite plain tomato sauce
1	buttered gratin dish

Preheat oven to 200°C (400°F).
Heat oil in a large sauté pan over high heat. Add chicken livers and sauté for 3 minutes on each side, or until well done. Slice livers, then place in the bottom of gratin dish.
Break eggs over livers and season with salt and pepper. Pour tomato sauce over eggs. Bake for 7 to 8 minutes.
Season to taste.

Mushroom Omelette

Serves 1

1	omelette
5 ml	(1 tsp) butter
6	mushrooms, thinly sliced
	salt
	freshly ground pepper

In a small sauté pan, melt butter over high heat. When butter begins to foam, reduce to medium high. Sauté mushrooms, uncovered, for 3 minutes. Stir frequently.
Season with salt and pepper.
Reserve 3 mushroom slices.
Spoon mushrooms into prepared omelette. Once omelette has been transferred to heated dish, make 3 incisions in omelette and decorate by inserting reserved mushroom slices.
Serve at once.

Mushroom Omelette

Chapter IV

Salad Dressing • Salads
Vegetables • Rice

Chick Pea Vinaigrette

Serves 4

1	tin chick peas
15 ml	(1 tbs) fresh chopped chives
15 ml	(1 tbs) fresh parsley, chopped
2	dried shallots, finely chopped
	juice of 1/2 lemon
30 ml	(2 tbs) wine vinegar
5 ml	(1 tsp) Dijon mustard
45 ml	(3 tbs) corn oil
	salt and pepper to taste

Drain chick peas. Place in a serving bowl. Mix in remaining ingredients. Chill for 2 hours before serving.

Mayonnaise

Yield: 250 ml (1 cup)

2	egg yolks
5 ml	(1 tsp) Dijon mustard OR 2 ml (1½ tsp) powdered English mustard
175 ml	(3/4 cup) vegetable or olive oil
5 ml	(1 tsp) wine vinegar
	salt
	freshly ground pepper
	lemon juice to taste

In a small mixing bowl, whisk egg yolks and mustard together until thick.
Add oil, drop by drop, whisking constantly.
As soon as mixture becomes thick, the flow of oil can be increased.
Incorporate vinegar, salt, and pepper to taste, and lemon juice.

In order to keep the mayonnaise for 5 to 6 days, mix in 5 ml (1 tsp) of hot water, cover with buttered wax paper and refrigerate. The hot water will prevent the mayonnaise from separating.

Green Mayonnaise

Add 15 ml (1 tbs) finely chopped fresh parsley to 250 ml (1 cup) mayonnaise before serving.

Roquefort Dressing

Yield: 300 ml (1-1/4 cups)

Use this dressing for salads and cold green vegetable hors d'oeuvre.

125 g	(1/4 lb) Roquefort cheese, soft and mashed
1 ml	(1/4 tsp) salt
	freshly ground pepper
5 ml	(1 tsp) Dijon mustard
15 ml	(1 tbs) dried shallot, finely chopped
5 ml	(1 tsp) fresh parsley, finely chopped
45 ml	(3 tbs) wine vinegar
105 ml	(7 tbs) olive oil
	juice of 1/4 lemon
30 ml	(2 tbs) heavy cream
2	drops Tabasco sauce

In a mixing bowl, blend salt, pepper, mustard, shallots, parsley, and wine vinegar. Mix with a whisk.
Add olive oil in a thin stream, whisking constantly.
Add Tabasco sauce.
Blend in lemon juice, cheese, and cream with a whisk.
Correct seasoning.

Vinaigrette Dressing for Potatoes

Yield: 4 potatoes

2 ml	(1/2 tsp) salt
	pepper to taste
5 ml	(1 tsp) imported mustard (such as Dijon)
30 ml	(2 tbs) wine vinegar
1	dried shallot, finely chopped
1	garlic clove, peeled, crushed, and chopped (optional)
45 ml	(3 tbs) vegetable or olive oil
	few drops of lemon juice
1	raw egg yolk (optional)

Blend all ingredients together in a small bowl.
Pour and toss over warm largely diced 2 cm (3/4 in) potatoes.

Technique: Mayonnaise

1 In a small mixing bowl, place egg yolks and mustard.

2 Add few drops of lemon juice.

3 Mix well. Add oil, drop by drop, whisking constantly. As soon as mixture becomes thick, the flow of oil can be increased.

Technique: Roquefort Dressing

1 In a mixing bowl, blend salt, pepper, mustard, shallot, parsley and wine vinegar.

2 Add olive oil in a thin stream, whisking constantly.

3 Blend in lemon juice, cheese and cream with a whisk. Correct seasoning.

Mayonnaise

Plum Sauce, Chinese Style

Yield: 500 ml (2 cups)

250 ml **(1 cup) Chinese plum sauce***
250 ml **(1 cup) white vinegar**
      few drops of lemon juice
      sugar (optional)

Combine all ingredients together in a mixing bowl.
Serve this sauce with butterfly shrimp, egg rolls, etc.

* Plum sauce can be obtained in stores that carry canned and dried Chinese cooking ingredients.

French Dressing with Ailloli

Serves 4

Serve this dressing with salads, cold vegetable hors d'oeuvre and cold poached fish.

175 ml **(3/4 cup) French dressing**
30 ml **(2 tbs) ailloli sauce**

Whisk the ailloli sauce into the French dressing. Serve.

French dressing, see page 50.
Ailloli, see page 80.

French Dressing with Garlic

Serves 4

Serve with salads, and cold vegetable hors-d'oeuvre.

1 ml   **(1/4 tsp) salt**
      freshly ground pepper to taste
5 ml   **(1 tsp) Dijon mustard**
15 ml **(1 tbs) dried shallot, finely chopped**
5 ml   **(1 tsp) fresh parsley, finely chopped**
45 ml **(3 tbs) wine vinegar**
2   **garlic cloves, crushed and finely chopped**
105-
135 ml **(7-9 tbs) olive oil**
      juice of 1/4 lemon

Using a whisk, combine all ingredients in a mixing bowl, with the exception of oil and lemon juice.
Add oil in a thin stream, whisking constantly.
Add lemon juice, blend well and correct seasoning.
This dressing will keep for 2 to 3 weeks if covered and refrigerated.
Shake dressing well before using.

Technique: French Dressing with Garlic

1 Place salt, pepper, mustard, shallot and parsley into a bowl.

2 Add garlic.

3 Add wine vinegar.

Salads

Chick-Pea Salad

Serves 4

1	540 ml (19 oz) can of chick-peas
1	red pepper, diced
2	dry shallots, chopped
1	clove of garlic, smashed and chopped
30 ml	(2 tbs) Dijon mustard
75 ml	(5 tbs) olive oil
15 ml	(1 tbs) chopped parsley
	lemon juice
	salt and pepper

Drain and place chick-peas in a bowl. Add peppers, shallots, garlic and mustard. Season with salt and pepper; mix well.

Add lemon juice, parsley and oil; mix and marinate for 1 hour.

Serve on lettuce leaves. Garnish with olives.

Caesar Salad

Serves 4

2	*garlic cloves, smashed and chopped*
1	*tin of anchovies, drained and chopped*
1	*egg, cooked 1 minute in boiling water*
90 ml	*(6 tbs) olive oil*
1	*large head of romaine lettuce, washed and dried*
250 ml	*(1 cup) garlic croutons*
50 ml	*(1/4 cup) grated parmesan cheese*
6	*slices of crisp bacon, chopped*
	juice of 1 lemon
	salt and pepper

Place garlic in a salad bowl. Add anchovies and coddled egg; mix well.

Sprinkle with lemon juice; mix again.

Add olive oil, in a thin stream, whisking constantly.

Break lettuce leaves into bite size pieces and place in salad bowl. Add croutons, grated cheese and bacon. Toss well. Correct seasoning. Serve.

Garlic Croutons, see page 134.

Salade St. Georges

Serves 4

1	*Boston lettuce, broken into bite size pieces*
1	*romaine lettuce, broken into bite size pieces*
50 ml	*(1/4 cup) cooked crisp bacon bits*
15 ml	*(1 tbs) fresh parsley, chopped*
5	*anchovy fillets, rinsed, drained and finely chopped*
1	*hard boiled egg, sliced*
1	*endive, broken into bite size pieces*
250 ml	*(1 cup) small cooked shrimp*
1	*small green pepper, cut into thin strips*
125 ml	*(1/2 cup) garlic croutons*
75 ml	*(1/3 cup) basic vinaigrette*

Arrange lettuce leaves in a large salad bowl.

Add endive pieces.

Top with remaining ingredients. Toss and season to taste.

Toss in vinaigrette and correct seasoning if necessary.

Garlic Croutons, see page 134.
Basic Vinaigrette, see page 50.

127

Mushroom Salad

250 g	(1/2 lb) fresh white mushrooms, washed, drained, dried, and finely sliced*
45 ml	(3 tbs) lemon juice
50 ml	(1/4 cup) scallions, sliced
45 ml	(3 tbs) olive oil
	salt and pepper
30 ml	(2 tbs) sour cream

Place mushrooms in a bowl and add all the remaining ingredients. Stir well and marinate for 1 hour.
Stir in sour cream just before serving.

* Remember use only fresh white mushrooms in this recipe.

The Everyday Salad

Serves 4

2	heads of Boston lettuce, cleaned
2	hard boiled eggs, cut in four
6	anchovy fillets, drained and chopped
15 ml	(1 tbs) fresh parsley, finely chopped
2	tomatoes, cut into wedges
2	cooked chicken breasts, skinned, deboned, and cut into 5 cm (2 in) pieces
	salt
	freshly ground pepper
125 ml	(1/2 cup) vinaigrette

Discard any wilted leaves from the lettuce. Dry leaves in a lettuce drier or on paper towels.
Break leaves into bite size pieces.
Mix all ingredients except salt, pepper, and vinaigrette, in a wooden salad bowl. Season salad to taste and toss in vinaigrette.

Vinaigrette, see page 50.

The Everyday Salad

Tomato Salad

Serves 4

4	large tomatoes, thinly sliced
15 ml	(1 tbs) fresh parsley, finely chopped
1	dry shallot, finely chopped
	salt and freshly ground pepper
30 ml	(2 tbs) wine vinegar
75 ml	(5 tbs) olive oil

Place tomato slices on a serving platter.
Mix remaining ingredients together, then
pour over tomatoes.
Set aside for 1 hour before serving.

Macaroni Salad

Serves 4

500 ml	(2 cups) cooked macaroni
2	hard boiled eggs, chopped
2 ml	(1/2 tsp) Dijon mustard
24	black olives, cut in two
1	stalk of celery, diced
1/2	red pepper, diced

50 ml	(1/4 cup) mayonnaise
	salt and pepper
	chopped parsley
	juice of 1/2 lemon

Place cooked macaroni in a bowl. Add chopped eggs and lemon juice; mix well. Season with salt and pepper. Add mustard; mix again.

Add remaining ingredients; mix and serve.

Mayonnaise, see page 119.

Boiled Beef Salad

Serves 4

500 g	*(1 lb) leftover boiled beef*
2	*tomatoes, cut in 4*
250 ml	*(1 cup) rice, cooked*
1	*onion, finely chopped*
2	*hard boiled eggs, peeled and finely chopped*
1	*ripe avocado, peeled and cut into strips*
50 ml	*(1/4 cup) vinaigrette*
15 ml	*(1 tbs) sour cream*
	lemon juice to taste
	salt and pepper
	romaine lettuce

Mix vinaigrette, sour cream, and lemon juice together. Set aside.

Cut beef into strips. Mix beef, rice, onion, egg, and avocado together. Add vinaigrette and season to taste.

Line a salad bowl with the cleaned and dried lettuce leaves.

Spoon beef mixture into bowl and garnish with tomato wedges.

Vinaigrette, see page 50.

Green Salad

Serves 4

1	*small romaine lettuce*
1	*small Boston lettuce*
	salt and pepper
30 ml	*(2 tbs) wine vinegar*
75-90 ml	*(5-6 tbs) corn oil*
5 ml	*(1 tsp) chives*
	juice of 1/4 lemon
1 ml	*(1/4 tsp) thyme*
1 ml	*(1/4 tsp) tarragon*
1 ml	*(1/4 tsp) basil*

Place herbs, chives, vinegar, salt, and pepper in a mixing bowl.

Gradually whisk in the oil, in a thin stream. Whisk in lemon juice and correct seasoning.

Break lettuce into bite size pieces and place into a salad bowl.

Toss in dressing, season, and serve.

For picnics: prepare dressing ahead of time and transport in a sealed container.

Rice and Artichoke Heart Salad

Wash and throughly dry lettuce. Place in a plastic bag and it will remain crisp for 24 hours.

Rice and Artichoke Heart Salad

Serves 4

375 ml	*(1 1/2 cups) cooked white rice*
125 g	*(1/4 lb) cooked green beans*
2	*dry shallots, chopped*

1	can of artichoke hearts, drained and cut in two
30 ml	(2 tbs) Dijon Mustard
45 ml	(3 tbs) wine vinegar
90 ml	(6 tbs) olive oil
15 ml	(1 tbs) chopped parsley
	lettuce leaves, washed and dried
	several drops of lemon juice
	sliced hard boiled eggs
	salt and pepper

Arrange lettuce leaves on a service platter. Set aside.

Place rice in a bowl. Add green beans, shallots and artichoke hearts. Season with salt and pepper.

Sprinkle with lemon juice; mix.

Add mustard; mix again.

Add vinegar and oil; incorporate well. Sprinkle with chopped parsley. Arrange rice salad on the lettuce leaves. Garnish with sliced eggs.

Serve.

133

Technique: Garlic Croutons

Garlic Croutons

Yield: 500 ml (2 cups)

500 ml *(2 cups) day old French bread, cut into cubes*
45 ml *(3 tbs) corn or olive oil fresh chopped garlic, to taste*

Place croutons on a cookie sheet. Broil, 20 cm (8 in) away from the top element, until browned. Turn frequently.
Heat oil in a sauté pan over high heat. When oil is very hot, add croutons and cook for several minutes.
Add garlic and cook for 1 to 2 minutes. Stir constantly.
Place croutons in a sealed container and refrigerate. They will keep for 1 to 2 weeks.

1 Place croutons on a cookie sheet and broil.

2 Add croutons to hot oil.

3 Add garlic.

Pol's Potato Salad

Serves 4

4	*medium size potatoes, scrubbed*
15 ml	*(1 tbs) chives, finely chopped*
30 ml	*(2 tbs) wine vinegar*
60 ml	*(4 tbs) olive oil*
15 ml	*(1 tbs) onions, finely chopped*
	salt and freshly ground pepper

Drop potatoes into a large saucepan three quarters filled with boiling, salted water. Cook over high heat.

When potatoes are done, transfer to a large heavy saucepan and dry the outsides over medium heat.

Remove saucepan from heat. Set aside for 15 minutes.

Peel potatoes. Cut into large cubes.

Place all ingredients in a bowl. Toss well. Cover the salad with wax paper and refrigerate for at least 4 hours.

Vegetable Julienne Salad

Serves 4

125 g	(1/4 lb) green beans
2	carrots, peeled and cut into julienne style
1	stalk of celery, cut into julienne style
1	green pepper, cut into julienne style
1/2	red pepper, cut into julienne style
50 ml	(1/4 cup) mayonnaise
15 ml	(1 tbs) sour cream
2	apples, peeled, quartered and sprinkled with lemon
50 ml	(1/4 cup) slivered almonds
	lemon juice
	salt and pepper
	lettuce leaves, washed and dried

Cook the green beans for 5 minutes in a saucepan containing 500 ml (2 cups) of salted boiling water.

Add remaining vegetables and continue to cook for 5 minutes.

Cool vegetables under cold water, drain well and pat dry.

Place vegetables in a bowl. Season with salt and pepper. Add mayonnaise and sour cream. Sprinkle with lemon juice; mix well.

Arrange lettuce leaves on a service platter. Place vegetable salad on lettuce leaves. Sprinkle with almonds. Garnish with apples. Serve.

Mayonnaise, see page 119.

Roquefort Salad

Serves 4

1	*large head of romaine lettuce*
90 g	*(3 oz) Roquefort or blue cheese*
1	*egg yolk*
5 ml	*(1 tsp) Dijon mustard*
45 ml	*(3 tbs) vinegar*
1	*small clove of garlic, smashed and chopped*
120 ml	*(8 tbs) olive oil*
15 ml	*(1 tbs) 10% cream*
	lemon juice
	salt and pepper

Break lettuce leaves into bite size pieces and place in a salad bowl. Season with salt and pepper. Set aside.

Place 3/4 of cheese in a bowl. Add egg yolk; blend well.

Add mustard and vinegar; mix with a whisk.

Add garlic and olive oil, in a thin stream, whisking constantly. Season to taste. Incorporate cream.

Pour vinaigrette over lettuce. Sprinkle with lemon juice; mix well.

Dice remaining cheese. Sprinkle over salad. Serve.

Leeks Vinaigrette

Serves 4

4	medium leeks OR 8 small leeks
	juice of 1/2 lemon
5 ml	(1 tsp) dry shallots
1 ml	(1/4 tsp) salt
1 ml	(1/4 tsp) pepper
5 ml	(1 tsp) Dijon mustard
5 ml	(1 tsp) freshly chopped parsley
5 ml	(1 tsp) freshly chopped chives
45 ml	(3 tbs) wine vinegar
100 ml	(7 tbs) corn oil
1	hard boiled egg (for garnish, optional)

Trim and discard most of the green section from the leeks. Slice through each leek, lengthwise almost to the base.

Rotate each leek by one quarter turn and slice through once again, lengthwise.

Spread out the leaves and clean thoroughly under cold running water. Tie leeks together, in two bunches, with kitchen string.

Pour lemon juice into a saucepan filled with boiling, salted water. Add leeks and blanch for 30 minutes at a simmer.

Once leeks are done, place under cold running water for 4 to 5 minutes. Discard string and drain on paper towel. Set aside.

Place all vinaigrette ingredients, except oil, in a bowl. Whisk together until creamy.

Gradually whisk in oil and correct seasoning.

Arrange leeks on a serving platter.

Pour the vinaigrette over leeks and refrigerate for 1 to 2 hours before serving.

Slice egg in two. Scoop out yolk and force yolk through a fine sieve.

Sprinkle the yolk onto the top part of the leeks. Sieve egg white and sprinkle on the base of the leeks.

Serve with lemon wedges.

Leeks Vinaigrette

Vegetables

Sauteed Zucchini

Serves 4

2	large zucchini, thinly sliced
30 ml	(2 tbs) corn oil
	salt and pepper
15 ml	(1 tbs) fresh parsley, chopped

Heat oil in a heavy, sauté pan.
When oil is very hot, sauté zucchini over high heat until browned. Stir frequently.
Season to taste and sprinkle with parsley.

Fresh Beans

Serves 4

625 g	(1¼ lb) string beans, washed and trimmed
30 ml	(2 tbs) butter
	salt and pepper

Drop beans in a large saucepan, three quarters filled with salted, boiling water.
Cover and blanch for 12 minutes.
Cool beans under cold running water for at least 4 minutes. Drain.
Melt butter in a heavy, medium saucepan over medium heat. Add beans when butter begins to foam, and reduce heat to low.
Cook, uncovered, for 5 to 6 minutes.
Season with salt, pepper, then serve.

Potato Gnocchi

Serves 4

1 kg	(2 lb) potatoes
250 ml	(1 cup) all purpose flour, sifted
2	eggs
2	egg yolks
	pinch of nutmeg
	dash of pepper
5 ml	(1 tsp) salt

Boil potatoes in salted water until tender.
Drain and cool. Peel.
Pass potatoes through a ricer or sieve.
Beat flour, eggs, egg yolks, nutmeg, pepper, and salt into potatoes.
Work mixture into small balls, about the size of a walnut. Should you have trouble working the mixture, dust your hands with flour.
Heat a large amount of water in a large stock pot. Lightly salt.
Drop potato balls* into simmering water.
Cook for about 10 minutes or until they rise to the surface.
Serve with tomato or mushroom sauce and sprinkle with gruyère or parmesan cheese before serving.
* Do not crowd the potato balls. It is best to cook them in 2 or 3 shifts.

Deep Fried Bananas

Batter for about 6 bananas

Bananas prepared in this manner are delicious served with chicken or seafood.

250 ml	(1 cup) all purpose flour
1 ml	(1/4 tsp) salt
30 ml	(2 tbs) vegetable oil
300 ml - 45 ml	(1¼ cups - 3 tbs) cold water
2	egg whites

Combine all ingredients except egg whites.
Refrigerate uncovered for 30 minutes.
Beat egg whites until very stiff then fold thoroughly into chilled batter.
Peel yellow bananas, cut lengthwise, then crosswise, resulting in four pieces per banana.
Dip each piece into batter, then deep fry in oil at 180°C (350°F).
Lift pieces from oil with a slotted spoon when crisp and golden.
Drain on paper towel a minute before serving.

Steamed Broccoli

Serves 4

1	bunch broccoli, cut into 2,5 cm (1 in) pieces
	lemon juice to taste
15 ml	(1 tbs) butter
	salt and pepper

Steam broccoli for 6 minutes, if frozen for 4 minutes.
Season to taste, sprinkle with lemon juice, and top with melted butter.

Spinach au Gratin

Serves 4

2	packages fresh spinach
1	garlic clove, chopped
	salt and lemon pepper to taste
15 ml	(1 tbs) butter
	pinch of nutmeg
375 ml	(1½ cups) warm thin white sauce
125-175 ml	(1/2-3/4 cup) grated cheddar cheese

Wash spinach, then trim off stalks.
Steam spinach for 3 to 4 minutes. Refresh spinach under cold running water.
Form leaves into balls and press firmly to squeeze out excess water.
Chop finely.
Melt butter in a saucepan. Add garlic, spinach, salt, lemon pepper, and nutmeg.
Cover and cook over medium heat for 3 to 4 minutes.
Stir in white sauce and simmer for 3 to 4 minutes.
Correct seasoning. Divide mixture between four oiled coquille St-Jacques shells or place in a gratin dish. Top with grated cheese and broil until bubbly and browned.

White Sauce Thin, see page 41.

Eggplant Turkish Style

Serves 4

4	medium eggplants OR 2 large
2	small tomatoes, peeled and diced
30 ml	(2 tbs) corn oil
1	onion, peeled and diced
2	garlic cloves, crushed and finely chopped
15 ml	(1 tbs) parsley, chopped
	pinch of cayenne pepper
1 ml	(1/4 tsp) basil
1 ml	(1/4 tsp) oregano
250 ml	(1 cup) cooked, leftover rice
375 ml	(1½ cups) cooked, leftover lamb, ground
50 ml	(1/4 cup) seasoned breadcrumbs
	salt and pepper

Preheat oven to 180°C (350°F).
Cut each eggplant in half, lengthwise.
With a sharp paring knife, score the flesh deeply in a criss-cross pattern. Score a deep line into the flesh, 0,65 cm (1/4 in) from the skin.
Brush oil over the flesh and set eggplants into an oiled baking dish. Bake for 40 minutes.
When done, scoop out the flesh, leaving 0,65 cm (1/4 in) layer of flesh in the shell. Set shells aside.
Chop flesh. Heat 30 ml (2 tbs) oil in a small sauté pan, over high heat.
Add onion and cook over medium heat until transparent. Stir occasionally.
Add tomatoes and continue to cook until most of the liquid has evaporated.
Add garlic, parsley, cayenne pepper, basil, oregano, and chopped eggplant flesh. Season with salt and pepper.
Cook over medium heat until eggplant flesh becomes transparent. Add rice and lamb.
Fill shells with the mixture. Sprinkle with breadcrumbs. Set shells back in the baking dish.
Bake for about 30 minutes.

Carrots, with Hollandaise Sauce

Serves 4

5	carrots peeled and cut into small sticks
15 ml	(1 tbs) sugar
1	mint leaf
1	Hollandaise sauce recipe
	salt and white pepper
	lemon juice

Preheat oven to 200°C (400°F).
Pour 750 ml (3 cups) water in a saucepan.
Season with salt. Sprinkle with lemon juice and bring to boil.
Add carrots, sugar and mint leaf; cover and cook 10 to 12 minutes.
As soon as the carrots are cooked, drain well and place in an ovenproof casserole.
Cover with hollandaise sauce.
Broil for 2 minutes. Serve.

Hollandaise Sauce, see page 50.

Carrots with Hollandaise Sauce

Potato Chips

Potato Chips

Serves 4

5 to 6	large potatoes, peeled and washed
	salt
	peanut oil, in deep-fryer, heated to 180°C (350°F)

With a vegetable slicer, slice the potatoes as thinly as possible.
Soak sliced potatoes in cold water, drain and dry well with paper towel.

Deep fry, a few at a time, in hot oil. Drain and place in a bowl.
Season with salt. Serve.

Potato Surprise

Serves 4

12	small potatoes
45 ml	(3 tbs) butter
25	fresh mushrooms, washed and dried

Potato Surprise

2	**chopped shallots**
1	**package of small shrimp**
15 ml	**(1 tbs) chopped parsley**
125 ml	**(1/2 cup) grated mozzarella cheese**
	salt and pepper

Preheat oven to 200°C (400°F).
Cook the potatoes in the oven.
As soon as the potatoes are cooked, remove from the oven. With a paring knife, cut off a 0,65 cm (1/4 in) thick top slice from each potato.
Scoop out half of the potato flesh. Set aside the potato shells and let cool.
Heat butter in a frying pan over medium heat. Add mushrooms, shallots and shrimp. Season with salt and pepper; cook 3 to 4 minutes.
Add parsley and cheese; mix well; cook for 2 minutes. Season to taste.
Stuff potatoes with the mixture. Sprinkle with grated cheese.
Broil for 3 minutes. Serve.

Surprise Baked Potatoes

Serves 6

6	Idaho potatoes
45 ml	(3 tbs) butter
	salt and pepper
	nutmeg to taste
1	egg, beaten
50 ml	(1/4 cup) cream
125 ml	(1/2 cup) gruyère or cheddar cheese, grated

Pierce potatoes in several locations with a fork. Bake, unpeeled, until tender. Preheat oven to broil.

Cut off a 0,65 cm (1/4 in) slice from the top of each potato.

Scoop out most of the flesh. Force flesh through a fine sieve or through the fine blade of a food mill.

Mix butter, salt, pepper, nutmeg, egg, and cream with potato flesh.

Place mixture in a pastry bag with a star tip. Force mixture into 6 potato shells. Use any remaining mixture as a garnish.

Sprinkle on cheese.

Set shells in an oiled baking dish and broil until golden brown.

Mushrooms Provençale

Serves 4

250 g	(1/2 lb) mushrooms, sliced
45 ml	(3 tbs) butter
1	dried shallot, finely chopped
1	garlic clove, finely chopped
15 ml	(1 tbs) fresh parsley, finely chopped
	salt and freshly ground pepper

Melt butter in a sauté pan over high heat. Add mushrooms, when butter begins to foam, and reduce heat to medium. Cook, uncovered for 5 minutes. Stir occasionally.

Add shallot, garlic, parsley, and season to taste.

Cook for another 3 minutes, stirring occasionally.

Surprise Baked Potatoes

Spiced Tomatoes

Serves 4

4	tomatoes, cut into 2.5 cm (1 in) slices
45 ml	(3 tbs) corn oil
50 ml	(1/4 cup) scallions, diced
30 ml	(2 tbs) brown sugar
2 ml	(1/2 tsp) paprika
	pinch of ground cloves
	salt and pepper

Mix brown sugar, cloves, paprika, salt, and pepper together.

Heat oil in a sauté pan. Sauté tomatoes for 5 minutes.

Add scallions. Sprinkle half of spice mixture over tomatoes. Turn slices over and cook for another 5 minutes.

Add remaining spice mixture, turn slices again. Cook for 2 minutes.

Serve at once.

Fried Won Ton

40	won ton skins*
250 g	(1/2 lb) lean pork, finely minced
	egg, beaten
	salt and pepper
1 ml	(1/4 tsp) monosodium glutimate
5 ml	(1 tsp) water
1 ml	(1/4 tsp) mixed herbs (selection optional)
	pinch of sesame oil (optional)
	oil for deep fryer

Blend pork, egg, water, and seasonings together.

Place 2 ml (1/2 tsp) of mixture on one corner of each won ton skin. Roll diagonally.

Deep fry won tons in preheated oil at 180°C (350°F), until golden brown.

Serve hot with plum or cherry sauce.

* Won ton skins can be founded in any chinese food store or in some of the leading supermarkets.

Buttered Flageolets

Serves 4

500 g	(1 lb) dried flageolets or small kidney beans
75 ml	(5 tbs) butter
1	onion, finely chopped
1	clove
	pinch of thyme
1	bay leaf
	salt and pepper
15 ml	(1 tbs) fresh parsley, chopped
15 ml	(1 tbs) fresh chives, chopped

Place beans in a saucepan. Add cold water 5 cm (2 in) above the beans. Soak beans for 12 hours; discard water.

Add the same amount of water to the saucepan. Set beans aside.

Melt 30 ml (2 tbs) butter in a small sauté pan. Cook onions over medium heat until transparent.

Add onions, clove, thyme, bay leaf, salt, and pepper to the saucepan containing the beans.

Place saucepan over high heat. Bring to a boil, then reduce to low.

Simmer for 1½ hours or until tender.

Mix remaining butter, parsley, and chives with the beans.

Braised Endives

Serves 4

12	endives, carefully washed
60 ml	(4 tbs) butter
	juice of 1 lemon
250 ml	(1 cup) hot basic chicken stock
	salt and pepper
30 ml	(2 tbs) flaked almonds

Preheat oven to 180°C (350°F).

Drop endives into a large saucepan, three quarters filled with salted, boiling water. Cover and blanch for 8 minutes over high heat.

Cool endives under running water for at least 4 minutes.

Drain and set endives into a buttered baking dish.

Dot endives with 45 ml (3 tbs) butter. Pour lemon juice and chicken stock over endives. Season to taste.

Cover dish with aluminum foil and bake for 30 minutes.

Transfer endives to a heated serving platter.

Place baking dish over high heat and reduce liquid by two thirds. Pour liquid over endives.

Melt remaining butter in a sauté pan over medium heat. Add almonds when butter begins to foam, and cook until golden. Stir frequently.

Spoon almonds over endives and serve.

Chicken Stock, see pages 33-34.

Technique: Braised Endives

1 Drop endives into a large saucepan, 3/4 filled with salted, boiling water. Cover and blanch for 8 minutes.

2 Cool endives for 4 minutes. Drain.

3 Place endives into a buttered baking dish.

4 Dot endives with butter. Add lemon juice and chicken stock. Cover and bake.

5 Transfer endives to a heated serving platter.

Asparagus Crêpe

Serves 4

750 ml	(3 cups) water
500 g	(1 lb) fresh asparagus
4	crêpes
375 ml	(1½ cups) hot white sauce
	lemon juice
	nutmeg
	paprika
	salt and pepper

Preheat oven to 180°C (350°F).
Pour water into a saucepan. Season with salt. Sprinkle with lemon juice; bring to boil.

Peel and cut off ends of asparagus. Place asparagus in boiling water; cover and cook 10 to 12 minutes.

As soon as the asparagus are cooked, drain and pat dry.

Divide asparagus between the 4 crêpes. Roll each crêpe and place in a buttered baking dish. Pour white sauce over the crêpes. Sprinkle with nutmeg. Cook 10 minutes in the oven.

Sprinkle with paprika. Serve.

White Sauce, see page 40.

Marinated Hot Vegetables

Serves 4 to 6

2	large potatoes, peeled and cut into large cubes
1	Spanish yellow pepper, cut into large cubes
1	stalk of celery, cut into large cubes
1	green or red pepper, cut into large cubes
24	fresh whole white button mushrooms, washed and dried
30 ml	(2 tbs) chopped shallots
15 ml	(1 tbs) Dijon mustard
45 ml	(3 tbs) wine vinegar
90 ml	(6 tbs) olive oil
15 ml	(1 tbs) chopped parsley
	lemon juice
	salt and pepper

Cook the potatoes for 8 to 9 minutes in boiling salted water. Add remaining vegetables and continue to cook for 7 minutes.

As soon as the vegetables are cooked, drain well and place in a bowl. Add mustard and remaining ingredients. Season well. Let cool.

Serve with pickles and toasted bread.

151

Zucchini Italian Style

Serves 4

2	*medium zucchini, washed* *salt and pepper* *peanut oil in a deep fryer, heat* *to 160°C (325°F)*

Slice zucchini in half, lengthwise. Cut into 1.2 cm (1/2 in) slices. Deep fry until golden brown. Drain on paper towel, then season with salt and pepper.

Potatoes au Gratin

Serves 4

4	*large potatoes, scrubbed*
1	*egg yolk*
45 ml	*(3 tbs) milk OR cream* *salt and white pepper* *pinch of nutmeg*
175 ml	*(3/4 cup) grated cheese*
30 ml	*(2 tbs) melted butter*

Parboil potatoes until tender.
Place in a large, heavy saucepan over medium heat and dry. Remove saucepan from heat and allow potatoes to cool for 15 minutes.
Peel and purée potatoes into a bowl.
Beat egg yolk with milk (cream) and mix into potatoes. Season with salt, pepper, and nutmeg. Mix in 125 ml (1/2 cup) grated cheese.
Spoon mixture into a buttered gratin dish. Sprinkle with remaining cheese and pour in melted butter.
If potatoes are hot when you add the cheese, simply broil until nicely brown.
If potatoes are cold, bake for 20 minutes at 200°C (400F); then broil for several minutes until brown.

Potatoes au Gratin

Spinach Crêpe

Serves 4

4	*packages of fresh spinach, washed and trimmed*
30 ml	*(2 tbs) butter*
1/2	*clove of garlic, smashed and chopped*
1 ml	*(1/4 tsp) nutmeg*
750 ml	*(3 cups) hot thin white sauce*
8	*crêpes*
50 ml	*(1/4 cup) spiced breadcrumbs*
	lemon juice
	melted butter
	salt and pepper

Preheat oven to 200°C (400°F).
Place the spinach in a large saucepan. Season with salt. Sprinkle with lemon juice.

Add 250 ml (1 cup) water; cover and cook 4 to 5 minutes. Refresh the spinach under cold running water.

Form the spinach into balls and press firmly, in order to squeeze out any excess water.

Chop the spinach finely. Set aside.

Melt butter in a frying pan. Add garlic and chopped spinach. Sprinkle with nutmeg; cover and cook 3 minutes.

Add white sauce. Season well; simmer 2 to 3 minutes.

Stuff the crêpes, roll and place in a buttered baking dish. Garnish with remaining spinach. Sprinkle with breadcrumbs and melted butter.

Cook 8 to 10 minutes in the oven. Serve.

White Sauce Thin, see page 41.

Ratatouille

Ratatouille

Serves 4

1	*small eggplant, peeled and sliced*
4	*small zucchini, thinly sliced*
2	*onions, peeled and thinly sliced*
4	*tomatoes*
50 ml	*(1/4 cup) corn oil*
	salt and pepper
	pinch of basil
2	*garlic cloves, crushed and finely chopped*
	pinch of coriander seeds
15 ml	*(1 tbs) fresh parsley, chopped*

Preheat oven to 180°C (350°F).

Blanch tomatoes in boiling water for 1 minute. Cool under cold running water. Peel and chop.

Heat half of the oil in a large ovenproof sauteuse. Add eggplant and cook over low heat for 12 to 15 minutes. Transfer to a bowl.

Heat remaining oil in the sauteuse. Cook onions and zucchini for 6 to 7 minutes over medium heat. Stir frequently.

Add tomatoes, garlic, salt, pepper, basil, and coriander seeds.

Add eggplant and cover. Cook in the oven for 30 minutes.

Garnish with parsley and serve.

155

Deep Fried Onion Rings

Serves 4

1	*large Spanish onion*
2	*egg whites*
250 ml	*(1 cup) flour*
	salt
	lemon pepper

Heat corn oil in a deep fryer to 180°C (350°F).
Slice onion into 0,65 cm (1/4 in) rings.
Mix flour, salt, and lemon pepper together.
Beat egg whites until they form stiff peaks.

Dip each onion ring into egg whites, then into the flour mixture.
Deep fry onion rings, several at a time, until golden.
Drain on paper towel and sprinkle with salt and lemon pepper.

Stuffed Tomatoes

Serves 4

8	*medium tomatoes*
45 ml	*(3 tbs) corn oil*
1	*onion, finely chopped*

Deep Fried Onion Rings

375 ml	(1½ cups) cooked rice
250 g	(1/2 lb) fresh mushrooms, finely chopped
60 ml	(4 tbs) 35% cream salt and pepper
1 ml	(1/4 tsp) cumin
1 ml	(1/4 tsp) parmesan cheese

Preheat oven to 190°C (375°F).
Cut a 0,65 cm (1/4 in) slice off the top of each tomato. Reserve the lids.
Scoop out tomato flesh with a spoon, leaving 0,65 (1/4 in) thick shell. Season insides with salt and pepper. Set aside.
Coarsely chop tomato flesh.

Heat oil in a large sauté pan over high heat. When hot, sauté onion for 3 to 4 minutes.
Add mushrooms, season, and continue to cook for 2 minutes. Add cumin, tomato flesh, rice and season again. Cook for 3 to 4 minutes at high heat.
Remove pan from heat and stir in cream. Spoon mixture into shells; season to taste. Set shells into a baking dish, just large enough to contain them. Top with cheese and place lids on top.
Increase oven to 200°C (400°F) and bake for 15 minutes.

Mexican Succotash

Serves 10

500 ml	(2 cups) frozen corn kernels
375 ml	(1½ cups) frozen peas, thawed
1	small zucchini, diced
1	small cucumber, diced
1	green pepper, seeded and diced
1	red pepper, seeded and diced
1	small onion, peeled and diced
45 ml	(3 tbs) corn oil
2	garlic cloves, crushed
45 ml	(3 tbs) fresh parsley, chopped

Place the corn in a steamer and cook for 2 minutes.
Add peas, zucchini, cucumber, peppers, and steam for 5 to 6 minutes. Set aside.
Heat oil in a deep saucepan. Cook garlic for 4 to 5 minutes. Discard garlic.
Cook onions, in the saucepan, until transparent.

Increase heat to high, and add vegetables.
Sauté until reheated.
Season with salt, pepper, and garnish with parsley.
Serve at once.

Breaded Tomatoes

Serves 4

4	*medium tomatoes*
2	*eggs*
50 ml	*(1/4 cup) corn oil*
	salt and pepper
125 ml	*(1 cup) seasoned breadcrumbs*

Mix eggs and oil together in a bowl.
Cut each tomato into 3 slices.
Season tomato with salt and pepper. Coat each slice with the egg mixture then with breadcrumbs.
Heat 30 ml (2 tbs) corn oil in a sauté pan.
When oil is hot, add tomatoes and sauté 5 or 6 at a time. Cook until golden brown.
Add more oil if required.

Dutchess Potatoes

Serves 4

4	large potatoes, scrubbed
2	egg yolks
45 ml	(3 tbs) milk
	salt and white pepper
	nutmeg to taste

Preheat oven to broil.

Drop potatoes into a large saucepan three quarters filled with salted, boiling water.

Cook over high heat until tender.

Transfer to a large, heavy saucepan and dry over medium heat.

Remove saucepan from heat and allow potatoes to stand for 15 minutes. Peel and rub potatoes through a sieve into a bowl.

Beat egg yolks and milk into potatoes. Season with salt, pepper, and nutmeg.

Spoon mixture into a pastry bag and form into desired shapes on a buttered baking dish.

Broil 15 cm (6 in) away from the top element, until brown.

Stuffed Green Peppers

Serves 4

4	large green peppers
500 g	(1 lb) Labrador shrimp, unfrozen and drained
6	slices of bacon, chopped
1	medium Spanish onion, chopped
2	garlic cloves, crushed and chopped
3	tomatoes, peeled and chopped
20 ml	(1½ tbs) corn oil
2	slices of white bread, trim crust, soak in 125 ml (1/2 cup) milk, then chop
2 ml	(1/2 tsp) oregano
	juice of 1/2 lemon
	salt and pepper

Preheat oven to 190°C (375°F).

Cut the tops off green peppers. Remove white fibers, seeds, and rinse well.

Plunge peppers in salted boiling water containing lemon juice. Cover and simmer for 5 minutes.

Drain, then arrange peppers in a buttered dish. Set aside.

Heat 5 ml (1 tsp) oil in a saucepan. When hot, add bacon and cook for 4 minutes.

Add onion, garlic, tomatoes, oregano, salt and pepper. Cook for 5 to 6 minutes.

Add bread and mix well. Remove mixture and set aside.

Pour remaining oil in the saucepan. When hot, sauté shrimps for 1 minute. Season with salt and pepper.

Return vegetable mixture to the saucepan; stir well.

Fill green peppers (do not pack) with the mixture.

Bake for 15 minutes.

Serve with your favorite tomato sauce.

Stuffed Onions

Serves 4

4	medium Spanish onions
1	can, 454 g (16 oz) stewed tomatoes, drained and coarsely chopped
250 g	(1/2 lb) mushrooms, chopped
375 g	(3/4 lb) sausage meat*
6	slices of bacon, chopped
125 ml	(1/2 cup) chicken stock, hot
20 ml	(1½ tbs) corn oil
5 ml	(1 tsp) parsley
2 ml	(1/2 tsp) tarragon
2	garlic cloves, crushed and chopped
	salt and pepper
2	celery stalks, chopped

Preheat oven to 190°C (375°F).

Peel onions. Cut off a thin slice from the top of each onion. Discard slices.

Cook onions in a saucepan containing about 5 cm (2 in) of boiling salted water. Cook for 25 minutes over medium low heat.

Drain and cool onions under cold running water for about 5 minutes.

Using a knife, core the center of the onions

about 0,65 cm (1/4 in) from the edge. Spoon out the centers, chop, and set aside. Place onion shells in a buttered baking dish; set aside.

Heat 5 ml (1 tsp) oil in a sauté pan over high heat. When hot, sauté bacon for 4 to 5 minutes. Add sausage meat and garlic. Season generously with salt and pepper. Cook for 7 minutes. Mix well, then remove mixture from pan and set aside.

Add remaining oil to pan. When hot, add chopped onions, mushrooms, celery, parsley, tarragon, and tomatoes. Stir, season to taste, and cook for 8 minutes.

Return meat to the pan, mix well, and correct seasoning.

Fill onions with mixture (do not pack). Pour chicken stock into the baking dish. Add stuffed onions and bake for 20 minutes.

Serve.

NOTE: If sausage meat is unavailable, use Farmer's sausages and remove meat from the casing.

Chicken Stock, see pages 33-34.

Parisienne Potatoes

Serves 4

6	*large potatoes, peeled and scrubbed*
60 ml	*(4 tbs) butter*
	salt and pepper
15 ml	*(1 tbs) fresh parsley, finely chopped*

Scoop out pieces of potato with a round vegetable scooping spoon. Try to make them as round as possible.

Place potato balls in cold water and let stand for 10 minutes.

Dry on paper towel.

Melt butter in a sauté pan over medium heat. When butter begins to foam, add potato balls and cook, uncovered, over low heat. Stir frequently.

When potatoes are golden brown, season with salt and pepper. Garnish with parsley and serve.

Technique: Parisienne Potatoes

1 Place potato balls in cold water and let stand for 10 minutes. Dry on paper towel.

2 Melt butter in a sauté pan over medium heat. Add potato balls and cook.

Mushroom Tomatoes

Serves 4

4	*large tomatoes*
15 ml	*(1 tbs) chopped parsley*
15 ml	*(1 tbs) fresh chives, chopped*
2	*garlic cloves, crushed and finely chopped*
45 ml	*(3 tbs) corn oil*
250 g	*(1/2 lb) mushrooms, finely chopped*
125 ml	*(1/2 cup) cheddar cheese, grated*
	salt and pepper

Preheat oven to 190°C (375°F).
Cut a 1,2 cm (1/2 in) slice from the tops of the tomatoes. Scoop out the flesh, leaving 0,65 cm (1/4 in) thick shell.
Season the insides with salt and pepper. Set aside.
Coarsely chop tomato flesh.
Place 15 ml (1 tbs) oil in a sauté pan over high heat. Add tomato flesh, herbs, garlic, salt, and pepper. Cook over high heat until the liquid evaporates. Stir frequently.
Heat remaining oil in another pan. Add mushrooms and sauté for 2 to 3 minutes over high heat.
Mix ingredients from both pans together.

Correct seasoning. Spoon mixture into tomato shells.
Set shells in an oiled baking dish just large enough to contain them.
Sprinkle with grated cheese and bake for 20 minutes.

Lyonnaise Potatoes

Serves 4

| 4 | potatoes, boiled, cooled, and cut into 1,2 cm (1/2 in) slices |
| 15 ml | (1 tbs) butter |

Lyonnaise Potatoes

30 ml	(2 tbs) vegetable oil
1	large onion, thinly sliced
	salt and pepper
15 ml	(1 tbs) parsley, finely chopped

Heat butter and oil in a sauté pan over high heat. When foam subsides, add potatoes and reduce heat to medium. Brown on one side.
Turn potatoes over, add onion, and continue to cook for 5 to 6 minutes.
Season to taste and garnish with parsley.

163

Rice Pilaf

Serves 4

250 ml	(1 cup) long grain converted rice
15 ml	(1 tbs) butter
15 ml	(1 tbs) onion, finely chopped
375 ml	(1½ cups) hot basic chicken stock
2 ml	(1/2 tsp) chervil
	pinch of thyme
	bay leaf
	salt and freshly ground pepper

Preheat oven to 180°C (350°F).
Place rice in a strainer and rinse under cold running water for several minutes. Drain and set aside.
In a heavy, ovenproof casserole, melt butter over medium heat. When butter foams, add onion. Cook for 2 to 3 minutes, stirring frequently.
Add rice, cook for 2 to 3 minutes. Stir frequently and do not brown.
Add chicken stock, herbs, salt, and pepper.
Bring to a boil over high heat. Cover and cook in the oven for 18 to 20 minutes. Stir rice before serving.

Chicken Stock, see pages 33-34.

Rice à l'Égyptienne

Serves 6

250 ml	(1 cup) long grain converted rice
15 ml	(1 tbs) butter
15 ml	(1 tbs) finely chopped onion
375 ml	(1½ cups) hot chicken stock
2 ml	(1/2 tsp) chervil
	pinch of thyme
	bay leaf
	salt and pepper
30 ml	(2 tbs) vegetable oil
75 ml	(1/3 cup) diced chicken liver
75 ml	(1/3 cup) diced cooked ham
75 ml	(1/3 cup) sliced mushrooms

Preheat oven to 180°C (350°F).
Place rice in a strainer and rinse under cold running water. Drain and set aside.
In a heavy, ovenproof casserole, melt butter over medium heat. When foaming, cook chopped onion for 2 to 3 minutes. Stir frequently.
Add rice and cook for 2 to 3 minutes. Stir frequently.
Add chicken stock, herbs, and season with salt and pepper. Bring to a boil over high heat. Cover and cook in the oven for 10 minutes.
While rice is in the oven, heat oil in a sauté pan over high heat. When hot, add liver and ham. Reduce heat to medium and cook for 2 to 3 minutes.
Add mushrooms and cook for another 2 to 3 minutes. Season to taste and remove pan from heat.
Add contents of sauté pan to rice. Mix, cover and cook in the oven for 8 to 10 minutes.

Chicken Stock, see pages 33-34.

Rice à l'Orientale

Serves 4

Best served with fish and seafood.

250 ml	(1 cup) rice, washed and drained
1	large red onion, thinly sliced
75 ml	(5 tbs) butter
5 ml	(1 tsp) saffron
500 ml	(2 cups) hot chicken stock
	salt and pepper
1	bay leaf
60 ml	(4 tbs) parmesan cheese, grated

Preheat oven to 160°C (325°F).
Melt 60 ml (4tbs) butter in an ovenproof casserole over medium high heat.
When butter becomes hot, add onion and cook for 2 to 3 minutes. Add rice, season to taste and cook for 3 to 4 minutes or until rice completely absorbs butter.
Pour chicken stock into the casserole, add bay leaf, and cover. Cook in the oven for 25 minutes.
5 minutes before the rice is cooked, add saffron, and continue to cook.
When cooked, stir in cheese and butter with a fork.

Chicken Stock, see pages 33-34.

Fluffy White Rice

Serves 4

250 ml	(1 cup) rice
2 ml	(1/2 tsp) salt
1	bay leaf
1.2 l	(5 cups) water
30 ml	(2 tbs) butter
15 ml	(1 tbs) parsley
	salt and pepper

Preheat oven to 180°C (350°F).
Wash and drain rice.
Pour water into a saucepan, add salt and bay leaf. Bring to a boil over high heat. Stir in rice, cover, and boil for 15 minutes. Drain rice, set in a buttered ovenproof mold. Cover with kitchen paper and place in the oven. Cook for 20 minutes.
Remove mold from oven, stir in butter with a fork, and season to taste. Serve with parsley as a garnish.

Rice à la Grecque

Serves 6

250 ml	(1 cup) long grain converted rice
15 ml	(1 tbs) butter
15 ml	(1 tbs) finely chopped onion
375 ml	(1½ cups) hot chicken stock
2 ml	(1/2 tsp) chervil
	pinch of thyme
	bay leaf
	salt and pepper
2	pork sausages
15 ml	(1 tbs) vegetable oil

Preheat oven to 180°C (350°F).
Set sausages in a saucepan three quarters filled with boiling water. Cook for 5 minutes over high heat. Drain and set aside.
Place rice in a strainer and rinse under cold running water. Drain and set aside. In a heavy, ovenproof casserole, melt butter over medium heat. When foaming, cook onion for 2 to 3 minutes. Stir frequently.

Fluffy Whrite Rice

Add rice and cook for 2 to 3 minutes, stirring frequently. Pour in chicken stock, herbs, and season with salt and pepper. Bring to a boil over high heat. Cover and cook in the oven for 10 minutes.
Cut sausages into 1,2 cm (1/2 in) pieces. While rice is cooking, heat oil in a sauté pan over high heat.
When oil is hot, add sausages. Reduce heat to medium and cook for 3 to 4 minutes. Add sausages to rice, cover, and continue to cook for 8 to 10 minutes.

Chicken Stock, see pages 33-34.

Riz d'Athènes

Serves 4

Ideal to serve with shish kebabs.

250 ml	*(1 cup) rice, washed and drained*
375 ml	*(1½ cups) hot chicken stock*
60 ml	*(4 tbs) butter*
1	*small onion, chopped*
1/2	*small lettuce head, chopped*
1	*red pepper, diced*
125 ml	*(1/2 cup) frozen peas*
	salt and pepper
5 ml	*(1 tsp) parsley*
1	*bay leaf*

Melt 30 ml (2 tbs) butter in an ovenproof casserole over medium heat. When hot, add onion and cook for 2 to 3 minutes. Stir in rice, cook for 2 to 3 minutes, and season to taste.

Preheat oven to 180°C (350°F).

Add chicken stock, drop in bay leaf, and cover. Cook in the oven for 16 minutes.

5 minutes before rice is cooked, melt remaining butter in a sauté pan over medium high heat.

Sauté lettuce, red pepper, and peas. Season, mix, and cook for 4 minutes. Add parsley. Mix vegetables with rice and cook for 1 more minute before serving.

Chicken Stock, see pages 33-34.

Risotto à la Milanaise

Serves 4

250 ml	(1 cup) rice, washed and drained
45 ml	(3 tbs) tomato paste
125 ml	(1/2 cup) mushrooms, sliced
75 ml	(5 tbs) butter
1	large red onion, thinly sliced
500 ml	(2 cups) hot chicken stock salt and pepper
1	bay leaf
60 ml	(4 tbs) parmesan cheese, grated

Preheat oven to 160°C (325°F).
Melt 60 ml (4tbs) butter in an overproof casserole over medium heat.
When butter foams, cook onion for 2 to 3 minutes. Add rice, season to taste, and continue to cook 3 to 4 minutes or until rice completely absorbs butter.
Pour in chicken stock, add bay leaf, and cover. Cook in the oven for 25 minutes.
8 minutes before the rice is cooked, melt remaining butter in a sauté pan. Sauté mushrooms over high heat for 2 to 3 minutes.
Mix tomato paste and mushrooms into rice. Continue to cook for 5 minutes.
When rice is cooked, stir in cheese with a fork. Serve.

Chicken Stock, see pages 33-34.

Risotto à la Piémontaise

Serves 4

250 ml	(1 cup) rice, washed and drained
1	large red onion, thinly sliced
75 ml	(5 tbs) butter
500 ml	(2 cups) hot chicken stock
60 ml	(4 tbs) parmesan cheese, grated salt and pepper
1	bay leaf

Preheat oven to 160°C (325°F).
Melt butter in an ovenproof casserole over medium high heat. When butter foams, add onion and cook for 2 to 3 minutes.
Add rice, season to taste, and cook for 3 to 4 minutes or until rice absorbs butter.

Add chicken stock, bay leaf, and correct seasoning.
Cover and cook in the oven for 25 minutes.
When rice is cooked, flake with a fork and stir in cheese and 15 ml (1 tbs) butter. Serve.

Chicken Stock, see pages 33-34.

Gruyère Rice

Serves 4

750 ml	(3 cups) cooked rice, hot
50 ml	(1/4 cup) gruyère cheese, grated* salt

Preheat oven to 180°C (350°F).
Mix rice and cheese together until cheese melts. Season to taste.
Place rice in a gratin dish. Cook in the oven for 10 minutes. Serve.

* The cheese can be replaced by another such as cheddar, emmenthal, etc.

Seafood Rice

Serves 4

30 ml	(2 tbs) vegetable oil
1	onion, finely chopped
1/2	branch of celery, diced
250 ml	(1 cup) long grain rice, washed and drained
375 ml	(1½ cups) hot chicken stock
250 g	(8 oz) shrimp, shelled
250 g	(8 oz) scallops
90 g	(3 oz) crab meat
1	clove of garlic, smashed and chopped
1	zucchini, thinly sliced
125 g	(1/4 lb) fresh mushrooms, thinly sliced
15 ml	(1 tbs) soy sauce lemon juice salt and pepper

Preheat oven to 180°C (350°F).
Heat 15 ml (1 tbs) oil in a ovenproof casserole. Add onions and celery; cover and cook for 2 minutes.

Seafood Rice

Add rice; mix and cook 2 minutes. Season with salt and pepper.

Add chicken stock; cover and cook in the oven for 18 minutes.

5 to 6 minutes before the end of cooking, heat remaining oil in a frying pan. Add seafood and garlic; cook 2 to 3 minutes over high heat.

Add zucchini, mushrooms and soy sauce; cook 2 minutes. Incorporate seafood and vegetables into rice. Finish cooking process.

Sprinkle with lemon juice. Serve with sliced lemon.

Chicken Stock, see pages 33-34.

Chapter V
Fish and Crustaceans

Broiled Fillet of Porgy with Shallot Butter

Serves 4

4	227 g (8 oz) porgy fillets
30 ml	(2 tbs) vegetable oil
	salt
	freshly ground pepper
	juice of 1/2 lemon
60 ml	(4 tbs) shallot butter

Preheat oven to broil.
Wash fillets under cold running water and dry with paper towel.
Brush fillets with the oil. Season with salt and pepper.
Arrange fillets in a baking dish.
Broil, 15 cm (6 in) away from top element for 7 minutes on each side. Baste occasionally with vegetable oil.
Remove baking dish from oven. Season again with salt and pepper. Squeeze lemon juice over the fillets.
Place 15 ml (1 tbs) shallot butter on each fillet. Return fillets to the oven and broil until shallot butter has melted.

Turbot au Gratin

Serves 4

375 ml	(1½ cups) basic fish court bouillon (stock)
1 kg	(2 lb) turbot fillets
375 ml	(1½ cups) white sauce, hot
250 g	(1/2 lb) mushrooms, sliced
1	dry shallot, finely chopped
15 ml	(1 tbs) parsley
1 ml	(1/4 tsp) fennel
75 ml	(5 tbs) white wine
15 ml	(1 tbs) butter
	salt and pepper
250 ml	(1 cup) parmesan cheese, grated

Butter a sauté pan. Add fillets, fish stock, salt, and pepper.
Cover with a sheet of buttered wax paper.
Bring to a boil and quickly turn fillets over.
Remove from heat and let stand for 2 minutes. Transfer to a baking dish.
Melt butter in a saucepan over high heat.

When butter begins to foam, add shallots and parsley. Cook for 1 minute.
Add mushrooms to saucepan, season to taste, and cook for 3 to 4 minutes over medium heat.
Add wine and reduce by 2/3.
Stir in white sauce, fennel, and season to taste.
Shower the sauce over fillets and sprinkle with cheese. Set dish in the oven preheated at broil for 3 to 4 minutes. Serve.

Court Bouillon, see page 33.
White Sauce, see page 40.

Pickerel à la Coker

Serves 4

4	250 g (1/2 lb) pickerel fillets
250 ml	(1 cup) milk
1 ml	(1/4 tsp) salt
250 ml	(1 cup) flour
45 ml	(3 tbs) butter
15 ml	(1 tbs) olive oil
30 ml	(2 tbs) capers
	salt and freshly ground pepper
15 ml	(1 tbs) fresh parsley, finely chopped
	juice 1/2 lemon

Preheat oven to 180°C (350°F).
Wash fillets under cold running water and drain on paper towel.
In a mixing bowl, combine milk and 1 ml (1/4 tsp) salt.
Dip fillets into the salted milk and then in the flour. Gently shake off excess flour. Set fillets aside on a sheet of wax paper.
Heat 30 ml (2 tbs) butter and olive oil in a sauté pan with an ovenproof or metal handle, over high heat. When foam subsides, add fillets and reduce heat to medium.
Cook, uncovered, for 4 to 5 minutes on each side. Season with salt and pepper.
Place the pan in the oven, uncovered, and bake fillets for 5 to 6 minutes, or until flesh is firm to the touch.
Transfer fillets to a heated platter.
Discard fat from sauté pan. Melt remaining butter and brown over medium heat for 1 minute.
Add lemon juice, capers, and parsley.
Pour sauce over fillets and serve at once.

Poached Salmon with Mousseline Sauce

Serves 4

4	slices of salmon, 2,5 cm (1 in) thick
	court bouillon
	salt and freshly ground pepper
250 ml	(1 cup) mousseline sauce

Arrange salmon slices in the bottom of a baking dish. If you have a fish poacher, place the fish on the grid and lower it to the bottom of fish poacher.

Cover salmon with court bouillon.
Cover, bring to a slow simmer over medium heat. Simmer for 15 to 20 minutes.
Transfer salmon to a heated serving platter; season.
Serve with the mousseline sauce.

Court Bouillon, see page 33.
Mousseline Sauce, see page 47.

Barbecued Salmon

Serves 4 to 6

1	1.4 kg (3 lb) piece of salmon*

172

Poached Salmon with Mousseline Sauce

50 ml	(1/4 cup) corn oil
	salt and pepper
	juice of 1 lemon
50 ml	(1/4 cup) butter
5 ml	(1 tsp) fresh parsley, chopped

Mix oil and juice of 1/2 lemon together; set aside.

Season salmon with salt and pepper. Brush generously with oil/lemon mixture.

Arrange fish on a fish barbecue rack. Set salmon, skin side down, on a hot grill at low position.

Sear skin side, then turn. Sear again. Baste fish generously and raise grill by 8 cm (3 in).

Continue to cook fish until it flakes with a fork. Turn and baste frequently during cooking process.

While fish is cooking, place a small saucepan on the grill. Melt butter, then mix in remaining lemon juice, salt, pepper, and parsley.

Pour sauce over individual portions of fish.

* Have your fishmonger split the piece of salmon down the spine.

Cod au Gratin

Serves 4

1 kg	*(2 lb) cod fillet*
	court bouillon
500 ml	*(2 cups) hot white sauce thick*
	salt
	freshly ground white pepper
	dash of cayenne pepper
125 ml	*(1/2 cup) grated cheese*

Preheat oven to broil.

Wash cod under cold running water.

Place cod in a buttered pan, season with salt and pepper. Cover with court bouillon.

Cover the pan with a sheet of buttered fireproof paper. Press the paper down so that it covers the cod.

Bring to a boil over medium heat. Reduce heat to low and simmer for 30 minutes or 15 minutes per 500 g (1 lb).

When fish is almost done, pour 30-45 ml (2-3 tbs) court bouillon (hot) into a medium size saucepan. Reduce for 1 minute over high heat.

Add white sauce, mix well, then season with salt, pepper, and cayenne pepper. Remove pan from heat.

Transfer cod to a buttered baking dish. Pour the sauce over cod and top with grated cheese.

Broil 15 cm (6 in) away from top element for 6 to 7 minutes.

Court Bouillon, see page 33
White Sauce Thick, see page 41.

Mussels à la Crème

Serves 4

2.3 kg	(5 lb) fresh mussels in the shell well washed and scrubbed
45 ml	(3 tbs) butter
30 ml	(2 tbs) dried shallots, finely chopped
250 ml	(1 cup) dry white wine
	salt
	freshly ground pepper
	pinch of thyme
2 ml	(1/2 tsp) chervil
250 ml	(1 cup) heavy cream
5 ml	(1 tsp) fresh parsley, finely chopped
30 ml	(2 tbs) kneaded butter (manié butter)

Place mussels, butter, shallots, wine, salt, pepper, thyme, and chervil in a large pot. Cover and cook over high heat until the shells open. Remove mussels from the pot and reserve liquid.

In a small saucepan, combine the reserved liquid, cream, and parsley. Reduce the liquid, over high heat for 6 to 8 minutes. Correct the seasoning.

Remove mussels from shells and arrange on a heated platter.

Thicken the sauce with kneaded butter and pour over mussels.

Kneaded Butter, see page 14.

Lake Trout Baked in Foil

Serves 4

1.4 kg	(3 lb) lake trout, cleaned
45 ml	(3 tbs) butter
1	onion, thinly sliced
2	dried shallots, finely chopped
1	carrot, thinly sliced
	salt and freshly ground pepper
1 ml	(1/4 tsp) thyme
1	bay leaf
	several fennel seeds
50 ml	(1/4 cup) dry white wine
60 ml	(4 tbs) water
	juice of 1/2 lemon
1	parsley sprig
	lemon wedges

Preheat oven to 180°C (350°F).
Melt butter in a saucepan over high heat.
When butter begins to foam, reduce heat to medium. Cook onion, shallot, carrot, herbs, uncovered for 4 minutes. Stir frequently.

Season with salt and pepper. Add wine, water, lemon juice, and parsley sprig.

Bring to a boil over high heat, then reduce to medium and simmer for 5 minutes. Remove saucepan from heat; set aside.

Wash trout under cold running water. Drain on paper towel.

Place trout in the middle of a large sheet of foil. Fold foil loosely over trout and secure one end.

Pour ingredients from the saucepan into the open end, then seal tightly.

Transfer trout to a baking dish. Bake for 45 minutes or 15 minutes per 500 g (1 lb).

Remove trout from the oven. Open one end of the foil and pour cooking liquid into a bowl. Reserve.

Unwrap trout and carefully transfer to a heated serving platter. Pour the reserved

liquid over the trout and top with the vegetables.

Decorate with lemon wedges.

Fillet of Perch with Mushrooms

Serves 4

8	*125 g (1/4 lb) perch fillets*
1	*egg*
250 ml	*(1 cup) milk*
1 ml	*(1/4 tsp) salt*
250 ml	*(1 cup) flour*
45 ml	*(3 tbs) clarified butter or vegetable oil*
	salt and freshly ground pepper
15 ml	*(1 tbs) butter*
250 g	*(1/2 lb) mushrooms, sliced*
	juice of 1/2 lemon
15 ml	*(1 tbs) fresh parsley, finely chopped*

Wash perch fillets under cold running water, then drain on paper towel.

Lightly beat egg in a mixing bowl. Add milk and 1 ml (1/4 tsp) salt; mix well.

Dip fillets into salted milk and then in the flour. Gently shake off excess flour.

Set aside on a sheet of wax paper.

Heat clarified butter in a sauté pan over high heat. When hot, add fillets and sauté, uncovered, for 4 minutes on each side. Season with salt and pepper.

Transfer fillets to a heated serving platter. Discard excess fat from pan. Melt remaining butter in the pan, over high heat. When butter begins to foam, reduce to medium and add mushrooms. Cook for 5 minutes, stirring occasionally. Add lemon juice, parsley, and season to taste.

Spoon over fillets and serve at once.

Clarified Butter, see page 13.

Baked Salmon in Foil

Serves 4 to 6

1	*1-1.4 kg (2-3 lb) whole salmon, center cut*
60 ml	*(4 tbs) butter*
5	*parsley sprigs*
2 ml	*(1/2 tsp) fennel*
50 ml	*(1/4 cup) water*
2	*bay leaves*
	juice of 2 lemons
	salt and pepper

Preheat oven to 200°C (400°F).

Clean and wash salmon under cold running water. Dry thoroughly.

Fill the cavity with 30 ml (2 tbs) butter, fennel, parsley, bay leaves, salt, pepper, and juice of 1 lemon.

Tie salmon with kitchen string and place in foil.

Place remaining butter over fish, shower with lemon juice and water, and season generously to taste.

Wrap salmon securely in the foil. Place in a baking dish and bake 17 to 20 minutes per 500 g (1 lb).

Unwrap salmon and arrange on a serving platter. Shower the fish with the cooking juices.

Decorate with fresh parsley and lemon slices. Serve at once.

Brochette of Mussels

Serves 4

16	*mussels*
16	*large mushrooms*
3	*green peppers, cut into 3.8 cm (1½ in) pieces*
16	*cherry tomatoes*
125 ml	*(1/2 cup) corn oil*
2	*garlic cloves, crushed*
	pepper
15 ml	*(1 tbs) fresh parsley, chopped*
	juice of 1 lemon
	seasoned breadcrumbs

Alternate the mussels, mushrooms, tomatoes, and pieces of green pepper on large skewers.

Arrange the brochettes into a stainless steel baking dish.

Mix corn oil, garlic, parsley, pepper, and lemon juice together. Pour over the brochettes.

Cover with a sheet of wax paper and refrigerate for 1 hour. Turn brochettes occasionally.

Roll brochettes in breadcrumbs.

Place brochettes on a hot oiled grill set at low position over the coals.

Sear on both sides. Raise grill by 7.5 cm (3 in), then cook for 2 to 3 minutes more.

Poached Halibut with Mushroom Sauce

Serves 4

4	*slices of halibut, 2,5 cm (1 in) thick*
	court bouillon
	salt and freshly ground pepper

THE SAUCE

250 g	*(1/2 lb) mushrooms, sliced*
30 ml	*(2 tbs) butter*
1	*dried shallot, finely chopped*
250 ml	*(1 cup) hot basic white sauce thin*
30 ml	*(2 tbs) hot court bouillon*
	salt and freshly ground pepper

Arrange fish in the bottom of a baking dish. If you have a fish poacher, place fish on the grid, and lower to the bottom of poacher.

Cover fish with court bouillon. Cover and bring to a slow simmer over medium heat. Simmer for 15 to 20 minutes.

While halibut is cooking, melt 30 ml (2 tbs) butter in a medium size heavy saucepan, over high heat. When butter begins to foam, add shallots, reduce to medium and cook, uncovered for 1 minute.

Add mushrooms; continue to cook for 3 to 4 minutes. Stir occasionally.

Mix in white sauce and 30 ml (2 tbs) court bouillon. Season to taste.

Transfer halibut to a serving platter. Season and pour sauce over the fish.

Court Bouillon, see page 33.
White Sauce Thin, see page 41.

Technique: Poached Halibut with Mushroom Sauce

1 Arrange fish in the bottom of a baking dish. Cover with court bouillon and cook.

2 Melt butter in a saucepan. Add shallots cook 1 minute.

3 Add mushrooms; continue to cook 3 to 4 minutes. Stir occasionally.

4 Mix in white sauce and 30 ml (2 tbs) court bouillon. Season to taste.

5 Transfer halibut to a serving platter. Season and pour sauce over the fish. Serve.

Salmon Poached in Court Bouillon

Serves 4

4	slices of salmon, 2.5 cm (1 in) thick
	court bouillon
45 ml	(3 tbs) butter
	juice of 1/2 lemon
15 ml	(1 tbs) fresh parsley, finely chopped
	salt and freshly ground pepper

Place salmon in the bottom of a baking dish. If you have a fish poacher, place the fish on the grid and lower it to the bottom of the poacher.

Cover salmon with court bouillon. Cover and bring to a slow simmer over medium heat. Simmer for 15 to 20 minutes.

Transfer salmon to a heated serving platter and season.

Pour 30 ml (2 tbs) court bouillon into a small saucepan. Reduce over high heat for 1 minute. Whisk in butter, then remove from heat.

Add lemon juice and parsley to the sauce, then pour over salmon.

Court Bouillon, see page 33.

Lake Trout Amandine

Serves 4

4	*284 g (10 oz) lake trout, cleaned*
1	*egg*
250 ml	*(1 cup) milk*
1 ml	*(1/4 tsp) salt*
250 ml	*(1 cup) flour*
45 ml	*(3 tbs) clarified butter or vegetable oil*
	salt and freshly ground pepper
15 ml	*(1 tbs) butter*
30 ml	*(2 tbs) flaked almonds juice of 1/2 lemon*
15 ml	*(1 tbs) fresh parsley, finely chopped*

Preheat oven to 180°C (350°F).
Wash trout under cold running water, then drain on paper towel. Season the insides with salt and pepper.
Lightly beat egg in a large mixing bowl. Add milk and 1 ml (1/4 tsp) salt; mix well. Dip trout in salted milk, then in flour. Gently shake off excess flour. Set aside on a sheet of wax paper.

Heat clarified butter in a sauté pan over high heat. When hot, add trout and sauté, uncovered, for 4 to 5 minutes on each side. Season with salt and pepper.

Place pan in the oven and bake trout, uncovered, for 5 to 6 minutes.

Transfer trout to a heated platter.

Discard excess fat from pan. Add remaining butter and brown for 1 minute over medium heat.

Add almonds and cook 1 minute. Add lemon juice and parsley.

Pour sauce over the trout and serve.

Clarified Butter, see page 13.

Fillet of Sole Nouvelle Cuisine Style

Serves 4

750 g	*(1¹/₂ lb) sole fillets*
1	*celery stalk, thinly sliced*
1	*cucumber, peeled and thinly sliced*
15 ml	*(1 tbs) butter*
	salt and pepper
	juice of 1/2 lemon
30 ml	*(2 tbs) dry white wine (or dry white vermouth)*

Melt butter in a saucepan over medium heat. When melted, add celery and cucumber.

Cover, increase to high heat. As soon as steam appears, reduce to low and steam vegetables for 5 minutes.

Arrange fillets in a buttered baking dish just large enough to hold them. Sprinkle with lemon juice and wine. Season.

When vegetables are done, season, and spoon over fillets.

Cover dish with a sheet of wax paper. Press paper so that it touches the surface of the ingredients.

Set pan over low heat and cook until fish is done. Timing should be about 4 to 5 minutes. Serve.

Filet of Sole Nouvelle Cuisine

Cod à l'Espagnole

Serves 4

1 kg	(2 lb) cod
30 ml	(2 tbs) butter
1	green pepper, seeded and thinly sliced
250 g	(1/2 lb) mushrooms, sliced
	pinch of thyme
2 ml	(1/2 tsp) tarragon
2 ml	(1/2 tsp) chervil
	pinch of fennel seeds
8	tomato wedges
1	bay leaf
	salt
	freshly ground pepper
125 ml	(1/2 cup) dry white wine
250 ml	(1 cup) water
	juice of 1/2 lemon
15 ml	(1 tbs) parsley, finely chopped

Preheat oven to 180°C (350°F).

Melt butter in a sauté pan over high heat until it begins to foam. Add green pepper, mushrooms, thyme, tarragon, chervil, and fennel seeds.

Reduce heat to medium, and cook uncovered for 4 minutes. Stir occasionally. Add tomatoes, bay leaf, and continue to cook for 1 minute. Season to taste and remove pan from heat.

Wash cod under cold running water; pat dry with paper towel.

Season cod with salt and pepper. Arrange in a buttered baking dish. Pour the contents from the pan over the cod.

Add wine, water, and correct the seasoning.

Cover baking dish with aluminum foil.

Bake for 30 minutes.

Transfer cod to a heated serving platter. Place baking dish over high heat and reduce the sauce for 3 to 4 minutes. Add lemon juice and discard bay leaf.

Pour the sauce over the fish. Garnish with chopped parsley.

Technique: Cod à l'Espagnole

1 Melt butter in a sauté pan. Add green pepper, mushrooms and spices; cook for 4 minutes. Stir occasionally.

2 Add tomatoes and bay leaf; continue to cook for 1 minute.

3 Arrange cod in a buttered baking dish. Pour the tomato mixture over the fish.

Perch au Gratin

Serves 4

750 g	(1¹/₂ lb) perch fillets
30 ml	(2 tbs) corn oil
250 g	(1/2 lb) mushrooms, finely chopped
15 ml	(1 tbs) parsley, chopped
	lemon juice
	salt and pepper
125 ml	(1/2 cup) breadcrumbs

Preheat oven to broil.
Sauté mushrooms in corn oil for 2 to 3 minutes. Season and mix in parsley.
Butter a gratin dish.
Season fillets and place in the gratin dish. Spread mushrooms over fish.
Sprinkle mushrooms with breadcrumbs, lemon juice, and several drops of oil.
Broil in the middle of the oven for 10 to 12 minutes.

Coquilles St. Jacques

Serves 4

500 g	(1 lb) raw scallops
2	dried shallots, finely chopped
50 ml	(1/4 cup) dry white wine
50 ml	(1/4 cup) water
	salt
	freshly ground pepper
250 ml	(1 cup) hot white sauce thick
	dash of cayenne pepper
30 ml	(2 tbs) thin cream
50 ml	(1/4 cup) grated gruyère cheese

Preheat oven to broil.

In a sauté pan, combine scallops, shallots, wine, water, salt, and pepper to taste. Cover with buttered wax paper. The paper must touch the surface of the ingredients. Bring to a boil over high heat. Reduce heat to medium and simmer for 5 minutes.

Remove scallops from the pan and transfer to a heated platter. Reduce remaining liquid by 2/3 over high heat. Reduce heat to medium, and blend in white sauce. Season with salt, pepper, and cayenne pepper. Simmer, uncovered, for 8 to 10 minutes.

Add scallops and cream to the sauce. Pour mixture into four coquille St. Jacques shells.

Sprinkle each shell with cheese. Broil 15 cm to 20 cm (6 to 8 in) away from top element for 8 to 10 minutes.

White Sauce Thick, see page 41.

Scampi Served in a Scallop Shell

Serves 4

20	uncooked scampi in the shell
	18 to 24 scampi per 500 g (1 lb)
375 ml	(1½ cups) water
	salt
	freshly ground pepper
5 ml	(1 tsp) white vinegar
125 ml	(1/2 cup) mayonnaise
5 ml	(1 tsp) curry powder
	juice of 1/4 lemon

Coquille St-Jacques

Scampi Served in Scallop Sheel

5 ml   *(1 tsp) fresh parsley, finely*
          chopped
4   *lemon wedges*

In a medium saucepan, bring the cold water, salt, vinegar, and scampi to a boil, over high heat.
Remove saucepan from heat and cool scampi under running water for at least 4 minutes.

With a pair of kitchen scissors, cut the inner shells of the scampi and remove scampi from the shell.
In a mixing bowl, combine scampi, mayonnaise, curry powder, lemon juice, and parsley.
Correct seasoning.
Spoon the mixture into the individual shells* and garnish with a lemon wedge.

Boiled Lobster

NOTE: If you wish, serve scampi mixture in salad bowl.

Boiled Lobster

1   *live lobster*
1   *basic fish stock recipe*

Plunge the live lobster into a large stock-pot three-quarters filled with boiling fish stock.

The cooking time is as follows:
for a 500 g (1 lb) lobster: 16 minutes;
for a 750 g (1½ lb) lobster: 19 minutes.

If you are cooking more than one lobster, they should be plunged into the boiling liquid one at a time.

Basic Fish Stock, see page 33.

Technique: How to Cook Shrimp

THERE ARE TWO WAYS TO COOK SHRIMP:

1 Wash shrimp under cold running water. Drop into a large saucepan filled with cold salted water* and 15 ml (1 tbs) white vinegar.
Bring water to boil over high heat. Once water reaches boiling point, the shrimp are cooked.
Immediately cool under running water for at least 4 minutes.

2 Wash shrimp under cold running water. Drop into a saucepan filled with boiling salted water and 15 ml (1 tbs) white vinegar.
Simmer for 3 minutes.
Immediately cool under running water for at least 4 minutes.
Should you wish to refrigerate the shrimp, do not remove the shell. Before using shrimp, shell and devein. To devein, slit shrimp along the back and remove black or white intestinal vein. Wash under cold running water.

* Court bouillon can be substituted.

Frog's Legs Provençale

Serves 4

1.1 kg	(2¹/₂ lb) frog's legs [9 per 500 g (1 lb)]
375 ml	(1¹/₂ cups) milk salt and pepper
250 ml	(1 cup) flour
60 ml	(4 tbs) butter
15 ml	(1 tbs) vegetable oil
3	garlic cloves, crushed and finely chopped
5 ml	(1 tsp) fresh parsley, finely chopped juice of 1/2 lemon

Wash frog's legs under cold running water. Fold legs along the joints and secure wider tip of leg, between opposite bone and ligament.

Combine milk, 1 ml (1/4 tsp) salt, and pepper in a mixing bowl. Soak frog's legs in bowl for 1 hour.
Dip legs in flour and gently shake off excess. Set legs on a sheet of wax paper.
Heat 30 ml (2 tbs) butter and 15 ml (1 tbs) oil in a sauté pan over medium heat. When foam subsides, add legs. For a crisp skin, cook for 7 to 8 minutes each side.
Should you prefer a softer skin, cook 4 minutes each side. Place in the oven for 4 to 5 minutes at 180°C (350°F).
When frog's legs are done, transfer to a heated serving platter.
Season with salt and pepper.
Pour off excess fat from pan. Add remaining butter and set over medium heat. When foaming, add garlic, parsley, and pepper.
Simmer for 1 to 2 minutes. Add lemon juice to sauce.
Pour sauce over frog's legs and serve.

Frog's Legs Provençale

Seafood à la Nautilus

Serves 4

250 g	(1/2 lb) scallops, thawed
250 g	(1/2 lb) shrimp
250 g	(1/2 lb) mushrooms, cut into 4
15 ml	(1 tbs) butter
15 ml	(1 tbs) dry shallots, chopped
	salt and pepper
5 ml	(1 tsp) mixed herbs
375 ml	(1½ cups) dry white wine
	juice of 1/4 lemon
250 ml	(1 cup) water
	beurre manié*, or
	10 ml (2 tsp) cornstarch, mixed
	with 15 ml (1 tbs) cold water

Butter a deep sauté pan. Add scallops, shrimp, mushrooms, shallots, herbs, lemon juice, wine, water, salt, and pepper.
Cover with a sheet of buttered wax paper. Bring to a boil and cook for 2 minutes. Remove pan from the heat.
Set aside for 3 minutes, then remove scallops, shrimp, and mushrooms.
Return pan to stove over high heat. Bring to a rapid boil. Reduce liquid until 375 ml (1½ cups) remain. Whisk in beurre manié while liquid is boiling.
Remove pan from the heat and add scallops, shrimp, and mushrooms. Season with salt, pepper, and lemon juice if necessary.

Seafood Brochette

* 30 ml (2 tbs) soft butter mixed with 15 ml (1 tbs) flour.

Kneaded Butter, see page 14.

Seafood Brochette

Serves 4

4	*wooden skewers*
4	*cherry tomatoes*
2	*perch filets, cubed*
12	*shrimps*
12	*scallops*
4	*green onions, cut into sticks*
1	*green pepper, cubed*
2	*slices of fresh pineapple, diced*

30 ml	*(2 tbs) oil*
15 ml	*(1 tbs) soy sauce*
	juice of 1/2 lemon
	salt and pepper

Preheat oven to 200°C (400°F).
On a skewer, alternate vegetables, fish, seafood and pineapple. Set aside.
Combine oil, lemon juice and soy sauce in a small bowl.
Brush brochettes with mixture. Season with salt and pepper. Place brochettes in a roasting pan. Broil, 15 cm (6 in) away from the broiling element, for 3 minutes on each side.
Bruch brochettes during cooking process.
Serve with rice and chutney sauce.

193

Fillet of Sole with Nuts

Fillet of Sole with Nuts

Serves 4

4	sole fillets
125 ml	(1/2 cup) slivered almonds
125 ml	(1/2 cup) chopped nuts
2	beaten eggs
50 ml	(1/4 cup) milk
15 ml	(1 tbs) vegetable oil
30 ml	(2 tbs) butter
	lemon juice
	salt and pepper

Preheat oven to 190°C (375°F).
Pour beaten eggs into a bowl. Add milk and whisk.
Spread almonds and nuts on a plate and mix well.

Season fish with salt and pepper. Dip fish into egg mixture then roll into nut mixture.
Heat butter and oil in a large frying pan over medium heat. Add fish; cook 3 minutes on each side.
Place in the oven and cook 3 to 4 minutes. Sprinkle with lemon juice. Serve with vegetables.

Sole Bretonne

Serves 4

8	125 g (4 oz) sole fillets
375 ml	(1½ cups) milk

Sole Bretonne

2	*eggs*
	salt
	freshly ground pepper
375 ml	*(1½ cups) flour*
90 ml	*(6 tbs) butter*
250 g	*(1/2 lb) mushrooms, cut in four*
375 g	*(3/4 lb) cooked shrimp, peeled, deveined, and coarsely chopped*
15 ml	*(1 tbs) capers*
15 ml	*(1 tbs) fresh parsley, finely chopped*
	juice of 1/2 lemon

Wash sole under cold running water and dry with paper towel.

In a mixing bowl, blend milk and eggs together with a whisk. Season fillets, then dip into the mixing bowl, then into the flour. Shake off excess flour.

Melt 60 ml (4 tbs) butter in a sauté pan over high heat. When the foam subsides, add fillets and reduce to medium.

Cook, uncovered, for 5 minutes on each side.

Season fillets and transfer to a heated serving plate.

Pour off excess fat from the pan.

Add remaining butter. Cook mushrooms, uncovered, for 2 minutes over medium heat. Stir occasionally. Add shrimp and cook for 2 minutes stirring occasionally. Season with salt and pepper. Add capers, parsley, lemon juice, and pour over the sole.

Lobster Newburg

Serves 4

2	750 g (1½ lb) lobsters, cooked*
15 ml	(1 tbs) butter
1	dry shallot, finely chopped
	paprika
6	mushrooms, cut into quarters
75 ml	(1/3 cup) Madeira wine OR cognac
125 ml	(1/2 cup) hot court bouillon
250 ml	(1 cup) heavy cream
15 ml	(1 tbs) heavy cream
	salt
	freshly ground pepper
30 ml	(2 tbs) kneaded butter (manié butter)
1	egg yolk

Shell the tail, claws, and body of the lobster. Reserve the greenish-brown tomalley (or liver) and the coral.

Cut the lobster flesh into 2 cm (3/4 in) pieces, on an angle.

In a heavy, medium size saucepan, melt butter over high heat. When it begins to foam, add lobster and shallot. Sprinkle with paprika.

Reduce heat to medium and cook, uncovered for 3 minutes. Stir frequently. Transfer lobster to a heated platter.

* Plunge live lobsters, one at a time, into a large stockpot three-quarters filled with boiling salted water. Cook for 19 minutes, then cool under running water.

THE SAUCE:

Increase the heat to high under the saucepan. Sauté mushrooms, uncovered for 4 minutes. Stir constantly.

Add wine and bring to a boil over high heat. Reduce wine for 2 minutes.

Add court bouillon and reduce for 3 to 4 minutes.

Add 250 ml (1 cup) heavy cream, bring to a boil, continue to cook for another 3 to 4 minutes.

Whisk in the kneaded butter over high heat.

Add the lobster and juices to the sauce. Correct seasoning.

In a small bowl, combine egg yolk, remaining cream, tomalley and coral. Stir into sauce.

Serve Lobster Newburg over a bed of rice.

Kneaded Butter, see page 14.
Court Bouillon, see page 33.

Salmon Loaf

Serves 4

Serve with an egg sauce or a dill & caper sauce.

45 ml	(3 tbs) butter
500 ml	(2 cups) cooked salmon, finely flaked
250 ml	(1 cup) cooked rice
3	hard boiled eggs, in thick slices
2	egg yolks
4	scallions, chopped
625 ml	(2½ cups) mushrooms, finely sliced
30 ml	(2 tbs) flour
125 ml	(1/2 cup) fish or light chicken stock
	salt and pepper
1	garlic clove, crushed and chopped

Generously butter a 1 l (4 cups) loaf pan with 15 ml (1 tbs) of butter. Set aside.

Melt 30 ml (2 tbs) butter in a sauté pan. When butter begins to foam, add scallions and garlic. Stir a few times, then add mushrooms. Cook over high heat for 4 minutes. Season to taste.

Remove pan from heat and transfer ingredients to a large bowl. Add flour and stock.

Mix in salmon, rice, and hard boiled eggs. Blend in egg yolks, one at a time, mixing well. Correct seasoning.

Transfer mixture to loaf pan. Set into a bain-marie (low pan filled with water), and place in the center of the oven. Bake for about 1 hour and 15 minutes.

Chicken Stock, see pages 33-34.
Dill and Caper Sauce, see page 41.

Lobster Newburg

Scallop Skewers

Scallop Skewers

Serves 4

125 g	(1/4 lb) large scallops
25	large mushrooms
2	broccoli stems, cut in 2,5 cm (1 in) pieces
2	large carrots, sliced salt and pepper
45 ml	(3 tbs) water juice of 1/2 lemon
45 ml	(3 tbs) garlic butter

Blanch broccoli and carrots in salted boiling water for 4 minutes. Drain and set aside.

Butter a saucepan and add scallops.

Pour the water and lemon juice over fish. Season with salt and pepper.

Cover and seal the inside of the pan with kitchen paper. Cook over medium for 2 minutes.

Remove scallops; discard liquid.

Place ingredients on skewers in the following order: a piece of broccoli, carrot, scal-

Grilled Cod

lop, and mushroom. Repeat procedure until all ingredients have been used. Season and brush with garlic butter.

Place skewers on a barbecue or shallow frying pan and cook for 2 minutes on each side.

Serve with lemon wedges.

Garlic Butter, see page 16.

Grilled Cod

Serves 4

4	198 g (7 oz) cod
60 ml	(4 tbs) corn oil
	juice of 1 lemon
5 ml	(1 tsp) paprika
	salt and pepper

Mix corn oil, lemon juice, and paprika together in a small bowl.

Preheat oven to broil.

Place fish in a baking pan. Brush fish with the oil mixture and season to taste.

Broil cod for 6 minutes, turn, and broil again for 4 minutes.

Transfer to a serving platter and serve with a lime butter sauce.

Broiled Lobster au Persil

Serves 4

1	750 g (1½ lb) lobster, cooked*
	juice of 1/2 lemon
6	slices of garlic butter 0,65 cm (1/4 in) thick
90 ml	(6 tbs) breadcrumbs
	salt
	pepper from the mill
5 ml	(1 tsp) fresh parsley

Preheat oven to broil.

Shell the tail and claws from the lobster.

Split lobster in half, lengthwise and place in an ovenproof baking dish.

Put 3 slices of garlic butter on each half. Season to taste and sprinkle with parsley. Add lemon juice and sprinkle with bread-crumbs.

Broil 15 cm (6 in) away from top element for about 10 minutes.

Garnish with parsley sprigs and lemon wedges.

* If possible, when you buy the lobster, have your fishmonger boil it for 7 minutes.

Or, plunge live lobster in a large stock-pot, three-quarters filled with boiling salted water and cook for 7 minutes. Re-move and set aside until cooled.

Garlic Butter, see page 16.

Alaska Crab Legs

Serves 4

1.8 kg	(4 lb) crab legs, cut into 12 cm (5 in) pieces
250 g	(1/2 lb) garlic butter, room temperature

Preheat oven to 190°C (375°F).

Break crab shells every 5 cm (2 in).

Fill a pastry bag with garlic butter. Force butter inside crab shells, through the fissures.

Set crab in a baking dish. Cook in the oven for 15 minutes. Serve with lemon wedges.

Garlic Butter, see page 16.

Broiled Lobster au Persil

Poached Salmon with Vegetables

Poached Salmon with Vegetables

Serves 4

4	salmon steaks
1	branch of celery, thinly sliced
1	bay leaf
3	sprigs of parsley
2	carrots, peeled and cut into julienne style
1	zucchini, cut into julienne style
30 ml	(2 tbs) butter
15 ml	(1 tbs) chopped parsley
	juice of 1½ lemon
	salt and pepper

Place salmon steaks into a roasting pan and cover with cold water. Season with salt and sprinkle with lemon juice. Add celery, bay leaf and parsley.

Bring to boil and remove from the stove. Let salmon steaks simmer in the hot liquid for 15 minutes.

Place carrots and zucchini into a small saucepan. Add 250 ml (1 cup) water. Season with salt; cover and cook for 3 minutes over high heat. Drain.

Place butter, parsley and lemon juice into a small casserole. Cook until butter is completely melted.

Arrange salmon steaks in a service platter. Garnish with vegetables. Pour melted butter over fish. Serve.

Shrimp and Tomato Sauce

Serves 4

30 ml	*(2 tbs) corn oil*
2	*garlic cloves, finely chopped*
500 ml	*(2 cups) canned tomatoes, drained and coarsely chopped*
250 g	*(1/2 lb) Matane shrimp, defrosted*
	salt and pepper

Shrimp and Tomato Sauce

50 ml	*(1/4 cup) parmesan cheese, grated*

Heat 15 ml (1 tbs) oil in a deep sauté pan. When very hot, add shrimp and sauté for 1 minute. Set aside.

Heat remaining oil in the same pan. Add tomatoes and garlic.

Season with salt and pepper. Evaporate liquid over high heat. Stir frequently.

Add shrimp to pan. Pour mixture over your choice of pasta and sprinkle with grated cheese.

Shrimp with Peas

Serves 3 to 4

500 g	(1 lb) raw shrimp, peeled and deveined
500 g	(1 lb) peas, frozen variety, defrosted
10 ml	(2 tsp) cornstarch
1	egg white
10 ml	(2 tsp) dry sherry
5 ml	(1 tsp) salt
30 ml	(2 tbs) corn oil
1	scallion, cut into 5 cm (2 in) pieces
3	slices fresh ginger root, cut into thin slices

Lightly coat shrimp with cornstarch. Mix in egg, sherry, and salt.

Place a large sauté pan over high heat for 30 seconds. Add oil so that it evenly coats bottom.

Add scallion and ginger root. Fry, while stirring constantly, for 30 seconds. Remove and discard. Immediately add shrimp and stir fry for 2 minutes, or until pink.

Add peas and stir fry for 3 minutes.

Season to taste and serve at once.

Deep Fried Fish

Serves 4

6	sole filets, washed, dried and cut into strips of 1.2 cm (1/2 in) wide
375 ml	(1½ cups) flour
3	eggs
250 ml	(1 cup) milk
5 ml	(1 tsp) vegetable oil
500 ml	(2 cups) breadcrumbs
	salt and pepper

Peanut oil in a deep-fryer heated to 180°C (350°F).

Season fish with salt and pepper and roll in flour.

Shrimp with Peas

Fish and Crustaceans

Place eggs in a bowl. Add milk; mix well.
Add vegetable oil and mix again.
Dip fish into milk and egg mixture and roll
in breadcrumbs.

Deep Fried Fish

Deep fry 3 minutes in hot oil.
Drain and serve with french fries.

Scampi au Gratin

Scampi au Gratin

Serves 4

32	scampi, (18-24 scampi per 500 g (1 lb))
	salt and pepper
	juice of 1 lemon
125 ml	(1/2 cup) garlic butter*, room temperature
125 ml	(1/2 cup) breadcrumbs

Preheat oven to 200°C (400°F).

Wash scampi under cold running water. Cut scampi, 3/4 of the way through, down along the back. Remove black or white intestinal vein. Open shells so that scampi will lie flat.

Set scampi, flat, in a buttered baking dish. Season with salt and pepper. Add lemon juice and dab 2 ml (1/2 tsp) garlic butter on each. Sprinkle with breadcrumbs. Broil, 15 cm (6 in) away from the top element, for 8 to 10 minutes.

* Shallot butter can be substituted.

Garlic Butter, see page 16.

Fish Loaf the Easy Way

Serves

This loaf is excellent served with hollandaise or egg sauce.

45 ml	(3 tbs) soft butter
45 ml	(3 tbs) breadcrumbs
3	slices of bread, remove the crust
60 ml	(4 tbs) 35% cream
1	onion, chopped
5	anchovy filets
2	chives, chopped
625 ml	(2½ cups) sole filets, chopped
1	fresh dill, chopped
	juice of 1/2 lemon
	salt and pepper
	pinch of lemon pepper
	pinch of cayenne pepper
	pinch of fennel
3	egg yolks
3	egg whites

Preheat oven to 180°C (350°F).
Generously butter a 1 *l* (4 cups) meat loaf pan. Sprinkle the bottom with breadcrumbs; set aside.
Pour cream in a bowl and soak bread for about 10 to 15 minutes.
Melt butter in a sauté pan. Sauté onions, anchovy filets, and chives for 3 to 4 minutes over medium heat. Remove ingredients and transfer to a large bowl.
Add bread and remaining ingredients, except eggs, to the large bowl.
Beat mixture with an electric hand beater for 4 minutes or until all ingredients are well incorporated. Add egg yolks, one at a time, continue to beat for several minutes.
In a separate bowl, beat egg whites until firm. Add to remaining ingredients and blend well.
Transfer mixture to the loaf pan. Set the pan into a bain-marie (low pan filled with water) and place in the center of the oven.
Cook for about 1 hour and 15 minutes.
NOTE: If the top of the loaf is firm when pressed with your finger, it is done.

Hollandaise Sauce, see page 50.

Lobster à la Lincoln

Serves 4

2	750 g (1½ lb) lobsters, cooked
45 ml	(3 tbs) butter
2	dry shallots, finely chopped
250 g	(1/2 lb) mushrooms, sliced
1	garlic clove, crushed and finely chopped
2 ml	(1/2 tsp) tarragon
375 ml	(1½ cups) hot basic thin white sauce
	salt and pepper
	Worcestershire sauce
5 ml	(1 tsp) english powdered mustard
50 ml	(1/4 cup) mozzarella cheese, grated
	parsley sprigs
	lemon wedges

Preheat oven to broil.
Shell tail and claws from lobsters. Split lobsters in half, lengthwise. Remove meat from shell and scrape clean.
Reserve liquid, tomalley, and coral.
Broil the shell 15 cm (6 in) away from the top element, for 5 to 6 minutes. Set empty shell aside.
Heat butter over high heat in a sauté pan. When foaming, add mushrooms, shallots, garlic, and tarragon. Reduce heat to medium. Cook for 4 minutes, stirring frequently.
Pour in white sauce, add lobster liquid, tomalley, and coral. Season to taste with salt and pepper. Add Worcestershire sauce and mix in mustard.
Set empty shells in a buttered baking dish. Spoon lobster mixture into shells*. Sprinkle with grated cheese.
Broil, 15 cm (6 in) away from the top element, for 6 minutes.
Garnish with parsley sprigs and lemon wedges.

* Or use a gratin dish.

White Sauce Thin, see page 41.

Lobster à la Lincoln

Filet of Sole with Mushrooms

Fillet of Sole with Mushrooms

Serves 4

4	sole fillets
250 ml	(1 cup) flour
30 ml	(2 tbs) melted butter
30 ml	(2 tbs) oil
250 g	(1/2 lb) mushrooms, washed and sliced
30 ml	(2 tbs) chopped shallots
15 ml	(1 tbs) chopped parsley
	lemon juice
	salt and pepper

Season fish with salt and pepper; then, roll in flour.

Melt butter in a frying pan. Add fish; cook, over medium heat, 2 minutes on each side. Remove from frying pan and transfer to service platter. Keep hot in the oven at 70°C (150°F).

Pour oil into the frying pan. Add mushrooms and shallots. Season with salt and pepper; cook 3 to 4 minutes.

Add chopped parsley. Sprinkle with lemon juice. Pour mixture over fish. Serve.

Shrimp Provençale

Shrimp Provençale

Serves 4

1 kg	*(2 lb) cooked shrimp, shelled and deveined*
	[15-20 shrimp per 500 g (1 lb)]
30 ml	*(2 tbs) vegetable or olive oil*
1	*796 ml (28 oz) can tomatoes, drained and coarsely chopped*
2	*garlic cloves, crushed and finely chopped*
2 ml	*(1/2) tarragon*
2 ml	*(1/2) oregano*
	salt and pepper
30 ml	*(2 tbs) butter*
15 ml	*(1 tbs) fresh parsley, finely chopped*

Heat oil in a heavy medium size saucepan set over high heat. When hot, add tomatoes, garlic, tarragon, and oregano. Reduce heat to medium and cook for 9 to 10 minutes. Stir occasionally. Season with salt and pepper.

Melt butter in a deep sauté pan over high heat. When foam subsides, add shrimp. Sauté for 2 minutes, stirring frequently. Mix tomato sauce with shrimp; correct seasoning.

Garnish with chopped parsley and serve.

211

Chapter VI
Fowl and Game
Meat and Variety Meats

Fried Chicken Legs

Serves 4

4	chicken legs, skinned
250 ml	(1 cup) flour
50 ml	(1/4 cup) 10% cream
3	beaten eggs
500 ml	(2 cups) breadcrumbs
30 ml	(2 tbs) peanut oil
	several drops Tabasco sauce
	salt and pepper

Preheat oven to 190°C (375°F).
Season chicken legs with salt and pepper, then flour.
Mix cream with beaten eggs. Sprinkle with Tabasco sauce. Dip chicken legs in the mixture and coat with breadcrumbs.
Heat oil in a sauté pan. Add chicken legs; cook 3 to 4 minutes on each side. Then, continue to cook in the oven for 10 to 12 minutes.
Serve with a barbecue sauce.

Chicken aux Olives

Serves 6

1	1.4 kg (3 lb) chicken, cut into 8 pieces
250 g	(1/2 lb) bacon, diced
36	pitted olives
7	anchovy fillets, diced
15 ml	(1 tbs) capers
5 ml	(1 tsp) parsley
250 ml	(1 cup) white wine
250 ml	(1 cup) hot chicken stock
	salt and pepper

Wash chicken pieces under cold running water. Dry thoroughly with paper towel. Season generously with salt and pepper. Place bacon in a saucepan over medium heat and cook until crisp. Remove and set aside.
Add chicken to remaining bacon fat and brown on both sides until golden. Cover, reduce heat to low, and cook for 40 minutes.
Add olives, anchovy filets, capers, parsley, and bacon. Cook for 1 to 2 minutes. Add wine and reduce by half over high heat.
Transfer chicken mixture to a warm serving platter.
Pour chicken stock into saucepan and cook for 3 to 4 minutes. Pour this clear sauce over chicken and top with parsley.

Chicken Stock, see pages 33-34.

Roast Chicken

Serves 4

1.4 kg	(3 lb) chicken
	salt and pepper
60 ml	(4 tbs) butter, room temperature
30 ml	(2 tbs) carrots, diced
30 ml	(2 tbs) onions, diced
15 ml	(1 tbs) celery, diced
2 ml	(1/2 tsp) chervil
2 ml	(1/2 tsp) fresh parsley, finely chopped
375 ml	(1½ cups) hot chicken stock

Preheat oven to 200°C (400°F).
Wash chicken under cold running water. Thoroughly dry both inside and out with paper towel. Season main cavity with salt and pepper. Place 15 ml (1 tbs) butter inside cavity and truss with kitchen string. Spread remaining butter over outside of chicken: season with salt and pepper.
Set chicken in a roasting pan in the oven. After chicken has been in oven for 15 to 20 minutes, reduce heat to 180°C (350°F). Baste occasionally.
Roast for 60 to 70 minutes, then transfer to a heated serving platter.
Add vegetables and chervil to the fat in roasting pan. Cook over medium heat for 3 minutes. Add chicken stock and season with salt and pepper.
Pour contents into a medium size saucepan. Bring to a boil over high heat and boil briskly for 4 to 5 minutes.
Strain and skim off as much surface fat as possible.
Serve sauce separate from chicken.

Chicken Stock, see pages 33-34.

Fried Chicken legs

Duck à l'Orange

Serves 2

1	1.4 kg (3 lb) duck
7	oranges
2	lemons
	salt
	freshly ground pepper
30 ml	(2 tbs) diced carrots
30 ml	(2 tbs) diced onions
15 ml	(1 tbs) diced celery
	bay leaf
	pinch of thyme
1 ml	(1/4 tsp) basil
500 ml	(2 cups) dry red wine
500 ml	(2 cups) hot basic brown sauce, thin
125 ml	(1/2 cup) sugar
45 ml	(3 tbs) white vinegar
125 ml	(1/2 cup) Curaçao
5 ml	(1 tsp) cornstarch

Preheat oven to 220°C (425°F).

Trim excess fat from the duck. Wash duck under cold running water. Thoroughly dry inside and out with paper towel.

Rub outside of duck with 2 oranges which have been cut in half. Save oranges for other use if desired.

Season the main cavity with salt and pepper. Cut 1 orange and 1 lemon into 4 wedges. Place inside the duck. Truss duck with white kitchen string.

Place duck in a roasting pan. Brown in the oven for 30 minutes.

Squeeze the juice of 1 orange over duck. Reduce oven heat to 180°C (350°F) and roast duck for 1½ hours. To be sure duck is cooked, pierce thigh with a fork. If no trace of blood is apparent, the duck is cooked.

Set duck aside on a heated platter.

Discard 2/3 of the fat in roasting pan. Place pan over medium heat. Add diced vegetables and herbs. Cook, uncovered for 5 minutes.

Add red wine, increase heat to high and reduce liquid by 2/3. Add brown sauce and season with salt and pepper. Bring to a boil and simmer over low heat for 2 minutes.

In a separate saucepan, place sugar and vinegar over high heat. Bring to a boil, then reduce to medium. As soon as mixture becomes dark brown, remove from heat.

Add the juice of 2 oranges and return to stove. When mixture becomes liquidy, pour into roasting pan. Strain sauce.

In a small dish, dissolve cornstarch in Curaçao, then mix into sauce.

Remove rind from 1 orange and 1 lemon. Plunge rind into a saucepan 3/4 filled with boiling water. Blanch for 3 to 4 minutes. Drain on paper towel.

Carve duck and arrange on a heated service platter. Pour any drippings from duck into sauce. Pour sauce over duck and garnish with blanched rinds.

Basic Thin Brown Sauce, see page 42.

Chicken Vol-au-Vent

Serves 4-6

1	1.4 kg (3 lb) chicken, poached with:
	2 celery stalks
	1 leek, sliced
	1 bouquet garni, consisting of:
	1 ml (1/4 tsp) thyme
	2 ml (1/2 tsp) chervil
	1 ml (1/4 tsp) basil
	1 clove
	2 sprigs fresh parsley
	1 celery stalk
60 ml	(4 tbs) butter
45 ml	(3 tbs) flour
500 ml	(2 cups) hot chicken stock
250 g	(1/2 lb) mushrooms, quartered
1	onion, quartered
1	small can of red pimento, diced
45 ml	(3 tbs) 35% cream (optional)
5 ml	(1 tsp) parsley
	salt and pepper

Wash chicken under cold running water. Place chicken and poaching ingredients listed in a stockpot. Cover with cold water; season with salt and pepper.

Bring liquid to a boil, reduce heat to low and simmer for 1 hour. Skim liquid occasionally.

Remove chicken and cool. Skin, debone, and dice. Set aside.

Chicken vol-au-vent

Melt 45 ml (3 tbs) butter in a saucepan over medium heat. When hot, add flour and cook for 3 minutes. Stir constantly with a whisk.

Gradually pour in chicken stock. Season with salt and pepper.

Reduce heat to low and continue cooking for 8 minutes.

Melt remaining butter in a sauté pan. When butter foams, add onions, mushrooms, and cook for 2 minutes. Season with salt and pepper.

Add red pimento and correct seasoning. Add parsley.

Transfer mushroom mixture to the saucepan. Mix in chicken and stir in cream. Serve.

This dish is excellent served in pastry shells, on toast, or over fluffy white rice.

NOTE: Do not discard the poaching liquid as it can be used in the making of soups or sauces.

Chicken Stock, see pages 33-34.

Cashew Chicken

Serves 4

2	chicken breasts
30 ml	(2 tbs) corn oil
250 ml	(1 cup) celery, thinly sliced
2	stalks of chinese cabbage, thinly sliced
250 ml	(1 cup) cashews
250 ml	(1 cup) warm chicken stock
1 ml	(1/4 tsp) powdered tarragon
2 ml	(1/2 tsp) chervil
30 ml	(2 tbs) cold water
5 ml	(1 tsp) cornstarch
	salt and pepper

Debone, skin, and wash chicken under cold running water. Thinly slice.

Heat oil in a wok or sauté pan, over high heat. When oil is very hot, sauté chicken for 3 to 4 minutes. Season generously with salt and pepper.

Set chicken aside on a warm platter.

Add celery, cabbage to the pan, and sauté for 4 minutes. Season. Add cashews, herbs, and continue to cook for 1 minute.

Add chicken stock and bring to a boil.

Combine cornstarch with water; add to pan. Simmer until liquid thickens.

Remove pan from stove, replace chicken, and correct seasoning.

Serve at once.

Chicken Stock, see pages 33-34.

Broiled Chicken Breast

Broiled Chicken Breast

Serves 4

2	*whole chicken breasts, cut into 2*
125 ml	*(1/2 cup) corn oil juice of 1 lemon*
5 ml	*(1 tsp) chervil*
1	*garlic clove, crushed salt and pepper*

Trim the fat and skin from chicken breasts. Place breasts in a dish.
Mix remaining ingredients together.

Pour mixture over chicken and cover with a sheet of oiled wax paper. Refrigerate for 2 to 3 hours and baste occasionally.
Preheat oven to broil.
Brush a small, ovenproof roasting dish with a bit of the marinade. Place in the oven 20-25 cm (8-10 in) away from the top element. As soon as the marinade becomes very hot, add chicken breasts, flesh side up. Broil for 40 minutes and baste frequently with remaining marinade. This will prevent the chicken from drying.
While broiling, leave the oven door ajar.

217

Duck Marinated in Red Wine

Serves 4

This is a two part recipe.

MARINADE:

1	**duck, about 2.3 to 2.7 kg (5 to 6 lb)**
1	**carrot, thinly sliced**
1	**onion, chopped**
2	**bay leaves**
1	**garlic clove, smashed and chopped**
2	**dry shallots**
1 ml	**(1/4 tsp) thyme**
5 ml	**(1 tsp) chopped parsley**
125 ml	**(1/2 cup) dry red wine**
45 ml	**(3 tbs) corn oil**
	salt and pepper

Clean duck and pat dry. Cut in four and remove skin.

Place duck in a large platter. Add vegetables, garlic, shallots and spices. Add oil and wine. Cover with wax paper and refrigerate for 24 hours.

Next day, remove duck from marinade. Dry duck and set aside.

Technique: Duck Marinated in Red Wine

1 Clean duck and pat dry. Cut in four and remove skin.

2 Place duck in large platter. Add vegetables, garlic, shallots and spices.

5 Add onions; continue to cook.

6 Meanwhile, pass reserved marinade through a sieve into a saucepan. Reduce by half over high heat.

COOKING PROCESS:

45 ml	*(3 tbs) butter*
1	*onion, finely chopped*
45 ml	*(3 tbs) flour*
1	*bay leaf*
1 ml	*(1/4 tsp) thyme*
1 ml	*(1/4 tsp) savory*
15 ml	*(1 tbs) cornstarch*
30 ml	*(2 tbs) cold water*

Preheat oven to 180°C (350°F).

Melt butter in an ovenproof casserole over high heat. When butter becomes hot, sauté duck for 5 minutes. Season with salt and pepper.

Add onions; continue to cook 4 to 5 minutes over medium heat. Turn duck occasionally.

Meanwhile, pass reserved marinade through a sieve into a saucepan. Reduce by half over high heat. Be sure to skim the foam that forms during reducing process.

Sprinkle flour over duck. Turn pieces until the flour adheres to the casserole.

Pour in marinade and add remaining spices; stir well. Cover and cook in the oven for 40 to 50 minutes.

Transfer duck to hot service platter. Return casserole to stove top.

Mix cornstarch with water. Incorporate mixture into sauce. Cook 2 minutes over medium heat.

Pour sauce over duck. Serve.

3 Add oil and wine. Cover with wax paper. Refrigerate for 24 hours.

4 Remove duck from marinade. Sauté duck in hot butter.

7 Sprinkle flour over duck; continue to cook.

8 Pour in marinade and add remaining spices. Cover and cook in the oven.

Roast Rabbit

Serves 6

1	1.8 kg (4 lb) domestic rabbit
	salt and pepper
125 ml	(1/2 cup) Dijon mustard
90 ml	(6 tbs) butter
30 ml	(2 tbs) flour
375 ml	(1½ cups) warm chicken stock
30 ml	(2 tbs) wine vinegar
1	bay leaf
30 ml	(2 tbs) fresh tarragon, OR
7 ml	(1½ tsp) dried tarragon

Preheat oven to 190°C (375°F).

Clean rabbit under cold running water, then dry well with paper towel.

Season rabbit with salt and pepper. Brush the inside and outside with mustard.

Melt 45 ml (3 tbs) butter in a large oven-proof dutch oven or saucepan over high heat. When butter is very hot, brown rabbit evenly on all sides.

Cook in the oven, uncovered, for 60 minutes.

In the meantime, prepare the sauce. Melt remaining butter in a small saucepan. Add flour and cook for 2 to 3 minutes over low heat. Stir constantly.

Gradually stir in chicken stock. Mix in wine vinegar, bay leaf, tarragon, salt, and pepper to taste. Simmer for 10 minutes, stirring occasionally.

Approximately 15 minutes before the rabbit is done, pour the sauce over rabbit and return to the oven. Complete cooking process, uncovered.

To test if the rabbit is done, insert a trussing needle or fork along the inside of the thigh. If no liquid is apparent, the rabbit is cooked.

Place rabbit on a carving board or serving tray. Strain sauce into a gravy boat. Correct seasoning if necessary, then serve.

Chicken Stock, see pages 33-34.

Duck Marinated in Red Wine

Coq au Vin

Coq au Vin

Serves 4

1.4 kg	(3 lb) chicken, cut into 8 pieces
250 ml	(1 cup) flour
45 ml	(3 tbs) clarified butter
90 g	(3 oz) lean pork, diced
	salt and pepper
60 ml	(4 tbs) cognac (optional)
2	dry shallots, finely chopped
2	garlic cloves, crushed and finely chopped
250 ml	(1 cup) dry red or white wine
375 ml	(1½ cups) hot basic thin brown sauce
	bouquet garni, consisting of:
1 ml	(1/4 tsp) thyme
	bay leaf
1 ml	(1/4 tsp) rosemary
1 ml	(1/4 tsp) basil
2 ml	(1/2 tsp) chervil
	fresh parsley
	celery
15 ml	(1 tbs) butter
15	small white onions, peeled
250 g	(1/2 lb) mushrooms, cut into 4
15 ml	(1 tbs) fresh parsley, finely chopped

Preheat oven to 180°C (350°F).

Wash chicken pieces under cold water and dry on paper towel. Dip pieces in flour and gently shake off excess.

Heat clarified butter in a casserole over high heat. Add chicken and pork; cook 8 minutes on each side, or until golden brown. Season with salt and pepper.

Add cognac, heat and ignite. Add shallots and garlic. Cook 1 minute over medium heat. Add wine and cook over high heat until wine is reduced by half.

Incorporate brown sauce. Add bouquet garni and season with salt and pepper. Bring to boil; cover and cook in the oven for 25 minutes.

Melt 15 ml (1 tbs) butter over high heat. Add onions and cook 2 minutes over medium heat. Stir occasionally. Add mushrooms and simmer 5 minutes. Season with salt and pepper.

Add onions and mushrooms to casserole.

Correct seasoning. Cover and return to the oven for 15 more minutes.

Discard bouquet garni before serving. Sprinkle with chopped parsley and serve from casserole.

Clarified Butter, see page 13.
Basic Thin Brown Sauce, see page 42.

Marinated Braised Duck

Serves 4

1	duck, cut into 4 pieces
	salt and pepper
150 ml	(5 oz) brandy
250 ml	(1 cup) dry red wine
1	small onion, thinly sliced
2 ml	(1/2 tsp) thyme
1	bay leaf
15 ml	(1 tbs) freshly chopped parsley
45 ml	(3 tbs) corn oil
45 ml	(3 tbs) flour
30 ml	(2 tbs) butter
250 g	(1/2 lb) mushrooms, cut in 2

Trim excess fat from the duck. Place duck in a stainless steel bowl; season with salt and pepper.

Pour red wine and brandy over duck. Add onion, thyme, bay leaf, and parsley to the bowl.

Cover the duck with a sheet of wax paper and refrigerate for 12 hours.

Preheat the oven to 180°C (350°F).

Remove duck from marinade and dry on paper towel.

Heat oil in an ovenproof casserole.

When hot, add duck and brown the pieces evenly.

Sprinkle duck with flour and cook an additional 6 to 8 minutes. Turn the pieces over frequently in order to brown the flour.

Pour marinade in a saucepan and bring to a boil over high heat. Once it begins to boil, gradually stir into casserole. Season with salt and pepper.

Cover casserole and cook in the oven for 1 hour.

Melt butter in a sauté pan. When foaming, add mushrooms and sauté for 5 minutes over high heat. Season mushrooms then transfer to the casserole.

Cover and return casserole to the oven. Cook for 15 more minutes.

Serve.

Technique: Coq au Vin

1 Cut chicken into 8 pieces.

2 Dip pieces in flour and gently shake off excess.

5 Add shallots and garlic. Season with salt and pepper.

6 Add wine and continue to cook.

3 Sauté chicken in hot butter.

4 Add cognac, heat and ignite.

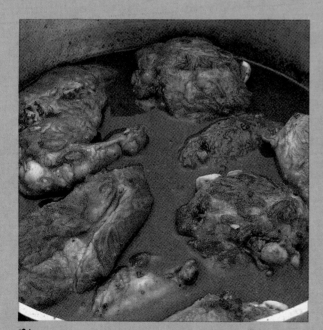

7 Add brown sauce. Cover and cook in the oven.

8 Add sautéed onions and mushrooms to the casserole.

Chicken à la Point

Serves 4

1.4 kg	(3 lb) chicken
	salt and pepper
75 ml	(5 tbs) unsalted, sweet butter
50 ml	(1/4 cup) cognac
125 ml	(1/2 cup) port wine
375 ml	(1½ cups) heavy cream
5 ml	(1 tsp) tarragon
5 ml	(1 tsp) kneaded butter (manié butter)
15 ml	(1 tbs) fresh parsley, finely chopped

Preheat oven to 150°C (300°F).

Wash chicken under cold running water. Thoroughly dry both inside and out with paper towel.

Season main cavity and outside chicken with salt and pepper.

Heat butter over low heat in a heavy ovenproof casserole. Once melted, add chicken, cover, and cook in the oven for 1½ hours. Chicken is done when nearly white.

Transfer chicken to a carving board. Discard fat from casserole but reserve drippings.

Set casserole on top of the stove. Add cognac to cooking liquid and ignite. Add wine and reduce over high heat for 2 minutes. Add cream, tarragon, and season to taste. Bring to a boil, cook 2 minutes, then whisk in kneaded butter.

Carve chicken and set slices on a heated serving platter.

Pour any drippings into sauce, then pour sauce over chicken. Sprinkle with chopped parsley.

Kneaded Butter, see page 14.

Chicken Normande

Serves 4

1	1.4 kg (3 lb) chicken, cut into 8 pieces
30 ml	(2 tbs) corn oil
	seasoned flour
1 ml	(1/4 tsp) tarragon
1 ml	(1/4 tsp) basil
125 ml	(1/2 cup) warm chicken stock

15 ml	(1 tbs) butter
2	apples, peeled, cored, and cut in two
	seasoned salt
	pepper from the mill
375 ml	(1½ cups) small onions, peeled

Trim the excess fat and skin from the chicken. Lightly coat chicken in seasoned flour.

Heat oil in an overproof casserole. When very hot, add chicken pieces and brown on all sides.

Sprinkle in herbs, dash of salt and pepper, and chicken stock. Cover and cook in the oven for 45 minutes.

In the meantime, steam onions for 4 to 5 minutes; set aside.

Melt butter in a small sauté pan. Sauté apples for 4 to 5 minutes, or until golden. About 10 minutes before chicken is cooked, add onions and apples to the casserole. Continue to cook until chicken is tender.

Chicken Stock, see pages 33-34.

Everyday Chicken

Serves 4

1.4 kg	(3 lb) chicken, cut into 8 pieces
250 ml	(1 cup) flour
	salt and pepper
45 ml	(3 tbs) clarified butter
1	onion, coarsely diced
1	green pepper, coarsely diced
	pinch of thyme
1	garlic clove, crushed and finely chopped
4	tomatoes, peeled and cut into 4 wedges

Wash chicken pieces under cold running water. Dry on paper towel.

Dip pieces in flour, then shake off excess. Season with salt and pepper.

Heat butter in a sauté pan over high heat. When hot, add chicken and brown for 8 minutes each side.

Add remaining ingredients and season with salt and pepper.

Cover, reduce heat to low, and cook for 30 minutes. Stir occasionally.

Clarified Butter, see page 13.

Everyday Chicken

Pineapple Chicken with Rum

Serves 4

1	1.4 kg (3 lb) chicken, cut into 8 pieces
	juice of 1 fresh lime
	salt and freshly ground pepper
125 ml	(1/2 cup) corn oil
1	onion, finely chopped
250 ml	(1 cup) pineapples, diced OR 375 ml (1½ cups) canned, drained, pineapples (unsweetened)
3	tomatoes, peeled and quartered
45 ml	(3 tbs) dark rum

Place chicken in a bowl.

Mix lime juice, 90 ml (6 tbs) corn oil, and pepper together. Pour over chicken.

Cover bowl with a sheet of wax paper and refrigerate for 1 hour. Brush chicken occasionally with marinade.

Preheat oven to 180°C (350°F).

Purée pineapples through a sieve, food mill, or blender. Set aside.

Heat remaining oil in an ovenproof saucepan or casserole. When oil is very hot, brown chicken pieces, a few at a time. Replace chicken in casserole, add rum and ignite. Remove chicken and set aside.

Cook onion in the casserole until transparent. Add tomatoes and sauté for 2 minutes. Add pineapple purée.

Replace chicken in casserole. Season and cover. Cook in the oven for 40 minutes. If you wish to obtain a thicker sauce, mix 15 ml (1 tbs) cornstach with 30 ml (2 tbs) water, and whisk into the liquid.

Pineapple Chicken with Rum

Cornish Hen Casserole

Chicken with Eggplant and Cheese

Serves 4

1	1.4 kg (3 lb) chicken, cut into 8 pieces
30 ml	(2 tbs) butter
	salt and pepper
1	bay leaf
	pinch of thyme
15 ml	(1 tbs) parsley
15 ml	(1 tbs) chives
2	garlic cloves, crushed and chopped
250 ml	(1 cup) hot chicken stock
1	eggplant, peeled and thinly sliced
45 ml	(3 tbs) corn oil
1	454 ml (16 oz) can stewed tomatoes, drained and coarsely chopped
	salt and pepper
50 ml	(1/4 cup) Gruyère cheese, grated

This is a two part recipe.

CHICKEN:

Wash chicken under cold running water. Season with salt and pepper.
Melt butter in a saucepan over high heat. When butter begins to foam, add chicken and brown for 8 minutes on each side. Add bay leaf and thyme.
Cover and cook over very low heat for 40 minutes, or if you prefer, in a preheated oven at 180°C (350°F) for 45 minutes.
Set chicken on a hot service platter. Return saucepan over high heat, and add remaining spices. Cook for 1 minute.
Add chicken stock to saucepan and cook for 3 minutes. Correct seasoning. Pour the sauce over the chicken.

Chicken Stock, see pages 33-34.

EGGPLANT AND CHEESE

Heat oil in a sauté pan over high heat. Cook eggplant and season with salt and pepper.
Reduce heat to low, cover, and cook for 30 minutes.

Stir in tomatoes and cook over medium for another 20 minutes. Correct seasoning. Sprinkle cheese over mixture, stir, and serve with the chicken.

Chicken New Orleans

Serves 4

1.4 kg	(3 lb) chicken, cut into 8 pieces
	salt and pepper
3	eggs
15 ml	(1 tbs) vegetable oil
375 ml	(1-1/2 cups) flour
375 ml	(1-1/2 cups) breadcrumbs
2	bananas
	peanut oil in a deep-fryer, preheated to 160°C (325°F)

Preheat oven to 200°C (400°F).
Wash chicken pieces under cold running water. Dry on paper towel.
In a mixing bowl, beat eggs and oil together.
Season chicken with salt and pepper. Dip pieces into flour, then beaten eggs, then in breadcrumbs.
Deep fry pieces until deep golden brown. Drain on paper towel and transfer to a baking dish. Cook in the oven for 8 to 10 minutes.
Peel bananas, cut in two, and split each half lengthwise. Dip pieces into flour, then eggs, and then breadcrumbs. Deep fry until golden.
Serve chicken with banana slices on a heated serving platter.

Cornish Hen Casserole

Serves 4

4	Cornish hens, thawed
125 g	(1/4 lb) unsliced bacon, diced
25	small onions
4	carrots, cut in 2,5 cm (1 in) pieces
375 ml	(1½ cups) hot chicken stock
15 ml	(1 tbs) parsley
1	bay leaf
	pinch of herbs
	salt and pepper

Preheat oven to 180°C (350°F).
Place bacon in an overproof casserole and cook over medium heat for 5 minutes. Remove bacon and set aside. Place hens in casserole and sear until golden brown. Season generously with salt and pepper. Cover and cook in the oven for 1 hour. While the hens are cooking, blanch onions and carrots in salted boiling water for 5 minutes.
Add bacon, onions, carrots, and bay leaf to the hens and continue the cooking process.
When the hens are done, transfer to a heated service platter. Spoon vegetables around hens.
Place casserole over high heat, add chicken stock and remaining spices. Reduce liquid by half and correct seasoning. Transfer sauce to a gravy boat and serve with the cornish hens.

Chicken Stock, see pages 33-34.

Pheasant Imperial

Serves 4

2	pheasants
125 ml	(1/2 cup) carrots, thinly sliced
125 ml	(1/2 cup) onions, thinly sliced
125 ml	(1/2 cup) celery, thinly sliced
3	cloves
60 ml	(4 tbs) corn oil
250 ml	(1 cup) dry white wine
45 ml	(3 tbs) wine vinegar
2	slices of lemon
1 ml	(1/4 tsp) thyme
2 ml	(1/2 tsp) parsley, finely chopped
1 ml	(1/4 tsp) savory salt and pepper
500 ml	(2 cups) chicken stock

Preheat oven to 150°C (300°F).
Clean pheasants and set aside.
Pour 30 ml (2 tbs) corn oil in a large saucepan over high heat. When hot, sauté all vegetables and season with salt and pepper. Reduce heat and simmer for about 10 minutes.
Add all remaining ingredients, except remaining oil and pheasants. Stir and cook for 12 minutes over low heat.
Pour remaining oil in a heavy ovenproof casserole. Place over high heat and when

hot, brown pheasants (whole) on all sides. Season well.
Pour the contents of the saucepan over the pheasants and correct the seasoning. Hermetically* seal the casserole.
Cook in the oven for approximately 1½ hours.

NOTE: Pheasants are cooked when the meat separates from the bone. Be sure to serve at once.

* Method for sealing casserole:
Mix 45 ml (3 tbs) flour with very little water in a small bowl. This will result in a very thick dough. Place the dough around the edge of the casserole, then set the cover on top. During the cooking process the dough will harden and hermetically seal the casserole.

Chicken Stock, see pages 33-34.

Chicken Arlésienne

Serves 4

1.4 kg	(3 lb) chicken, cut into 8 pieces
250 ml	(1 cup) flour salt and pepper
30 ml	(2 tbs) vegetable oil
1	onion, peeled and thinly sliced
1	garlic clove, crushed and finely chopped
2 ml	(1 tsp) tarragon
125 ml	(1/2 cup) dry white wine
3	tomatoes, peeled and cut into 4 wedges
1/2	small eggplant, peeled and thinly sliced

Preheat oven to 180°C (350°F).
Wash chicken pieces thoroughly under cold running water. Dry on paper towel. Season with salt and pepper. Dip in flour and gently shake off excess.
Heat oil in a sauté pan with an ovenproof handle or metal handle, over high heat. When hot, add chicken and cook for 8 minutes each side or until golden brown. Add onion, garlic, and tarragon. Cook for 2 minutes. Add wine and increase heat to high and reduce liquid by half.
Add tomatoes and eggplant, season with salt and pepper, and cover. Cook in the oven for 45 minutes.

Technique: Cornish Hen Casserole

1 Cook bacon in an ovenproof casserole for 5 minutes.

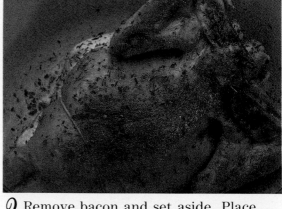

2 Remove bacon and set aside. Place hen in casserole and sear until golden brown. Season with salt and pepper.

3 Blanch onions and carrots in salted boiling water for 5 minutes.

4 Add bacon, onions, carrots and bay leaf to the hen; continue cooking process.

5 When the hens are done, transfer to a heated service platter. Spoon vegetables around hen.

6 Place casserole over high heat, add chicken stock and remaining spices.

Stuffed Cornish Hen

Serves 4

4	*Cornish hens, thawed, washed and pat dried*
30 ml	*(2 tbs) butter*
1	*chopped onion*
1	*chopped shallot*
125 g	*(1/4 lb) fresh mushrooms, washed and chopped*
375 ml	*(1½ cups) long grain rice, cooked*
15 ml	*(1 tbs) chopped parsley*
30 ml	*(2 tbs) clarified or melted butter*
125 ml	*(1/2 cup) dry white wine*
250 ml	*(1 cup) hot chicken stock*
15 ml	*(1 tbs) cornstarch*
2 ml	*(1/2 tsp) savory*
45 ml	*(3 tbs) cold water lemon juice salt and pepper*

Preheat oven to 190°C (375°F).

Heat butter in a saucepan over medium heat. Add onions and shallots; cook 2 minutes.

Add mushrooms; season with salt and pepper.

Add rice; mix well.

Add spices; mix again.

Stuff Cornish hens, tie and arrange in a roasting pan. Brush with melted butter.

Cook in the oven for 45 minutes or according to weight.

Transfer Cornish hens to a service platter. Keep hot.

Place roasting pan on stove top. Reduce cooking liquid over high heat. Add white wine; cook 3 to 4 minutes.

Add chicken stock; simmer 5 to 6 minutes. Sprinkle with lemon juice.

Mix cornstarch with cold water. Incorporate mixture into sauce; bring to boil.

Pour sauce over Cornish hens. Serve with green beans and sautéed potatoes.

Chicken Stock, see pages 33-34.
Clarified Butter, see page 13.

Stuffed Cornish Hen

Duck with Stuffed Olives

Duck with Stuffed Olives

Serves 4

1	2.2 kg (5 lb) duck
1	whole onion, peeled
1	celery stalk
1	onion finely chopped
250 ml	(1 cup) dry red wine
500 ml	(2 cups) hot brown sauce
15 ml	(1 tbs) tomato paste
250 ml	(1 cup) stuffed olives
	lemon juice
	salt and pepper

Preheat oven to 200°C (425°F).
Wash and pat dry duck. Remove excess fat. Season inside with salt and pepper, then insert a whole onion and one celery branch.
Tie and place duck in a roasting pan. Prick skin with a needle to allow fat to drip during cooking process.
Sear duck for 45 minutes in the oven. Every 15 minutes, remove accumulated fat in the bottom of the pan.
Then reduce oven to 180°C (350°F). Continue to cook duck for 45 minutes. Sprinkle duck with lemon juice during cooking process. Season with salt and pepper.
As soon as the meat is done, remove from the oven and transfer to a heated service platter.
Remove 3/4 of fat from the bottom of the pan.
Place roasting pan on stove top. Add chopped onions; cook 3 to 4 minutes.
Add red wine; continue to cook for 4 to 5 minutes.
Add brown sauce and tomato paste; mix well. Add stuffed olives; simmer 7 to 8 minutes.
Serve sauce with duck.

Brown Sauce, see pages 42-43.

Chicken Casserole

Serves 4

1.4 kg	(3 lb) chicken, cut into 8 pieces
250 ml	(1 cup) flour
	salt and pepper
45 ml	(3 tbs) clarified butter
1	dry shallot, finely chopped
250 g	(1/2 lb) mushrooms, cut into 4
250 ml	(1 cup) carrots, cut into thin strips
15	small white onions, peeled
125 ml	(1/2 cup) hot chicken stock
2 ml	(1/2 tsp) oregano

Preheat oven to 180°C (350°F).
Blanch carrots in a large saucepan filled with boiling salted water. Blanch for 7 minutes.
Remove from heat. Cool carrots under running water for at least 4 minutes. Drain and set aside.
Wash chicken pieces under cold running water. Dry on paper towel. Season with salt and pepper. Dip in flour and gently shake off excess.
Heat clarified butter in a sauté pan over high heat. When hot, add chicken and cook for 8 minutes each side or until golden brown, over medium heat. Add vegetables and cook for 1 to 2 minutes. Set chicken and vegetables in an oven-proof casserole.
Pour stock over contents and add oregano. Season, cover, and cook for 45 minutes. Correct seasoning and serve from casserole.

Chicken Stock, see pages 33-34.

Chicken Kiev

Serves 4

2	large chicken breasts
	salt and pepper
125 ml	(1/2 cup) frozen garlic butter
3	eggs
15 ml	(1 tbs) vegetable oil
250 ml	(1 cup) flour
500 ml	(2 cups) breadcrumbs
	peanut oil in deep-fryer, preheated to 160°C (325°F).

Debone and skin breasts: wash thoroughly under cold running water. Split breasts in two, lengthwise.
One by one, place breasts between 2 sheets of aluminum foil and flatten with a cleaver.
Season with salt and pepper. Place 15 ml (1 tbs) garlic butter at one end of breast and roll chicken over butter. As you roll,

tuck in edges towards middle. Secure rolls
with toothpicks.

Beat eggs and oil together. Dip rolls, one
at a time, into flour, then eggs, and then
breadcrumbs.

Deep fry in preheated oil until golden
brown.

Serve with tomato sauce.

Garlic Butter, see page 16.

Duck with Green Peppercorn

Serves 4

1	*2.2 kg (5 lb) duck*
30 ml	*(2 tbs) clarified butter*
2	*onions, finely chopped*
1	*carrot, peeled and diced*
1/2	*celery stalk, diced*
250 ml	*(1 cup) dry white wine*
500 ml	*(2 cups) hot brown sauce*
45 ml	*(3 tbs) green peppercorns*
125 ml	*(1/2 cup) 35% cream*
	lemon juice
	salt and pepper

Preheat oven to 200°C (400°F).

Trim excess fat from duck.

Cut duck into 4 pieces (2 breasts, 2 legs).
Season with salt and pepper.

Heat clarified butter in a sauté pan. Add
duck; sear 7 to 8 minutes on each side.
Sprinkle with lemon juice.

Add onions, carrots and celery. Cook in
the oven for 35 minutes. Brush duck during cooking process.

Remove from the oven. Add wine; continue to cook in the oven for 7 to 8 minutes.

Add brown sauce; cook in the oven for 10
to 12 minutes.

As soon as the meat is cooked, remove
from pan and transfer to a heated service
platter.

Strain sauce. Pour sauce into the pan.
Crush green peppercorns into cream.
Incorporate mixture to sauce. Sprinkle
with lemon juice.

Place duck into sauce; simmer 7 to 8 minutes. Serve.

Clarified Butter, see page 13.
Brown Sauce, see pages 42-43.

Duck with Green Peppercorn

Stuffed Beef Flank

Serves 4

1	500 g (1 lb) beef flanks
	salt and freshly ground pepper
250 ml	(1 cup) stuffing (vegetable)
15 ml	(1 tbs) vegetable oil
40 ml	(2½ tbs) butter
30 ml	(2 lbs) carrot, chopped
30 ml	(2 lbs) onion, chopped
15 ml	(1 tbs) celery, chopped
1	bay leaf
1 ml	(1/4 tsp) basil
	pinch of thyme
1	garlic clove, crushed and finely chopped
45 ml	(3 tbs) flour
375 ml	(1½ cups) hot brown beef stock
4	tomatoes, cut into 4, OR 375 ml (1½ cups) canned tomatoes, drained and coarsely chopped

Preheat oven to 180°C (350°F).

Split flanks in two, 0.65 cm (1/4 in) from the widest edge. Unfold and place flat. Pound with a meat cleaver.

Season and fill each flank with 1/2 of the stuffing. Roll and secure with kitchen string.

Heat 15 ml (1 tbs) oil in a sauté pan over high heat. When very hot, brown flanks on both sides. Set flanks in an ovenproof casserole and season with salt and pepper.

Add 30 ml (2 tbs) butter to the pan. When butter begins to foam, over high heat, add carrot, onion, celery, spices, and garlic. Reduce heat to medium and cook for 4 to 5 minutes. Stir occasionally.

Add flour and cook over low heat for 6 minutes. Stir constantly.

Remove pan from heat. Add 250 ml (1 cup) stock and mix with a wooden spoon.

Return pan over low heat. Add remaining stock, stir, and bring to a boil.

In a separate sauté pan, melt remaining butter over high heat. When foaming, add tomatoes and cook for 1 to 2 minutes. Stir frequently.

Pour tomatoes over meat.

Season sauce to taste, cover casserole and cook in the oven for 1½ hours.

Strain sauce before serving.

Brown Beef Stock, see page 34.
Stuffing, see page 18.

Brochettes of Beef

Brochettes of Beef

Serves 4

750 g	(1½ lb) beef tenderloin, cut into 3.8 cm (1½ in) cubes
	marinade
1	italian onion, cut into 2.5 cm (1 in) pieces
8	slices bacon, cut into 3
20	mushroom caps
	salt and freshly ground pepper
30 ml	(2 tbs) garlic butter

Cover beef with marinade and cover bowl with wax paper. Refrigerate for at least 12 hours.

On a skewer, alternate beef, onion, bacon, and mushroom caps.

Season brochettes with salt and pepper. Broil, 15 cm (6 in) away from the top element, or barbecue for:

4 minutes, medium rare;

12 minutes, well done;

Baste brochettes occasionally with the marinade.

When brochettes are almost done, spread 5 ml (1 tsp) garlic butter on each. Replace in the oven until butter melts.

Serve with rice.

Garlic Butter, see page 16.
Marinade, see page 26.

One for Three

Serves 4

45 ml	(3 tbs) butter
500 g	(1 lb) beef tenderloin, thinly sliced on an angle
1	small onion, peeled and thinly sliced
1	green pepper, seeded and thinly sliced
1	garlic clove, crushed and finely chopped
500 g	(1 lb) mushrooms, thinly sliced
2	water chestnuts, thinly sliced
8	tomato wedges
	salt
	freshly ground pepper

In a sauté pan, melt butter over high heat. When butter begins to foam, add beef. Sauté, uncovered for 3 minutes. Stir frequently. Set beef aside on a heated platter. Immediately add onion, green pepper, and garlic to pan. Sauté for 2 minutes, uncovered. Add mushrooms, continue to cook for 2 minutes, stirring frequently. Add water chestnuts and tomato wedges. Sauté for 1 minute, then season with salt and pepper.

Return meat along with meat juices to the pan. Rewarm for several seconds.

Correct seasoning. Arrange beef mixture over rice; serve at once.

Club Steak with Cognac

Serves 4

4	375 g (3/4 lb) club steaks
20 ml	(1½ tbs) peppercorns, coarsely smashed
45 ml	(3 tbs) clarified butter
45 ml	(3 tbs) cognac
	salt
30 ml	(2 tbs) butter
2	dried shallots, finely chopped

Press the smashed peppercorns into the meat.

Melt clarified butter in a heavy sauté pan over high heat. When hot, add steaks. Reduce heat to medium and cook steaks to taste.

5 minutes each side, medium rare;
6 minutes each side, medium;
7 minutes each side, well done.

Remove pan from heat and allow to cool for several minutes. Add cognac and ignite. After the flame has died, set steaks onto a heated serving platter. Season with salt.

Melt remaining butter in the pan. Cook shallots for 1 minute over medium heat. Pour contents of pan over steaks and serve.

Clarified Butter, see page 13.

Top Round Strogonoff

Serves 4

750 g	(1½ lb) top round, cut into thin strips on an angle
90 ml	(6 tbs) clarified butter
2	small onions, thinly sliced
250 g	(1/2 lb) mushrooms, sliced
5 ml	(1 tsp) paprika
3 ml	(3/4 tsp) tomato paste
60 ml	(4 tbs) hot basic brown thin sauce, OR
	60 ml (4 tbs) beef drippings
125 ml	(1/2 cup) sour cream
	salt
	freshly ground pepper
	juice of 1/2 lemon
	dash of cayenne pepper
15 ml	(1 tbs) fresh parsley, finely chopped

Melt clarified butter in a sauté pan over high heat. When hot, add onions. Reduce heat to low, cover, and cook for 8 to 10 minutes. Stir occasionally. Add mushrooms and cook, uncovered for 5 minutes. Stir occasionally.

Mix in paprika, sauce, tomato paste, and sour cream. Season to taste.

Remove pan from heat and set aside.

In a separate pan, melt remaining clarified butter over high heat. When hot, add beef and sauté over high heat for 3 minutes. Season beef, then mix into the sauce.

Squeeze in lemon juice and add cayenne pepper.

Serve over egg noodles and top with parsley.

Clarified Butter, see page 13.
Basic Thin Brown Sauce, see page 42.

Steak, Chinese Style

Serves 2

2	250 g (1/2 lb) steaks, club or filet mignon
45 ml	(3 tbs) butter
	salt
	freshly ground pepper
1	small onion, thinly sliced
1/2	green pepper, seeded and thinly sliced
12	mushrooms, sliced
1	garlic clove, crushed and finely chopped
1	tomato, cut into 4 wedges
15 ml	(1 tbs) soy sauce

Cut steaks into thin slices on an angle.

Heat 30 ml (2 tbs) butter in a sauté pan over high heat. When foam subsides, add steak.

Reduce heat to medium and cook for 3 minutes on each side. Season with salt and pepper, then transfer to a heated platter. Add remaining butter to pan. When foaming, cook onion for 1 minute.

Add green pepper and cook for 1 minute. Stir occasionally.

Add mushrooms and garlic; cook for 3 minutes. Stir occasionally.

Add tomato and continue to cook for 1 to 2 minutes. Season vegetables.

Add soy sauce.

Mix steak and drippings into the pan, then arrange over a bed of rice.

Serve at once.

Club Steak au Poivre

Serves 2

2	284 g (10 oz) club steaks, deboned
15 ml	(1 tbs) peppercorns, coarsely smashed
15 ml	(1 tbs) clarified butter
45 ml	(3 tbs) cognac
125 ml	(1/2 cup) hot brown thin sauce, OR
125 ml	(1/2 cup) roast beef drippings
125 ml	(1/2 cup) heavy cream salt
	freshly ground pepper
5 ml	(1 tsp) chopped parsley

Press smashed peppercorns into the meat.
Melt butter in a heavy sauté pan over high
heat. When hot, add steaks.
Reduce heat to medium and cook steaks
to taste.

5 minutes each side, medium rare;
6 minutes each side, medium;
7 minutes each side, well done.

Remove pan from heat and allow to cool for several minutes.

Add cognac and ignite. After the flame has died, set steaks onto a heated serving platter.

Add brown sauce to pan. Bring to a boil over high heat.

Reduce heat to medium, add cream, and simmer for 2 to 3 minutes.

Season to taste.

Add any drippings from the steaks to the sauce.

Pour the sauce over steaks and garnish with parsley.

Basic Thin Brown Sauce, see page 42.
Clarified Butter, see page 13.

Technique:
Steak au Poivre

1 Press smashed peppercorns into meat.

2 Sauté steak in a heavy sauté pan over high heat.

3 Add cognac and ignite.

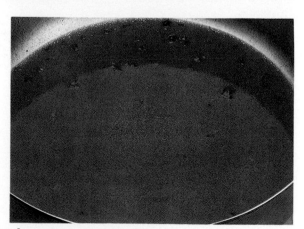

4 Add brown sauce to pan. Bring to a boil over high heat.

5 Add cream; simmer 2 to 3 minutes. Season to taste.

Technique: How to Roast Beef

Many cuts of beef ar suitable for roasting. The tastiest cut is the rib roast, as the ribs give an excellent flavor. Note that this particular cut is one of the more expensive. The eye of round, rump roast, and sirloin tip also serve well. As these cuts do not contain bone, they are more economical. A good cut of beef should be aged, by your butcher, for 2 to 3 weeks. This aging process tends to increase tenderness and flavor.

Always wrap your chosen cut in oiled wax paper. During summer months, a boneless cut will keep for 3 days, if covered and refrigerated. During winter months, the same cut will keep for 4 days.

Cuts with bones, will keep for 5 days, if covered and refrigerated.

Roast Beef

Serves 4

2.7 kg	(6 lb) rib roast, or 1.4 kg (3 lb) eye of roast, or 1.8 kg (4 lb) rump roast, or 1.4 kg (3 lb) sirloin tip
1 ml	(1/4 tsp) basil
1 ml	(1/4 tsp) thyme
2 ml	(1/2 tsp) chervil freshly ground pepper
15 ml	(1 tbs) vegetable oil salt
30 ml	(2 lbs) carrot, finely chopped
30 ml	(2 lbs) onion, finely chopped
15 ml	(1 tbs) celery, finely chopped dry shallot, finely chopped bay leaf
375 ml	(1½ cups) hot basic brown beef stock

Preheat oven to 240°C (450°F).

Cut a very thin strip from roast and cut into 1.2 cm (1/2 in) pieces. Mix basil, thyme, and chervil together in a small shallow bowl.

Roll pieces of beef in spices and set spices aside.

Using a paring knife, make small incisions, at least 1.2 cm (1/2 in) deep, in roast. Insert seasoned pieces of beef.

If you are cooking a rib roast, insert beef pieces between ribs. If the cut that you are using does not contain any fat, rub roast with vegetable oil.

Season roast with pepper. Do not use salt at this point, as it will tend to toughen meat.

Heat 15 ml (1 tbs) oil in a roasting pan, set in the oven. Heat for 3 to 4 minutes or until hot. Set roast in pan, fat side up, and cook in oven for 30 minutes.

Reduce heat to 180°C (350°F), and season with salt.

Total cooking time, including 30 minutes at 240°C (450°F).:

18 minutes per 500 g (1 lb), rare;
20 minutes per 500 g (1 lb), medium rare;
24 minutes per 500 g (1lb), well done.

Baste roast and discard fat every 15 minutes.

After cooking time is completed, remove and transfer roast to a carving board. Let stand for 15 minutes to complete cooking process and allow juices to settle.

During this time, remove all but 30 ml (2 tbs) fat from pan.

Try to retain most of the beef drippings. Add carrot, onion, celery, shallot, reserved spices, and bay leaf to pan. Cook over high heat for 5 to 6 minutes.

Add stock and season with salt and pepper. Pour contents into a medium size saucepan. Reduce sauce, over high heat for 4 to 5 minutes. Strain and skim off as much fat as possible.

Carve roast and pour meat drippings into sauce. Serve sauce separate from beef.

Brown Beef Stock, see page 34.

Rib Roast à la Française

Serves 4

1	rib roast (5 ribs)
250 ml	(1 cup) parisienne potatoes*
1	bunch asparagus tips
4	tomatoes, quartered
2	cucumbers, seeded and cut into 1.2 cm (1/2 in) slices
45 ml	(3 tbs) butter, (to sear roast)
125 ml	(1/2 cup) dry white wine
375 ml	(1½ cups) hot brown beef stock

	salt and pepper
1	*onion, chopped*
1	*celery stalk, chopped*

Preheat oven to 220°C (425°F).
Prepare and cook rib roast according to technique.
Blanch all vegetables, except tomatoes, for 5 minutes in boiling salted water. Drain and set aside.
Prepare sauce by adding onion and celery to pan, 10 minutes before roast is cooked.
Remove meat when done and place on a platter.
Extract 1/2 of the fat from pan and discard. Set roasting pan over high heat and add blanched vegetables. Cook for about 4 minutes.
Season to taste.
Add white wine and cook for 2 minutes.
Add tomatoes, stir in beef stock, and cook for 3 to 4 minutes over medium heat.
Spoon out vegetables and arrange around meat.
Pour sauce into a gravy boat and serve with roast.
* To do parisienne potatoes, peel potatoes and using a potato ball scooper, form round balls of potato.

Brown Beef Stock, see page 34.

Boeuf Bourguignon

Serves 4

1.4 kg	(3 lb) blade steak
	marinade
30 ml	(2 tbs) vegetable oil
15 ml	(1 tbs) butter
	salt and freshly ground pepper
1	bay leaf
2 ml	(1/2 tsp) chervil
1 ml	(1/4 tsp) thyme
2 ml	(1/2 tsp) tarragon
3	garlic cloves, crushed and
	finely chopped
2	dried shallots, finely chopped
60 ml	(4 tbs) flour

625 ml	(2½ cups) hot basic brown beef stock
227 g	(8 oz) salted pork, diced
18	white onions, peeled
250 g	(1/2 lb) mushrooms, cut in two
15 ml	(1 tbs) fresh parsley, finely chopped

Trim meat and cut into 3.8 cm (1½ in) cubes. Cover beef with marinade and cover bowl with wax paper. Refrigerate for at least 12 hours.

Preheat oven to 180°C (350°F).

Dry beef on paper towel. Strain marinade into a saucepan and reduce by 2/3 over high heat. Set aside.

Technique: Boeuf Bourguignon

1 Cover beef with marinade. Refrigerate.

2 Brown beef over high heat.

5 Stir in marinade. Season with salt and pepper.

6 Sauté pork for 3 to 4 minutes over high heat. Add onions; cook 4 minutes over medium heat.

Heat oil and butter in a heavy ovenproof casserole over high heat. When foam subsides, brown beef (a few pieces at a time) over high heat.

Season all the meat with salt and pepper.

Add herbs, garlic, and shallots. Reduce heat to medium and simmer for 1 minute.

Add flour and cook for 4 to 5 minutes, stirring constantly.

Remove casserole from heat. Add 250 ml (1 cup) beef stock and mix thoroughly with a wooden spoon.

Set again on top of the stove over low heat. Add remaining stock, 250 ml (1 cup) at a time, stirring constantly.

Stir in marinade, and season with salt and pepper.

Bring to a boil over high heat, then cover casserole and cook in the oven for 1 hour 15 minutes.

Sauté pork for 3 to 4 minutes in a sauté pan over high heat. Add onions, reduce heat to medium and cook for 4 minutes. Add mushrooms; cook for 4 minutes. Season and add to the casserole.

Cover casserole again and continue to cook in the oven for 1/2 hour.

Garnish this dish with chopped parsley and serve from the casserole.

Basic Brown Beef Stock, see page 34.
Marinade, see page 26.

4 Add beef stock.

3 Add spices. Sprinkle with flour and continue to cook.

7 Add mushrooms; cook for 4 minutes.

8 Add vegetable mixture to the meat.

Rolled Flank Fit for a King

Serves 10

3	*flanks*
500 g	*(1 lb) mushrooms, finely chopped*
45 ml	*(3 tbs) butter*
1	*small onion, finely chopped*
2 ml	*(1/2 tsp) thyme*
5 ml	*(1 tsp) chervil*
2 ml	*(1/2 tsp) basil*
2	*garlic cloves, finely chopped*
30 ml	*(2 tbs) fresh chives, chopped*
50 ml	*(1/4 cup) breadcrumbs*
1	*egg, beaten*
20 ml	*(1½ tbs) oil*
	salt and pepper

Melt butter in a sauté pan. Cook onion over medium heat for 2 minutes. Add mushrooms and spices; cook for 7 to 8 minutes. Season to taste.

Remove pan from heat and stir in breadcrumbs and egg.

Split flanks in half lengthwise, 0.65 cm (1/4 in) from the edge. Open flanks and place flat; pound with a meat cleaver.

Season with salt and pepper. Fill each flank with 1/3 of stuffing mixture. Roll meat and secure with kitchen string.

Heat 20 ml (1½ tbs) oil in a sauté pan. Brown flanks on all sides.

Season with salt and pepper.

Set flanks in a large ovenproof casserole. Season with salt and pepper.

THE SAUCE:

75 ml	*(5 tbs) butter*
30 ml	*(2 tbs) carrots, chopped*
30 ml	*(2 tbs) onion, chopped*
15 ml	*(1 tbs) celery, chopped*
1	*bay leaf*
1 ml	*(1/4 tsp) basil*
	pinch of thyme
1	*garlic clove, finely chopped*
90 ml	*(6 tbs) flour*
1.5 L	*(6 cups) hot beef stock*
250 ml	*(1 cup) dry wine, red*
375 ml	*(1½ cups) tomatoes, drained, and coarsely chopped*
30 ml	*(2 tbs) corn oil*
	salt and pepper

Brown Beef Stock, see page 34.

Melt butter in a sauté pan over high heat. Add vegetables, except tomatoes, and spices. Cook for 4 to 5 minutes. Stir constantly.

Mix in flour and cook for 6 minutes while stirring constantly.

Pour in beef stock; season with salt and pepper.

Bring sauce to a boil, then shower over flanks.

Reduce wine in the sauté pan by 3/4. Add wine to casserole and correct seasoning.

Sauté tomatoes in 30 ml (2 tbs) oil, then add to casserole.

Cover and cook in a preheated oven at 180°C (350°F) for 1½ hours.

Slice meat and arrange on a hot serving platter. Strain sauce then spoon over meat. Garnish with fresh parsley sprigs.

Technique: Rolled Flank Fit for a King

1 Beef flank.

4 Split flank in half lengthwise. Open flank and place flat; pound with a meat cleaver.

5 Season with salt and pepper. Fill with stuffing mixture.

8 Cook vegetables, except tomatoes, and spices in hot butter.

9 Add flour; continue to cook.

2 Cook onions and mushrooms in hot butter.

3 Remove pan from heat and stir in breadcrumbs and egg.

6 Roll meat and secure with kitchen string.

7 Heat oil in sauté pan. Brown flank on all sides. Season with salt and pepper.

10 Pour in beef stock; season with salt and pepper.

11 Reduce wine by 3/4.

Hamburger Victor

Serves 4

30 ml	(2 tbs) oil
1	chopped onion
900 g	(2 lb) minced lean beef
1	whole egg
15 ml	(1 tbs) chopped parsley
2 ml	(1/2 tsp) Worcestershire sauce
30 ml	(2 tbs) butter
3	potatoes, peeled and thinly sliced
1	onion, thinly sliced
4	slices of tomatoes
	salt and pepper

Heat 5 ml (1 tsp) oil in a frying pan. Add chopped onion; cover and cook 3 minutes over low heat.

Pour cooked onion into a mixing bowl. Add meat, egg, parsley and Worcestershire sauce. Season with salt and pepper; mix well.

Form 4 hamburger steaks. Set aside.

Melt butter in a frying pan. Add potatoes; season with salt and pepper. Cook 15 to 18 minutes over medium heat.

Five minutes before the end of cooking: Add sliced onion to the frying pan.

Heat remaining oil in a sauté pan. Add hamburger steaks; cook 4 minutes on each side.

Place one slice of tomato on each hamburger; continue to cook for 2 minutes.

Serve with potato and onion mixture.

Veal Kidneys with Madeira Wine

Serves 2

3	veal kidneys, peeled and trimmed of fat
30 ml	(2 tbs) clarified butter salt and pepper
250 g	(1/2 lb) mushrooms, cut into 4
1	dry shallot, finely chopped
250 ml	(1 cup) hot brown sauce, thin
125 ml	(1/2 cup) Madeira wine dash of cayenne pepper
15 ml	(1 tbs) heavy cream (optional)
15 ml	(1 tbs) fresh parsley, finely chopped

Veal Kidneys with Madeira Wine

Slice kidneys.

Heat clarified butter in a sauté pan over high heat. When very hot, sauté kidney for 3 to 4 minutes on each side.

Season with salt and pepper, and transfer to a heated platter.

Sauté mushrooms and shallot for 4 minutes over high heat. Stir frequently. Add brown sauce and wine. Bring to a boil, reduce heat to medium and simmer for several minutes.

Season sauce with cayenne pepper, salt, and black pepper.

Mix kidneys and cream into sauce. Garnish with parsley and serve.

Clarified Butter, see page 13.
Basic Thin Brown Sauce, see page 42.

257

Pot-au-Feu

Before serving: reheat vegetables in the hot bouillon.

Serve with seasoned mustard, pickles and garlic bread.

Goulash

Serves 4

30 ml	(2 tbs) vegetable oil
2	onions, chopped
1.5 kg	(3½ lb) blade steak, cubed
1	clove of garlic, smashed and chopped
30 ml	(2 tbs) paprika
45 ml	(3 tbs) flour
30 ml	(2 tbs) tomato paste
1.5 L	(6 cups) hot brown beef stock
15 ml	(1 tbs) fresh chopped parsley

buttered noodles
salt and pepper

Preheat oven to 180°C (350°F).

Heat oil in an ovenproof casserole. Add onions; cook for 3 minutes.

Add meat, garlic and paprika; sear 3 to 4 minutes, over high heat, on each side.

Add flour; mix well and cook for 2 minutes.

Add tomato paste and beef stock; stir and season to taste.

Cover and cook in the oven for 2 hours.

Serve with buttered noodles. Sprinkle with parsley.

Brown Beef Stock, see page 34.

Club Steak with Green Peppers,
Mushrooms, and Celery

Club Steak with Green Peppers, Mushrooms, and Celery

Serves 4

4	170 g (6 oz) club steaks
30 ml	(2 tbs) corn oil
	freshly ground pepper
	salt
2	green peppers, seeded and thinly sliced
250 g	(1/2 lb) mushrooms, thinly sliced
1	celery stalk, thinly sliced
2 ml	(1/2 tsp) thyme
1	garlic clove, finely chopped

Sprinkle steaks with pepper. Press the pepper into the surface of the meat.
Heat 15 ml (1 tbs) oil in a large sauté pan over high heat. When very hot, sear steaks for 3 minutes on one side. Do not disturb. Turn and sear the other sides for another 3 minutes.
Season with salt and continue to cook over medium high until cooked to taste. Turn meat every 2 to 3 minutes to avoid any crust from forming. When done, transfer to a heated platter.
Heat remaining oil in the pan. Add vegeta-

bles, garlic, thyme, salt, and pepper. Cover and cook for 4 minutes over medium low heat.

Serve steaks topped with the vegetables.

Swiss Style Chuck Steak

Serves 4

1.4 kg	(3 lb) chuck or blade steak
1	garlic clove, split in two
30 ml	(2 tbs) corn oil
1	onion, finely chopped
1	celery stalk, finely chopped
1	can, 796 ml (28 oz), stewed tomatoes, drained and coarsely chopped
250 ml	(1 cup) beef stock, hot
1	bay leaf
15 ml	(1 tbs) parsley
	salt and pepper

Preheat oven to 160°C (325°F).

Trim excess fat from the edges of the meat. Rub edges with garlic pieces.

Sear steak over high heat in an ovenproof casserole or roasting pan, containing 15 ml (1 tbs) hot oil. Remove meat when seared and set aside.

Heat remaining oil in casserole. Sauté chopped vegetables over medium heat for 5 minutes and season with salt and pepper.

Add tomatoes, beef stock, and spices.

Replace meat in casserole. Correct seasoning, cover, and cook in the oven for 1 hour 15 minutes.

Transfer meat to a service platter.

Purée liquid and vegetables through a food mill or blender. Serve over meat.

Brown Beef Stock, see page 34.

Skipper's Brochettes

Serves 4

500 g	(1 lb) round steak, cut into 2.5 cm (1 in) cubes
1	Spanish onion, diced
75 ml	(5 tbs) corn oil
2	celery stalks, largely diced
2	red peppers, diced
2	garlic cloves, crushed and chopped
5 ml	(1 tsp) seasoned salt
	pinch of mixed herbs
	juice of 1 lemon
	salt and pepper
60 ml	(4 tbs) garlic butter

Place cubes of meat in a stainless steel bowl. Add oil, seasoned salt, pepper, garlic, lemon, and mixed herbs. Mix well and refrigerate for 1 hour.

Insert ingredients on skewers in the following order: a piece of celery, red pepper, meat, onion, and repeat process until all ingredients are used.

Place skewers on the barbecue or under broil. Season and cook for 3 to 4 minutes on each side.

Melt garlic butter and brush over skewers just before serving.

Garlic Butter, see page 16.

Chicken Livers Chinese Style

Serves 4

45 ml	(3 tbs) corn oil
625 g	(1¼ lb) chicken livers, cut in half
1	small onion, sliced
1	green pepper, seeded and sliced
1	garlic clove, finely chopped
500 g	(1 lb) mushrooms, sliced
125 g	(1/4 lb) chinese snow pea pods
2	small tomatoes, cut in wedges
2	water chestnuts, thinly sliced (optional)
	salt and pepper

Heat oil in a deep sauté pan. Sauté livers over high heat until lightly browned on all sides (about 5 to 7 minutes). Season with salt, pepper, then transfer to a heated platter.

Sauté onion, green pepper, and garlic over medium heat for 2 minutes.

Add mushrooms and cook for 2 to 3 minutes. Sauté remaining ingredients for another 2 to 3 minutes.

Season generously with salt and pepper. Spoon vegetable mixture onto the heated platter, surrounding the livers.

Serve with steamed rice.

Technique: Beef Kidney Sautéed in Red Wine

1 Beef kidneys.

2 Remove fat from beef kidneys.

3 Slice beef kidneys.

4 Sauté kidneys in hot butter.

5 Sauté mushrooms in hot butter. Add parsley. Season with salt and pepper.

6 Add red wine; cook 3 to 4 minutes over high heat. Add brown sauce; stir and cook 7 to 8 minutes.

Beef Kidney Sautéed in Red Wine

Serves 4

60 ml	(4 tbs) butter
1	dry shallot, chopped
2	large beef kidneys, cleaned and sliced
15 ml	(1 tbs) flour
250 g	(1/2 lb) fresh mushrooms, diced
15 ml	(1 tbs) chopped parsley
250 ml	(1 cup) dry red wine
375 ml	(1½ cups) brown sauce
	salt and pepper

Melt 30 ml (2 tbs) butter in a sauté pan. Add shallot and kidney; cook over high heat, 2 to 3 minutes on each side.

Add flour; cook for 1 minute. Mix well. Remove kidney from sauté pan. Set aside. Melt remaining butter in sauté pan. Add mushrooms and parsley.

Season with salt and pepper; cook 3 minutes over high heat.

Stir in red wine; cook 3 to 4 minutes over high heat.

Add brown sauce; stir and cook 7 to 8 minutes.

Add beef kidneys; mix and simmer 3 to 4 minutes over low heat. Serve.

Basic Thin Brown Sauce, see page 42.

Grilled Sweetbreads with Béarnaise Sauce and Watercress

Serves 4

750 g	*(1¹/₂ lb) calf's sweetbreads*
125 ml	*(1/2 cup) melted clarified butter*
	salt and pepper
	fresh watercress
250 ml	*(1 cup) Béarnaise sauce*

Ahead of time, prepare sweetbreads according to the technique.

Preheat oven to 180°C (350°F).

Dip sweetbreads into melted clarified butter and set in a baking dish.

Season with salt and pepper. Cook in the oven for 35 minutes. Baste frequently with the butter.

Arrange sweetbreads on a heated service platter. Decorate with watercress.

Serve with Béarnaise sauce.

Clarified Butter, see page 13.
Béarnaise Sauce, see page 48.

Club Steak Bordelaise

Serves 2

2	*284 g (10 oz) club steaks, deboned*
15 ml	*(1 tbs) vegetable oil*
	salt
	freshly ground pepper
250 ml	*(1 cup) hot bourguignon sauce*
5 ml	*(1 tsp) fresh parsley, finely chopped*

Place oil in a very heavy sauté pan over high heat.

When oil begins to smoke, discard. Reduce heat to medium and immediately add steaks.

Cook steaks to taste.

   5 minutes each side, medium rare;
   6 minutes each side, medium;
   8 minutes each side, well done.

Season with salt and pepper.

Transfer to a heated platter and top with sauce.

Garnish with parsley.

Bourguignon Sauce, see page 46.

Club Steak Bordelaise

Chicken Livers Soubise

Serves 4

750 g	(1½ lb) chicken livers
2	large onions, liced
2	small cucumbers, peeled, seeded, and cut into 1,2 cm (1/2 in) slices
20 ml	(1-1/2 tbs) corn oil
30 ml	(2 tbs) butter
30 ml	(2 tbs) wine vinegar
375 ml	(1½ cups) white sauce, hot
2 ml	(1/2 tsp) parsley
2 ml	(1/2 tsp) nutmeg
	salt and pepper

Heat oil in a sauté pan over high heat. Add livers and season with salt and pepper.

Reduce to medium and cook for 7 minutes. Remove livers; set aside.

Melt butter in the sauté pan over high heat. When butter foams, add onions and season to taste.

Reduce heat to medium and cook for 8 minutes or until onions become golden. Four minutes before onions are cooked, add cucumbers.

Season again. Add vinegar and allow it to evaporate.

Pour in white sauce and sprinkle with nutmeg.

Return livers to the pan; cook for 2 minutes.

Sprinkle with parsley and serve with rice.

Basic White Sauce, see page 41.

Technique: Chicken Livers Soubise

1 Sauté livers in hot oil.

2 Cook onions in melted butter.

3 Add cucumbers and vinegar.

4 Pour in white sauce and sprinkle with nutmeg.

5 Return chicken livers to the pan; cook for 2 minutes.

6 This is the mixture after 2 minutes of cooking.

Calf's Liver on Skewers

Serves 4

750 g	(1½ tb) calf's liver
15 ml	(1 tbs) butter
16	mushroom caps
4	slices bacon, cut into 4
50 ml	(1/4 cup) clarified butter
	salt and pepper
125 ml	(1/2 cup) breadcrumbs
	parsley sprigs or fresh
	watercress

Preheat oven to broil.
Remove outside membrane from livers
and cut flesh into 5 cm (2 in) squares.
Heat butter in a sauté pan over high heat.
When foaming, add livers and mushroom
caps. Reduce heat to medium and cook for
2 to 3 minutes.
Drain contents on paper towel.
Alternate livers, mushroom caps, and
bacon on 4 skewers. Brush with clarified
butter and season. Roll in breadcrumbs.
Broil 15 cm (6 in) away from top element,
for 3 to 4 minutes on each side.
Decorae with parsley sprigs or watercress.
Serve with rice.

Clarified Butter, see page 13.

Lamb Shish Kebabs

Serves 4

750 g	(1½ lb) loin of lamb, cut into
	3.8 cm (1½ in) cubes
	marinade
8	bay leaves
2	large onions, cut into 4
250 g	(1/2 lb) cherry tomatoes
20	mushroom caps

AHEAD OF TIME: Cover lamb cubes with
marinade. Cover with wax paper and
refrigerate for 8 hours.
Preheat oven to broil.
Remove lamb from marinade. Alternate
lamb cubes and remaining ingredients on
4 skewers.
Broil or barbecue for 12 to 15 minutes.
Baste occasionally with marinade.
Serve over rice.

Marinade, see page 26.

Calf's Liver on Skewers

Veal Marsala

Serves 4

750 g	(1½ lb) veal scaloppini*
45 ml	(3 tbs) butter
125 ml	(1/2 cup) dry Marsala wine
50 ml	(1/4 cup) chicken stock
15 ml	(1 tbs) fresh chopped parsley
5 ml	(1 tsp) cornstarch
15 ml	(1 tbs) cold water
	seasoned flour
	salt and pepper

Lightly coat veal with flour.

Melt 30 ml (2 tbs) butter in a large sauté pan. Add veal, 3 to 4 pieces at a time, and cook on both sides over medium heat. Continue to cook until golden or done to taste.

Transfer veal to a warm serving platter. Add wine to pan. Increase heat to high and reduce by half.

Add chicken stock and bring to a boil. Scrape bottom of the pan.

Season with salt and pepper. Mix in parsley and remaining butter.

Mix cornstarch with cold water. Incorporate mixture to sauce.

Simmer for 1 minute.

Replace veal in pan. Do not allow sauce to boil as veal is being reheated.

Serve at once with buttered noodles.

* Veal scaloppini is from the «noix» (veal sirloin). Should be cut into 0.65 cm (1/4 in) thick, 6.3 cm (2½ in) diameter medaillons.

Chicken Stock, see pages 33-34

Technique: Veal Marsala

1 Lightly coat veal with flour.

2 Cook veal on both sides.

3 Add wine to pan. Note: For better results, remove veal from pan.

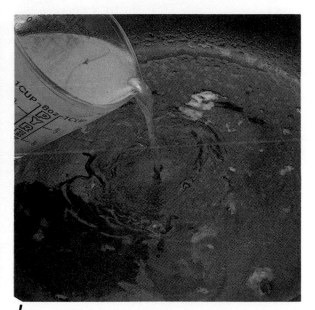

4 Add chicken stock and bring to boil.

Leg of Lamb Stuffed with Apples

Serves 4 to 6

45 ml	(3 tbs) melted butter
1	onion finely chopped
1	dry shallot, finely chopped
2	garlic cloves, smashed and chopped
30 ml	(2 tbs) chopped parsley
2	apples, hollowed, peeled and finely chopped
250 ml	(1 cup) small croûtons
1	leg of lamb, 2.3 to 2.7 kg (5 to 6 lb)
	salt and pepper
	pinch of thyme

SAUCE:

1	onion, diced
1	celery stalk, diced
45 ml	(3 tbs) flour
750 ml	(3 cups) hot brown beef stock
15 ml	(1 tbs) tomato paste

Preheat oven to 200°C (400°F).

Heat 15 ml (1 tbs) butter in a sauté pan. Add chopped onion, shallot, garlic, chopped parsley and thyme. Season with salt and pepper; cook for 3 minutes.

Add apples; mix well. Cover and cook 7 to 8 minutes over medium heat.

Add croûtons; mix and cook 2 to 3 minutes.

Season leg of lamb with salt and pepper. Stuff and tie leg of lamb, then place in a roasting pan. Brush with melted butter. Cook in the oven at 200°C (400°F) for 35 minutes.

Reduce oven heat to 190°C (375°F). Continue to cook the leg of lamb. Season lamb with salt and pepper. Brush with melted butter during cooking process.

Cooking time: 14 minutes per pound.

Ten minutes before end of cooking; add diced onions and celery to the roasting pan.

As soon as the leg of lamb is cooked, remove from roasting pan and set aside. Place roasting pan on stove top and add flour. Mix and cook 3 to 4 minutes to brown flour.

Add beef stock and tomato paste. Season to taste. Stir and cook 4 to 5 minutes. Strain sauce. Serve with leg of lamb.

Brown Beef Stock, see page 34.

Les Saucisses à l'Italienne

Serves 4

12	pork sausages, uncooked
284 g	(10 oz) spaghetti
30 ml	(2 tbs) butter
250 g	(1/2 lb) mushrooms, sliced
1	onion, thinly sliced
1	garlic clove, crushed and finely chopped
	salt
	freshly ground pepper
500 ml	(2 cups) hot quick tomato sauce

Preheat oven to broil.

Add sausages to a large saucepan three quarters filled with boiling water. Cook, uncovered for 5 minutes, over very high heat. Drain and set aside.

Add spaghetti to a stockpot half filled with boiling salted water. Cook, uncovered for 10 minutes, over very high heat.

Rinse spaghetti under running water for at least 6 minutes. Drain and set aside.

In a heavy, medium size saucepan, melt butter over high heat. When butter begins to foam, reduce heat to medium high. Add onion and sauté, uncovered, for 2 minutes. Stir frequently. Add mushrooms and garlic. Season with salt and pepper. Cook, uncovered, over high heat, for 5 to 6 minutes. Stir frequently. Add tomato sauce.

Bring sauce to a boil over high heat. Reduce to medium and simmer, uncovered, for 15 minutes.

Brown sausages, 15 cm (6 in) away from top element, for 3 to 4 minutes on each side.

Rewarm spaghetti by placing in a large sieve and immersing under hot water for 4 minutes.

Drain.

Spoon the spaghetti into four heated plates. Arrange 3 sausages in each plate over spaghetti. Spoon sauce over the sausages and spaghetti. Serve.

Leg of Lamb Stuffed with Apples

Braised Shoulder Of Veal

Serves 6 to 8

1	1.8 kg (4 lb) shoulder of veal*
30 ml	(2 tbs) corn oil
2	onions, diced
2	567 ml (20 oz) cans of tomatoes, drained and chopped
2	dry shallots, finely chopped
2	celery stalks, diced
125 ml	(1/2 cup) dry white wine
	salt and pepper
5 ml	(1 tsp) herbes de Provence
1	bay leaf

Preheat oven to 180°C (350°F).
Heat oil in a heavy ovenproof casserole.
When very hot, add veal.
Brown veal over medium high heat on all sides.
Set veal on a plate and season with salt and pepper.
Cook onions, shallots and celery in the casserole for 2 to 3 minutes. Add wine, increase heat to high, and reduce by half.
Add tomatoes, herbs, bay leaf, salt, and pepper. Replace veal in casserole and bring to a boil.
Cover and cook in the oven for 1½ to 2 hours or until tender.
When done, purée vegetables and liquid together. Serve sauce with the veal.

* Have your butcher debone the veal and roll the shoulder.

Rib Steak à la Bordelaise

Serves 4

4	steaks, 2.5 cm (1 in) thick
1	carrot, diced
1	celery stalk, diced
1	medium onion, diced
40 ml	(2½ tbs) corn oil
30 ml	(2 tbs) butter
45 ml	(3 tbs) flour
375 ml	(1½ cups) hot brown beef stock
250 ml	(1 cup) dry red wine
1	bay leaf
1	garlic clove, crushed and chopped

Rib Steak à la Bordelaise

1 ml	(1/4 tsp) thyme
2 ml	(1/2 tsp) parsley
	salt and pepper

Heat 15 ml (1 tbs) oil in a sauté pan over high heat. Add all diced vegetables, season with salt and pepper. Reduce heat to medium and cook for 7 minutes.

Add butter and spices; cook for 2 more minutes.

Sprinkle in flour and cook for 5 minutes or until flour has browned.

Add wine, increase heat to high, and cook for 4 to 5 minutes.

Add beef stock, season, and cook over medium for 8 minutes. During this time, prepare the steaks.

Heat remaining oil in a sauté pan over high heat. When hot, sear steaks for 3 minutes on each side. Reduce heat to medium, season, and cook until steaks are done to taste.

Pour sauce over steaks and serve.

Brown Beef Stock, see page 34.

Technique: Blanquette
of Veal

1 Cut veal into cubes.

2 Place veal in a large saucepan and cover with cold water. Bring to boil over high heat.

4 Set meat in another saucepan.

5 Add onion and carrots. Add leek, bouquet garni and chicken stock.

7 Melt butter in a saucepan. Add flour; cook 3 minutes.

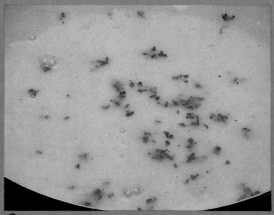

8 Add cooking liquid and blend well with a wooden spoon.

Blanquette of Veal

Serves 4

1 kg	(2 lb) shoulder of veal, cut into 3.8 cm (1½ in) cubes
1	onion, studded with 2 whole cloves
2	carrots, peeled
1	leek, cleaned
1	bouquet garni, consisting of:
2 ml	(1/2 tsp) thyme
1	bay leaf
2 ml	(1/2 tsp) tarragon
2 ml	(1/2 tsp) chervil
	fresh parsley
	celery
750 ml	(3 cups) hot chicken stock
90 ml	(6 tbs) butter
24	white onions, peeled
250 g	(1/2 lb) mushrooms, cut into 4
60 ml	(4 tbs) flour
1	egg yolk
30 ml	(2 tbs) heavy cream
15 ml	(1 tbs) fresh parsley, finely chopped
	salt and freshly ground pepper

3 Skim and strain meat.

6 Sauté onions and mushrooms in hot butter.

9 Incorporate egg yolk mixture to sauce.

Place veal in a large saucepan and cover with cold water. Bring to a boil over high heat. Skim and strain the meat.

Set meat in another saucepan. Add onion, carrots, leek, bouquet garni, and chicken stock. If necessary, add water to cover. Season with salt and pepper. Bring to a boil over high heat. Reduce heat to medium and simmer for 1 hour.

Heat 30 ml (2 tbs) butter in a sauté pan over high heat. When foaming, add white onions and reduce heat to medium. Cook, uncovered, for 2 minutes. Stir occasionally.

Add mushrooms and continue to cook for 2 to 3 minutes. Stir occasionally and season with salt and pepper.

Add contents of the pan to the veal and simmer, uncovered, for 15 minutes.

Discard onion studded with cloves, carrots, leek, and bouquet garni. Strain and transfer veal, mushrooms, white onions to a heated platter. Reserve cooking liquid. Melt 60 ml (4 tbs) butter in a heavy medium size saucepan over medium heat. When foaming, add flour. Cook for 3

Blanquette of Veal

minutes, stirring constantly. Remove from heat.

Add 250 ml (1 cup) reserved cooking liquid and blend well with a wooden spoon. Return to the stove over low heat.

Add remaining cooking liquid, 250 ml (1 cup) at a time, stirring constantly. Season with salt and pepper.

In a small bowl, mix egg yolk and cream together with a whisk. Whisk into the sauce.

Add veal and vegetables to the sauce and rewarm for several minutes.

Garnish with parsley before serving.

Chicken Stock, see pages 33-34.

Technique: Preparation of Sweetbreads

Fresh sweetbreads should be washed in cold water until white.

Drop sweetbreads in a stockpot filled with cold water. Add 30 ml (2 tbs) white vinegar to water.

Bring to a simmer over medium heat. Continue to simmer for 8 minutes.

Cool under running water for at least 5 to 6 minutes. Remove from water, drain, and trim.

Press sweetbreads between two weights for 2 to 3 hours.

Braised Sweetbreads

Serves 4

750 g	(1½ lb) calf's sweetbreads
	salt and pepper
250 ml	(1 cup) flour
45 ml	(3 tbs) butter
30 ml	(2 tbs) chopped onion
30 ml	(2 tbs) chopped carrot
15 ml	(1 tbs) chopped celery
1 ml	(1/4 tsp) chervil
	pinch of thyme
125 ml	(1/2 cup) dry white wine
250 ml	(1 cup) hot chicken stock

Ahead of time, prepare sweetbreads according to technique.

Preheat oven to 180°C (350°F).

Cut sweetbreads on an angle, into 5.0-7.6 cm (2-3 in) slices. Season with salt and pepper.

Dip sweetbreads into flour. Shake off excess.

Heat butter in a sauté pan with an ovenproof or metal handle, over high heat. When foaming, brown sweetbreads over medium heat for 2 to 3 minutes on each side.

Transfer to a heated platter and season. Add carrot, onion, celery and herbs to pan. Cook over medium heat for 3 minutes, stirring occasionally. Season with salt and pepper.

Pour wine over vegetables, increase heat to high, and reduce wine for 3 to 4 minutes.

Add chicken stock and sweetbreads to pan. Bring to a boil. Cover pan with aluminum foil and cook in the oven for 30 minutes.

Set sweetbreads on a heated service platter.

Set sauté pan over high heat. Cook for 3 to 4 minutes. Correct seasoning.

Pour sauve over sweetbreads. Serve.

Chicken Stock, see pages 33-34.

Croquettes of Veal

Serves 4

500 g	(1 lb) leftover cooked veal, minced*
15 ml	(1 tbs) butter
2	dry shallots, finely chopped
125 ml	(1/2 cup) mushrooms, finely chopped
	salt and freshly ground pepper
	pinch of nutmeg
250 ml	(1 cup) hot white sauce thick
250 ml	(1 cup) flour
3	beaten eggs
250 ml	(1 cup) breadcrumbs
	peanut oil in a deep-fryer, 160°C (325°F)

AHEAD OF TIME:

Heat butter in a sauté pan over high heat. When foaming, and shallots and reduce heat to medium. Cook for 1 minute.

Add mushrooms and cook for 3 to 4 minutes. Stir occasionally.

Add veal, cook for 2 minutes, then season with salt, pepper, and nutmeg.

Mix in white sauce; season to taste.

Spread contents in a buttered baking dish; cover with buttered wax paper.

Refrigerate overnight.

Roll 45 ml (3 tbs) of mixture at a time in the shape of a cylinder. Dip each croquette into flour, then beaten egg, and then into breadcrumbs.

Deep fry, a few at a time, until golden brown. Drain on paper towel.

White Sauce Thick, see page 41.

Meat and Variety Meats

Farmer's Sausage with Sautéed Vegetables

Serves 4

500 g	(1 lb) farmer's sausages, cut in 1.2 cm (1/2 in) slices
15 ml	(1 tbs) corn oil
1	small onion, sliced
1	green pepper, in thin slices
250 g	(1/2 lb) mushrooms, sliced
50 ml	(1/4 cup) chicken stock, hot

Heat oil in a sauté pan. Add sausages and brown over medium heat on both sides. Discard excess fat.

Add onion, green pepper, and cook for 2 minutes.

Add mushrooms and cook for 4 minutes. Stir occasionally.

Add chicken stock and reduce liquid by half.

Serve this dish over white rice.

Filet Mignon with Hollandaise Sauce

Serves 4

32	mushroom caps, washed and pat dried
30 ml	(2 tbs) butter
5 ml	(1 tsp) oil
4	filet mignons, 3.7 cm (1½ in) thick
375 ml	(1½ cups) hollandaise sauce lemon juice salt and pepper

Preheat oven to 200°C (400°F).

Place mushrooms in a small saucepan. Add 15 ml (1 tbs) butter and lemon juice. Season with salt and pepper; cover and cook 4 to 5 minutes. Set aside.

Heat oil and remaining butter in a sauté pan over medium heat. Add filets; cook 3 minutes on each side. Then continue to cook filets for 3 more minutes. Season with salt and pepper.

Transfer filet mignons to a heated service platter. Garnish with drained mushrooms. Top with hollandaise sauce.

Broil in the oven for 3 minutes.

Serve.

Hollandaise Sauce, see page 50.

Filet Mignon with Hollandaise sauce

Stuffed Paupiettes of Veal

Serves 4

4	170 g (6 oz) veal cutlets
	salt and pepper
125 ml	(1/2 cup) stuffing
250 ml	(1 cup) flour
45 ml	(3 tbs) butter

15 ml	(1 tbs) chopped carrot
15 ml	(1 tbs) chopped onion
15 ml	(1 tbs) chopped celery
1 ml	(1/4 tsp) oregano
375 ml	(1½ cups) hot tomato sauce

Preheat oven to 150°C (300°F).

Place each cutlet between 2 sheets of al-

288

uminum foil. Pound cutlets with a meat cleaver until thin.

Season veal with salt and pepper. Place 30 ml (2 tbs) stuffing on each cutlet. Roll veal over stuffing. As you roll veal, tuck edges in towards the middle.

Secure with kitchen string. Season veal, dip in flour, and shake off any excess.

Heat butter in a sauté pan with an oven-proof handle. When foaming, add veal rolls and reduce heat to medium. Brown veal and season with salt and pepper.

Add carrot, onion, celery, and oregano. Cook for 3 minutes. Pour in tomato sauce. Bring to a boil, cover, and cook in the oven for 15 minutes.

Serve with rice.

Stuffing, see page 18.

Technique: Stuffed Paupiettes of Veal

1 Stuff and roll each veal cutlet.

2 Secure veal with kitchen string. Season veal, dip in flour and shake off excess.

3 Brown veal in hot butter. Season with salt and pepper.

4 Add carrots, onions, celery and oregano. Cook for 3 minutes.

5 Add tomato sauce.

Braised Lamb Stew

Serves 4

1.4 kg	(3 lb) lamb shoulder, cut in 2.5 cm (1 in) cubes
	salt and pepper
75 ml	(5 tbs) corn oil
75 ml	(5 tbs) flour
1.2 L	(5 cups) warm brown beef stock
2	bay leaves
	pinch of thyme
2 ml	(1/2 tsp) lemon pepper
2	large onions, peeled
6	carrots, peeled
4	potatoes, peeled
3	celery stalks
1	567 ml (20 oz) can of tomatoes, drained, OR
	6 tomatoes quartered
15 ml	(1 tbs) butter

Preheat oven to 180°C (350°F).
Season lamb with salt and pepper.
Heat 45 ml (3 tbs) oil in an ovenproof casserole over high heat. When very hot, carefully drop half of the meat into casserole. Brown evenly on all sides. Turn meat using a pair of thongs every 3 minutes.
Remove seared lamb and place on a warm plate.

Add remaining oil to casserole. When hot, add remaining meat and brown.

Replace set aside meat in the casserole. Sprinkle with flour and cook again over high heat. Stir constantly until flour becomes golden brown and sticks to the bottom of the pan (about 6 minutes).

Gradually pour in beef stock, then add bay leaves. Add thyme, lemon pepper, salt, and pepper to taste.

Cover and cook in the oven for 40 minutes.

During cooking time, coarsely chop the vegetables and the tomatoes.

Heat butter in a sauté pan. When foaming, sauté onions and celery for 3 minutes over high heat.

Technique: Braised Lamb Stew

1 Brown meat evenly on all sides.

2 Sprinkle with flour and continue to cook.

3 Add beef stock and spices.

4 Sauté vegetables in hot butter.

5 Add onions, celery, carrots, potatoes and tomatoes to casserole.

Add tomatoes and cook over high until liquid evaporates. Season with salt and pepper.

Once lamb has cooked for 40 minutes, add onions, celery, carrots, potatoes, and tomatoes to casserole.

Cover and continue to cook in the oven for 30 to 40 minutes.

To keep this stew for 6 days, place in a stainless steel bowl. Cover with a sheet of wax paper pressed against the surface of the stew. Refrigerate.

To reheat stew, place in a preheated oven at 150°C (300°F), covered.

Brown Beef Stock, see page 34.

Leg of Lamb Boulangère

Serves 4

1	1.8 to 2.2 kg (4 to 5 lb) deboned leg of lamb
6	potatoes, peeled and thinly sliced
1	Spanish onion, thinly sliced
50 ml	(1/4 lb) clarified or melted butter
2	cloves of garlic, smashed and chopped
15 ml	(1 tbs) chopped parsley
1	bay leaf
	salt and pepper

Preheat oven to 220°C (425°F).

Cooking time: 12 to 13 minutes per pound.

Remove the fell or papery outer covering. Season leg of lamb with salt and pepper. Set aside.

Butter a roasting pan and add potatoes, onion, bay leaf and garlic. Season with salt and pepper; sprinkle with melted butter.

Place leg of lamb on top of vegetables. Cook in the oven at 220°C (425°F). As soon as the leg of lamb is seared, reduce heat to 190°C (375°F) and finish cooking process.*

Serve the leg of lamb with imported mustard.

Sprinkle with chopped parsley.

* Baste the leg of lamb with butter during cooking process.

Clarified Butter, see page 13.

293

Technique: Preparation of Calf's Brain

In a large stockpot, prepare the court bouillon consisting of:

2.5 L	*(10 cups) water*
45 ml	*(3 tbs) white vinegar*
5 ml	*(1 tsp) salt*
20	*whole peppercorns*
2	*bay leaves*
2 ml	*(1/2 tsp) thyme*
125 ml	*(1/2 cup) carrots, sliced*
50 ml	*(1/4 cup) onions, sliced*
2	*cloves*

Bring ingredients to a boil and simmer for 1½ hours. Very gently remove membrane covering brain.
Gently slide brain into stockpot and simmer over low heat for 10 minutes.
Cool brain under running water for 5 to 6 minutes.
Drain.

Cold Roast of Pork with Garlic

Serves 6 to 10

1	*loin of pork 1.8-2.7 kg (4-6 lb)*
30 ml	*(2 tbs) corn oil*
2	*garlic cloves, peeled and split in half*
1 ml	*(1/4 tsp) rosemary powder salt and pepper*

Preheat oven to 180°C (350°F).
Stud roast with the pieces of garlic. Do not debone.
Season with rosemary, salt, and pepper.
Heat oil in a roasting pan. Add roast and cook in the oven for 25-30 minutes per 500 g (1 lb).
Baste roast frequently during cooking. If there is not enough juices, add a bit of butter.
When cooked, remove and cool.
Chop bone with a meat cleaver. Wrap pork in foil and refrigerate.
Serve cold.

Veal Scaloppini Printanière (p. 294)

Deep-fried Pork Fingers

Deep-Fried Pork Fingers

Serves 4

1	*pork tenderloin*
250 ml	*(1 cup) flour*
2	*beaten eggs*
50 ml	*(1/4 cup) milk*
375 ml	*(1½ cups) breadcrumbs*
	salt and pepper
	peanut oil in a deep-fryer
	heated to 180°C (350°F).

Cut pork tenderloin into strips; season with salt and pepper. Roll in flour.
Mix beaten eggs and milk in a bowl. Dip pork strips into egg mixture, then coat with breadcrumbs.

Deep-fry, a few at a time, for 3 to 4 minutes.
Serve with ketchup and chips.

Pork Sausage with Risotto

Serves 4

500 g	*(1 lb) pork sausages*
15 ml	*(1 tbs) butter*
1	*small onion, minced*
250 ml	*(1 cup) long grain converted rice, rinsed and drained*
375 ml	*(1½ cups) hot chicken stock*
1	*bay leaf*
1 ml	*(1/4 tsp) salt*
2	*large tomatoes, seeded, peeled, coarsely chopped*

Preheat oven to 180°C (350°F).
Blanch sausages in lightly boiling water.
Drain, rinse; set aside.
Melt butter in an ovenproof casserole. Add onion and simmer until golden brown.
Stir in rice; cook for 1 minute.
Add chicken stock, bay leaf, spices, and season.
Bring to a boil on top of the stove, then cover with a tight fitting lid.
Place in the oven for 10 minutes.
Meanwhile, cook sausages in a sauté pan until browned on all sides.
Remove and set aside.
Sauté tomatoes in the same pan for 3 to 4 minutes.
Mix tomatoes into rice and arrange sausages on top. Cover casserole, bake for 10 minutes, then serve.
Chicken Stock, see pages 33-34.

Technique: Pork Sausage with Risotto

1 Melt butter in an ovenproof casserole. Add onion; simmer until golden brown.

2 Stir in rice.

3 Cook rice for 1 minute.

4 Add chicken stock and spices. Cover and cook.

5 Cooked rice.

Club Steak Nouvelle Cuisine

Serves 4

4	club steaks, 2.5 cm (1 in) thick, deboned
	fresh ground pepper, preferably green variety

45 ml	(3 tbs) corn oil
250 g	(1/2 lb) mushrooms, sliced
1	Spanish onion, thinly sliced
1 ml	(1/4 tsp) tarragon
1 ml	(1/4 tsp) parsley
5 ml	(1 tsp) French mustard
50 ml	(1/4 cup) chicken stock
	salt and pepper

300

Trim and generously pepper steaks. Heat half of the oil in a sauté pan. When very hot, quickly sear steaks on both sides. Salt steaks and cook over medium high heat for 7 minutes. Turn frequently. Transfer steaks to a hot service platter. Add remaining oil to pan. Sauté onion, mushrooms, and add salt and pepper.

Cover and cook over medium for 5 minutes.
Remove cover and add chicken stock. Sprinkle in tarragon and parsley.
Cook for 1 minute. Pass liquid and vegetables through a food mill.
Mix in mustard and serve over the steaks.

Chicken Stock, see pages 33-34.

Roast Loin of Pork

Serves 4

1.4 kg	(3 lb) loin of pork, deboned*
2	garlic cloves, peeled and cut into 4 slivers
	salt and pepper
30 ml	(2 tbs) vegetable oil
6	apples
15 ml	(1 tbs) carrot, diced
15 ml	(1 tbs) onion, diced
15 ml	(1 tbs) celery, diced
	pinch of thyme
2 ml	(1/2 tsp) rosemary
125 ml	(1/2 cup) hot chicken stock

Preheat oven to 220°C (425°F).
Using a paring knife, make small incisions in pork and insert slivers of garlic. Season pork with salt and pepper.
Pour oil into a roasting pan. Set in oven for 4 to 5 minutes, or until hot. Set pork in pan, along with reserved bones.
Return to oven for 20 minutes.
Reduce heat to 180°C (350°F). Total cooking time, including 20 minutes is 30 minutes per 500 g (1 lb).
Discard fat every 15 minutes.
Remove pan from oven and set roast on a carving board. Leave bones in pan.
Discard all but 30 ml (2 tbs) fat from pan. While roast is setting, peel and core apples. Cut each appel into 4.
Add apples, diced vegetables, and herbs to pan. Cook over medium high heat for 4 to 5 minutes. Discard bone and add chicken stock.
Season with salt and pepper and add any drippings from roast.
Skim off as much fat as possible.
Carve roast, and pour sauce over slices. Serve.
* Ask butcher to debone roast, but reserve bones for recipe.

Chicken Stock, see pages 33-34.

Technique: Roast Loin of Pork

1 Using a paring knife, make small incisions in pork and insert slivers of garlic. Season pork with salt and pepper.

2 Heat oil in roasting pan. Set pork in pan and sear in the oven.

3 When pork is cooked, transfer to a service platter. Add apples, diced vegetables and herbs to pan. Cover and cook 4 to 5 minutes.

4 Add chicken stock.

Ham Jardinière

Serves 6

This is a two part recipe.

1	ham, 1.8-2.7 kg (4-6 lb)*
10	cloves
125 ml	(1/2 cup) brown sugar
125 ml	(1/2 cup) hot chicken stock
1 ml	(1/4 tsp) nutmeg
30 ml	(2 tbs) honey
	juice of 1/2 lemon
	salt and pepper

Soak ham in cold water for 3 to 6 hours. For a country cured ham soak for 12 to 24 hours.

Set ham in a large stockpot filled with water and add the following ingredients:

2 onions
5 cloves
20 peppercorns
3 bay leaves

Bring to a boil, reduce heat to low, and simmer for about 18 minutes per 500 g (1 lb).

Remove ham, discard water, and pare off excess fat from ham.

Score ham in a diamond pattern. Set in a baking pan: set aside.

Preheat oven to broil.

Mix all remaining ingredients together, except cloves, in a saucepan. Cook over high heat for 5 minutes.

Remove and let cool for several minutes. Stud ham with cloves. Glaze top part of ham with cooled syrup and broil for 30 minutes. During last part of broiling process, prepare jardinière.

* If you purchase a pre cooked ham, skip soaking and simmering process.

JARDINIÈRE

1	celery stalk, diced
2	large carrots, diced
1	medium turnip, diced
250 g	(1/2 lb) snow pea pods
250 g	(1/2 lb) mushrooms, quartered
45 ml	(3 tbs) butter
5 ml	(1 tsp) parsley
	salt and pepper

Blanch celery, carrots, and turnip for 5 minutes. Cool under cold running water. Drain and set aside.

Blanch pea pods for 2 minutes: cool under cold water. Set aside.

Heat butter in a sauté pan. Once foaming, add all vegetables and sauté for 3 to 4 minutes. Season to taste with salt and pepper.

Serve with ham and garnish with fresh parsley.

Pork Chops, Mexican Style

Serves 4

PART 1: THE RICE

15 ml	(1 tbs) olive oil
250 ml	(1 cup) long grain rice, washed and drained
250 ml	(1 cup) chopped tomatoes
125 ml	(1/2 cup) hot chicken stock
1	red pepper, thinly sliced
1	clove of garlic, smashed and chopped
	crushed peppers
	salt and pepper

Preheat oven to 180°C (350°F).

Heat oil in an ovenproof casserole. Add garlic and red peppers; cook for 2 minutes. Add rice and crushed peppers; cook 2 minutes. Season to taste. Add tomatoes; continue to cook for 1 minute.

Add chicken stock; cover and cook in the oven for 18 minutes.

Chicken Stock, see pages 33-34.

PART 2: THE MEAT

15 ml	(1 tbs) vegetable oil
4	pork chops, excess fat removed
	salt and pepper

Fifteen minutes before the rice is cooked, heat oil in a frying pan. Add pork chops; cook 3 minutes on each side.

Season well. Continue to cook 5 to 6 minutes.

Serve with the rice and imported mustard.

Pork Chops, Mexican Style

Braised Short Ribs à la Martin

Serves 4

2.3 kg	*(5 lb) short ribs*
45 ml	*(3 tbs) corn oil*
1 L	*(4 cups) hot chicken stock*
1	*bay leaf*
2	*onions, largely diced*
2	*carrots, diced*
3	*celery stalks, diced*
2	*796 ml (28 oz) cans of tomatoes, drained*
2	*garlic cloves*
	pinch of thyme
	salt and pepper

Preheat oven to 180°C (350°F).
Heat 30 ml (2 tbs) oil in a sauté pan over high heat. When hot, add ribs. Do not overload the pan as it will cause the meat to boil.

Technique: Braised Short Ribs à la Martin

1 Short ribs cut into large pieces.

2 Sear ribs in hot oil.

3 Sauté diced vegetables.

4 Add tomatoes.

5 Pour tomatoes over ribs.

6 Add chicken stock.

Once all ribs have been seared, transfer to an ovenproof casserole. Season generously with salt and pepper; set aside.

Add remaining oil to sauté pan. Sauté diced vegetables, garlic, thyme, salt, and pepper over high heat for 7 minutes.

Add tomatoes to pan, season, and reduce heat to medium. Cook for 8 to 10 minutes.

Transfer tomatoes to casserole.

Pour chicken stock into casserole, stir, correct seasoning and add bay leaf.

Cover and bring to a boil over high heat. Cook in the oven for 1½ hours.

When ribs are done, remove from casserole and place on a hot platter.

Pass liquid and vegetables through a food mill using a fine disc.

Return puréed contents to casserole and add ribs. Serve from the casserole.

Chicken Stock, see pages 33-34.

Paté de Campagne

Yield: 1.2-1.4 kg (2½ - 3 lb)

500 g	*(1 lb) lean ground shoulder of veal*
250 g	*(1/2 lb) ground pork liver*
125 g	*(1/4 lb) ground pork fat*
6	*slices white bread, trim crust*
50 ml	*(1/4 cup) port wine*
15 ml	*(1 tbs) butter*
2	*dry shallots, chopped*
2	*eggs*
5 ml	*(1 tsp) thyme*
	salt and pepper
375 g	*(3/4 lb) larding fat, cut into thin strips*
2	*bay leaves*

Preheat oven to 180°C (350°F).

Place bread in a bowl. Cover with port wine and soak for 15 minutes.

Melt butter in a small pan. Cook shallots in the butter over low heat until transparent.

Place bread, port wine, shallots, and remaining ingredients, except larding fat and bay leaves, into a mixer. Blend for 15 minutes.

Line the inside of paté mold with 3/4 of larding fat.

Using blended ingredients, shape a spoon-full of the mixture into a small patty. Sauté the patty in a bit of butter until well done, and sample. If more salt and pepper is needed, correct seasoning of blended ingredients.

Transfer paté mixture to mold and pack down lightly. Smooth surface with a knife. Arrange bay leaves on top then seal with remaining larding fat.

Cover mold with a lid or with a sheet of parchment paper. Place mold in a roasting pan. Pour about 5 cm (2 in) fo water into the roasting pan.

Bake for 1¼ - 1½ hours.

To test if the paté is done, insert a stainless steel trussing needle into the middle of the paté. Leave the needle in place for 30 seconds then remove. If the needle is hot, the paté is done.

Remove paté from oven and place a heavy weight such as a heavy saucepan on the uncovered paté. Set aside at room temperature for 3 to 4 hours.

Remove the weight, cover, and refrigerate paté until cold.

Breaded Pork Chops

Serves 4

8	*pork chops, 2 cm (3/4 in) thick*
90 ml	*(6 tbs) melted butter*
	salt and pepper
250 ml	*(1 cup) seasoned breadcrumbs*
30 ml	*(2 tbs) corn oil*
	gherkins or dill pickles

Preheat oven to 180°C (350°F).

Season pork with salt and pepper. Brush well with melted butter and coat in breadcrumbs.

Heat oil in a sauté pan over high heat. When very hot, sear 4 chops on both sides. Set seared chops in an oiled baking dish. Sear remaining chops; add to baking dish. Bake pork for 17 minutes.

Sprinkle a bit of lemon juice over each chop and arrange on a warm platter.

Garnish with pickles and serve at once.

Breaded Pork Chops

Stuffed Pork Tenderloin (p. 315)

high heat. When foam subsides, immediately add tenderloins. Reduce heat to medium and brown on both sides. Transfer pork to a heated platter. Add chopped vegetables and herbs to pan. Cook for 2 to 3 minutes. Add flour and cook for 4 to 5 minutes. Stir constantly. Remove pan from heat. Add 250 ml (1 cup) chicken stock and mix well with a wooden spoon. Set pan over low heat and add remaining stock, while stirring constantly. Bring to a boil.

Return pork to pan, season and cover. Cook for 45 minutes in the oven. Serve.

Pork Brochette

Serves 4

| 4 | skewers |

Pork Brochette

4	large pork chops, deboned and cubed
1	green pepper, cubed
2	onions, quartered
20	fresh mushrooms caps, washed and dried
15 ml	(1 tbs) maple syrup
15 ml	(1 tbs) olive oil
	juice of 1 lemon
	salt and pepper

On a skewer, alternate, meat and vegetables. Season with salt and pepper.
Combine maple syrup, oil and lemon juice in a small bowl. Brush brochettes with the mixture. Season with salt and pepper. Cook on the barbecue, 5 minutes on each side.
Serve with a Tabasco barbecue sauce.

317

Technique: Marinated Pork Spareribs

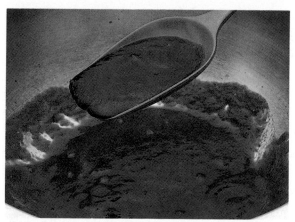

1 Pork spareribs.

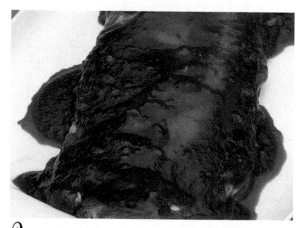

2 Combine soy sauce, garlic, oil, honey and vinegar in a bowl. Add chili sauce; mix well. Sprinkle with lemon juice and Tabasco sauce.

3 Pour mixture over spareribs.

Marinated Pork Spareribs

Serves 4

45 ml	(3 tbs) soy sauce
1	garlic clove, smashed and chopped
15 ml	(1 tbs) oil
30 ml	(2 tbs) honey
30 ml	(2 tbs) white vinegar

125 ml	(1/2 cup) chili sauce
125 ml	(1/2 cup) water
	lemon juice
	Tabasco sauce
	salt and pepper
1.8 kg	(4 lb) pork spareribs

Preheat oven to 190°C (375°F).
Combine soy sauce, garlic, oil, honey and vinegar in a bowl. Add chili sauce; mix well. Sprinkle with lemon juice and Tabasco sauce.

Pour mixture over pork spareribs. Refrigerate for 1 hour.

Place ribs in a baking dish. Brush with marinade. Cook in the oven for 30 minutes. Season with salt and pepper.

Add water and continue to cook for 25 minutes.

Serve.

Chapter VII
Desserts

Chocolate Quatre Quart

Serves 6 to 8

227 g	(8 oz) semi-sweet chocolate
250 g	(1/2 lb) unsalted butter, room temperature
4	medium eggs, room temperature
300 ml	(1¼ cups) granulated sugar
375 ml	(1½ cups) all purpose flour, sifted

Preheat oven to 190°C (375°F).
Butter and lightly sugar a square 20 cm (8 in) cake tin. Set aside.
Set chocolate and butter in a stainless steel bowl. Place bowl over a saucepan three-quarters filled with boiling water.
When chocolate has melted, set bowl aside and cool several minutes.
Break eggs into a mixing bowl. Add sugar and beat for about 1 minute or until foamy.
Fold chocolate mixture into eggs. Blend well. Fold in flour as well. Blend well.
Pour into cake tin. Bake in the oven for 45 minutes, or until a knife inserted comes out clean.
Cool cake for 3 to 4 minutes, then unmold onto a rack. Cool cake for at least 2 hours before cutting.

Zambia Salad

Serves 2

1	whole pineapple
250 ml	(1/2 pint) strawberries, washed, stemmed, and cut in two
20	fresh seedless grapes, stemmed
1	orange, peeled, sectioned, and seeded
45 ml	(3 tbs) granulated sugar
75 ml	(1/3 cup) kirsch
125 ml	(1/2 cup) heavy cream
15 ml	(1 tbs) icing sugar

Stawberry Pie

Slice pineapple in two; remove pulp. Reserve shells. Cut pulp into 1.2 cm (1/2 in) cubes.
Mix cubes, strawberries, grapes, orange sections, sugar, and kirsch together in a bowl. Cover with wax paper and refrigerate for 1 to 2 hours.
Beat cream until peaking. Fold in icing sugar.
Spoon cream mixture over fruits which have been arranged in reserved shells. Serve.

Caramel Custard

Serves 4 to 6

CARAMEL:

150 ml	(2/3 cup) granulated sugar
125 ml	(1/2 cup) water

CUSTARD:

500 ml	(2 cups) milk
5 ml	(1 tsp) vanilla
15 ml	(1 tbs) water
3	medium eggs, room temperature
3	egg yolks
125 ml	(1/2 cup) granulated sugar

Preheat oven to 180°C (350°F).
CARAMEL: Place sugar and water in a small saucepan over high heat. When mixture becomes light brown, pour into custard dishes.
CUSTARD: Bring milk, vanilla, and water to a boil in a medium saucepan.
In a mixing bowl, beat eggs and egg yolks lightly with a whisk. Add sugar and continue to beat until well blended.
Gradually add boiling milk to eggs, while whisking constantly. Strain through a fine sieve. Pour into custard dishes.
Place dishes in a baking pan with boiling water. The water should rise halfway along the dishes.
Set in the oven and bake for 40 to 45 minutes.
Remove when cooked, and chill before unmolding.
To unmold, lightly press edges of dish. Place a plate upside down over custard dish, and turn custard onto plate.

Thick Custard Cream

Yield: 300 ml (1¼ cups)

Serve with cakes, ice cream, iced soufflé, fruits, and rice pudding.

250 ml	(1 cup) boiled milk, cooked
4	egg yolks
125 ml	(1/2 cup) granulated sugar
15 ml	(1 tbs) vanilla

Beat egg yolks and sugar together in a medium size saucepan until foamy.
Mix in milk and vanilla.
Place over medium heat and stir constantly with a wooden spoon. Do not boil. Continue to stir until mixture thickens enough to coat the spoon.
Immediately transfer to a stainless steel bowl. Refrigerate for at least 24 hours before serving.

Basic Sweet Dough

Use for open pies, tartlets, and sweet cookies.

675 ml	(2¾ cups) all purpose flour, sifted
250 ml	(1 cup) icing sugar, sifted
125 ml	(1/2 cup) unsalted butter, room temperature
125 ml	(1/2 cup) shortening, room temperature
5 ml	(1 tsp) vanilla
2	medium size eggs, room temperature

Mix flour and icing sugar together in a bowl. Create a well in the middle.
Place butter and shortening in well. Add vanilla and cut with a pastry cutter until all flour has been absorbed.
Add eggs. Form dough into a ball. If dough is too dry, add 15-30 ml (1-2 tbs) ice water. Lightly dust dough with flour and wrap in wax paper. Refrigerate for 3 to 4 hours before using.
This dough will keep for 3 days, if wrapped and refrigerated. It will keep frozen for 3 months.
Pie shells should be baked at 200°C (400°F) for 10 minutes.

Basic Pie Dough

Use for apple pie, quiche lorraine, etc.

675 ml	(2¾ cups) all purpose flour, sifted
2 ml	(1/2 tsp) salt
250 ml	(1 cup) shortening, room temperature
125 ml	(1/2 cup) water

Place flour in a mixing bowl. Create a well in middle of flour.
Place salt and shortening in well. Cut with a pastry cutter until all flour has been absorbed.
Add water.
Form dough into a ball. Lightly dust dough with flour and wrap in wax paper. Refrigerate for 3 to 4 hours before using.
This dough will keep for 3 days. Be sure to wrap and refrigerate. It will also keep, frozen, for 3 months.
Dough must be room temperature before using. Bake pie shells at 200°C (400°F) for 10 minutes.

Peach Melba, Nouvelle Cuisine

Serves 4

375 ml	(1½ cups) fresh raspberries, washed and dried
5 ml	(1 tsp) lemon juice
50 ml	(1/4 cup) sugar
5 ml	(1 tsp) cornstarch
30 ml	(2 tbs) cold water
4	scoops of ice cream
	stewed peaches

Place raspberries, lemon juice and sugar in a saucepan; cover and bring to boil over low heat. Cook for 3 minutes.
Pass mixture through a sieve and return to saucepan.
Mix cornstarch with cold water. Incorporate to raspberry mixture. Bring to boil

Peach Melba Nouvelle Cuisine

and cook 1 minute. Stir and remove saucepan from stove top. Let cool.
Place 45 ml (3 tbs) stewed peaches in each dessert dish. And 1 scoop of ice cream. Top with raspberry sauce.
Serve.

Brownie Date Loaf

Serves 6

175 ml	*(3/4 cup) all-purpose flour*
2 ml	*(1/2 tsp) baking soda*
1 ml	*(1/4 tsp) salt*
250 ml	*(1 cup) dates, pitted and chopped*
125 ml	*(1/2 cup) brown sugar*
50 ml	*(1/4 cup) margarine*
50 ml	*(1/4 cup) water*
125 ml	*(1/2 cup) semi-sweet chocolate chips*
2	*beaten eggs*
45 ml	*(3 tbs) brandy*
50 ml	*(1/4 cup) buttermilk*

Brownie Date Loaf

125 ml	*(1/2 cup) chopped nuts*
1	*12 cm × 22 cm (5 × 9 in) loaf pan, buttered and floured*

Preheat oven to 180°C (350°F).
Sift flour, soda and salt; set aside.
Combine dates, brown sugar, margarine and water in a saucepan. Cook until dates are soft, stirring often.
Remove from heat. Pour mixture into a mixing bowl. Stir in chocolate chips. Add beaten eggs; mix with an electric beater for 1 minute.
Add half of sifted ingredients; mix well.
Incorporate brandy and buttermilk; blend thoroughly.
Stir in nuts.
Pour batter into loaf pan. Cook in the oven for 45 minutes.
Cool and unmold.
Sprinkle with icing sugar before serving (optional).

Technique: Brownie Date Loaf

1 Combine dates, brown sugar, margarine and water in a saucepan.

2 Cook until dates are soft, stirring often.

3 Pour mixture into a mixing bowl. Add chocolate chips and beaten eggs.

4 Add half of sifted ingredients.

5 Incorporate brandy and milk.

6 Add remaining sifted ingredients. Stir in nuts.

Zog's Baked Alaska

Serves 4

12	*lady fingers*
250 ml	*(1/2 pint) vanilla ice cream*
5	*egg whites*
150 ml	*(2/3 cup) granulated sugar*
75 ml	*(1/3 cup) cognac*
50 ml	*(1/4 cup) Grand Marnier*

Preheat oven to broil.

Butter a stainless steel platter and sprinkle with sugar.

Set 6 lady fingers, side by side, on platter. Be sure edges touch. Carefully place ice cream on top, and cover with remaining lady fingers.

Place in freezer.

Beat egg whites until very stiff. Gradually add sugar and continue to beat.

Remove platter from freezer. Using a spatula, spread half of egg mixture over lady fingers. Be sure all surfaces are sealed with egg whites.

Decorate surface with remaining egg whites.

Broil in the middle of the oven for 3 minutes, or until meringue is lightly browned.

Remove from oven.

Place cognac and Grand Marnier in a Turkish coffee server or small saucepan over high heat.

When hot, ignite and pour over baked alaska.

Serve immediately.

Coconut Pudding

Serves 4

500 ml	*(2 cups) milk*
22 ml	*(1½ tbs) cornstarch*
2	*separated eggs*
125 ml	*(1/2 cup) grated coconut*
125 ml	*(1/2 cup) sugar*
15 ml	*(1 tbs) lemon zest*

Preheat oven to 200°C (400°F).

Heat half of milk in a saucepan over low heat. Mix cornstarch and remaining milk.

Pour mixture into hot milk whisking constantly.

Add egg yolks, coconut, sugar and lemon zest; stir and cook 3 minutes until mixture thickens.

Pour pudding into gratin dish.

Beat egg whites until stiff.

Garnish pudding with egg whites.

Broil in the oven for 4 to 5 minutes.

Cool and serve with maple syrup.

Strawberry Pie

Serves 4 to 6

500 ml	*(2 cups) fresh strawberries, washed and stemmed*
30 ml	*(2 tbs) Cointreau*
30 ml	*(2 tbs) sugar*
1	*graham cracker pie crust, cooked*
	juice of 1/4 lemon
	whipped cream

Place strawberries in a bowl. Add Cointreau, lemon juice and sugar; marinate for 15 minutes.

Spread a thin layer of whipped cream on cooked pie crust. Cover with strawberries.

Sprinkle with syrup.

Garnish with remaining whipped cream. Serve.

Cantaloup Surprise

Serves 4

2	*cantaloups, cut in two*
1	*orange, peeled and cut into sections*
1	*banana, peeled and sliced*
45 ml	*(3 tbs) rum*
4	*egg whites*
50 ml	*(1/4 cup) sugar*
	lemon juice

Preheat oven to 200°C (400°F).

Scoop flesh from cantaloups with a melon-ball cutter.

Place cantaloups balls into a bowl. Add banana, orange and rum. Sprinkle with lemon juice; marinate for 30 minutes.

Cantaloup Surprise

In a stainless steel bowl, beat egg whites with an electric beater until stiff; then beat in sugar. Continue to beat for 1 minute.

Place meringue in a pastry bag fitted with a star nozzle.
Fill cantaloup shells with fruits. Decorate with meringue. Place under the broiler for 3 minutes.
Serve.

Creamy Pudding

Serves 4

250 ml	(1 cup) sugar
30 ml	(2 tbs) water
500 ml	(2 cups) milk
22 ml	(1½ tbs) cornstarch
2	beaten eggs
15 ml	(1 tbs) vanilla
30 ml	(2 tbs) Tia Maria (optional)

Pour water and half of sugar into a small saucepan. Cook over medium heat until mixture caramelizes.

Heat 250 ml (1 cup) milk in a saucepan. Add caramelized sugar whisking constantly.

Mix cornstarch and remaining sugar. Incorporate mixture to remaining milk.

Pour milk mixture into hot milk; cook 2 minutes over low heat.

Add beaten eggs, vanilla and Tia Maria; stir and cook 3 to 4 minutes over low heat, whisking constantly until mixture thickens.

As soon as mixture is cooked, pour into custard dishes and refrigerate for several hours.

Serve.

Apple Pudding

Serves 2

15 ml	(1 tbs) butter
50 ml	(1/4 cup) sugar
2	separated eggs
15 ml	(1 tbs) lemon zest
5 ml	(1 tsp) lemon juice
4	apples, hollowed, peeled and chopped
5 ml	(1 tsp) cinnamon pinch of clove
4	individual custard dishes

Preheat oven to 180°C (350°F).

Combine butter and sugar in a bowl with a wooden spoon.

Add egg yolks; mix well.

Add juice and lemon zest.

Add apples, cinnamon and clove; mix well.

Beat egg whites until stiff and incorporate to mixture.

Pour pudding into custard dishes; then place in a roasting pan containing 2,5 cm (1 in) hot water. Cook in the oven for 30 minutes.

Serve.

Chantilly Cream

Yield: 500 ml (2 cups)

250 ml	(1 cup) heavy cream, cold
45 ml	(3 tbs) icing sugar
5 ml	(1 tsp) vanilla

Beat cream and vanilla until mixture forms peaks.

Fold in icing sugar.

Peach Custard

Serves 6

3	peaches
500 ml	(2 cups) milk
90 ml	(6 tbs) honey
2	whole eggs
3	egg yolks

Preheat oven to 190°C (375°F).

Butter a 25 cm (10 in) round custard dish or soufflé dish.

Gently drop peaches into a saucepan filled with boiling water. Scald for 1 minute. Refresh peaches under cold running water and peel.

Slice in two and remove pits. Thinly slice flesh and set in the bottom of the dish.

Pour milk and honey into a saucepan. Bring to a boil over high heat.

Place eggs and yolks in a mixing bowl. Lightly beat with a whisk.

As soon as milk and honey begins to boil, remove from heat. Pour in a thin stream into egg mixture, whisking constantly.

Pour mixture over peaches. Place dish in a large baking pan containing 3,8 cm (1½ in) hot water. Bake for 40 minutes or until firm. Remove and cool.

When cool, press edges of custard to loosen, then unmold onto a serving platter. Slice and serve.

Crêpe Stuffed with Chestnut

Serves 4

250 ml	(1 cup) chestnut purée
125 ml	(1/2 cup) 35% cream
5 ml	(1 tsp) vanilla
30 ml	(2 tbs) icing sugar
4	crêpes
45 ml	(3 tbs) brown sugar
45 ml	(3 tbs) maple syrup

Preheat oven to 200°C (400°F).

Place chestnut purée in a bowl and mix well.

Pour 35% cream in a mixing bowl. Add vanilla; beat with an electric beater until stiff. Incorporate icing sugar with a spatula.

Incorporate whipped cream to the chestnut purée.

Fold crêpes and bring extremities to center to form little "baskets". Place in a gratin dish. Sprinkle with brown sugar and maple syrup. Place under broiler for 5 to 6 minutes. Serve.

Crêpes, see page 7.

Desserts

Flambéed Peaches in Orange Sauce

Serves 4

30 ml	(2 tbs) sugar
2	oranges
1	lemon
4	peach halves
30 ml	(2 tbs) dark rum

Place sugar, juice from oranges and lemon in a saucepan. Cook over high heat until mixture begins to thicken.

Cut peach halves in two or three slices; add to saucepan. Cook for 3 to 4 minutes. Set peaches on serving dishes. Add rum to saucepan, heat, and ignite. Once flame has died, pour over peaches.

Bread Pie

Serves 2 to 3

175 ml	(3/4 cup) flour
75 ml	(7 tbs) unsalted butter
45 ml	(3 tbs) cold water
125 ml	(1/2 cup) milk
60 ml	(4 tbs) sugar
5 ml	(1 tsp) liquor
2	eggs
45 ml	(3 tbs) powdered almonds
5 ml	(1 tsp) butter
125 ml	(1/2 cup) white breadcrumbs
	pinch of salt

Preheat oven to 200°C (400°F).
Cooking time: 30 minutes.
Sift flour and salt into a bowl. Add 75 ml (5 tbs) butter. Incorporate ingredients with a pastry knife.
Add cold water and form a ball. Refrigerate for 1 hour.
Roll dough and line a pie plate.

NOTE: Freeze remaining dough.
Pour milk into a bowl. Add sugar, liquor, eggs and butter; mix with a whisk.
Add almonds and breadcrumbs; mix well.
Pour mixture into pie crust. Cook in the oven for 30 minutes. Serve.

Lorna's Lemon Bread Cake

Can be served for tea, as a dessert, or on picnics.

	juice of 1 lemon
375 ml	(1½ cups) flour, sifted
5 ml	(1 tsp) baking powder
2 ml	(1/2 tsp) salt
125 ml	(1/2 cup) soft butter
250 ml	(1 cup) granulated sugar
2	eggs
125 ml	(1/2 cup) milk
	rind of 1 lemon

Butter and flour a 23 cm × 8 cm (9 × 3 in) loaf pan; set aside.
Preheat oven to 180°C (350°F).
Finely grate lemon rind and squeeze out lemon juice. Set aside.
Mix flour, baking powder, and salt together in a bowl. Stir in lemon juice; set aside.
Blend sugar and butter in a separate bowl. Mix into flour mixture.
Add eggs, milk, and lemon rind to batter. Beat until well blended.
Pour into loaf pan. Bake for 1 hour.

Strawberry Sundae

Serves 4

375 g	(3/4 lb) frozen strawberries
125 ml	(1/2 cup) semi-sweet chocolate chips
250 ml	(1 cup) small marshmallows
	juice of 1/2 lemon
	juice of 1 orange
	vanilla ice cream

Defrost strawberries and place in a saucepan. Add lemon juice and orange juice; cook 7 to 8 minutes over very low heat. Remove from stove. Set aside.
Place 30 ml (2 tbs) strawberries in each sundae dish. Sprinkle with chocolate chips. Add several marshmallows. Top with ice cream.
Repeat to fill dish.
Decorate with chocolate chips and marshmallows. Refrigerate 1 hour. Serve.

Strawberry Sundae

Almond Cake

Serves 6

125 ml	(1/2 cup) margarine
250 ml	(1 cup) sugar
3	eggs
300 ml	(1¼ cups) all-purpose flour
2 ml	(1/2 tsp) baking powder
1 ml	(1/4 tsp) salt
30 ml	(2 tbs) cognac
50 ml	(1/4 cup) powdered almonds
5 ml	(1 tsp) almond extract
1	21 cm (8¼ in) square mold, 6 cm (2¼ in) deep, buttered and floured

Preheat oven to 180°C (350°F).

Cream margarine, sugar and 1 egg in a mixing bowl. Beat with an electric mixer for 2 minutes.
Sift flour, salt and baking powder together. Add half of sifted ingredients to egg mixture.
Add remaining eggs; beat for 1 minute.
Add remaining sifted ingredients; beat for 1 minute.
Incorporate cognac; beat 1 minute.
Add powdered almonds; blend well.
Add almond extract; mix well.
Pour batter into cake mold. Cook in the oven for 40 minutes.
When cake is done, remove from the oven and set aside for 5 minutes.
Unmold and cool.
Spread cake with your favorite frosting.

Technique: Almond Cake

1 Cream margarine, sugar and 1 egg in a mixing bowl. Beat with an electric mixer for 2 minutes.

2 Add dry ingredients, eggs and cognac. Add powdered almonds.

Almond Cake

Strawberries Romanoff

Strawberries Romanoff

Serves 4

1 l	*(4 cups) strawberries, washed, drained and hulled*
50 ml	*(1/4 cup) sugar*
30 ml	*(2 tbs) Cointreau*
375 ml	*(1½ cup) 35% cream*
50 ml	*(1/4 cup) icing sugar orange juice*

Place strawberries in a bowl. Sprinkle with sugar and orange juice; mix well.
Add Cointreau; refrigerate for 1 hour.
In a stainless steel bowl, whip cream with an electric beater until stiff. Incorporate icing sugar with a spatula.

Pour whipped cream over strawberries and juice. Incorporate delicately with a spatula.
Serve in dessert glass cups.

Cherries Jubilee

Serves 4

Can be served over ice cream.

398 ml	*(14 oz) can Bing cherries, drained*
50 ml	*(1/4 cup) granulated sugar*
125 ml	*(1/2 cup) water*
125 ml	*(1/2 cup) kirsch*
5 ml	*(1 tsp) cornstarch*

Place sugar and water in a saucepan over high heat. Bring to a boil, reduce heat to medium and simmer for several minutes.

Chocolate Mousse

Place chocolate, butter and Tia Maria in a stainless steel bowl. Place bowl on top of saucepan containing 500 ml (2 cups) boiling water. Melt chocolate while stirring with a wooden spoon.

Remove bowl from saucepan. Incorporate egg yolks; mix with a whisk.

Return bowl to saucepan. Cook until mixture thickens, stirring constantly with a whisk.

Remove from stove top. Set aside.

In a stainless steel bowl, beat egg whites with an electric beater until stiff. Add icing sugar; beat for 30 seconds.

Incorporate egg whites to cool chocolate mixture; mix delicately to obtain a marbled mousse.

Serve in dessert dish.

Add cherries and simmer for 2 to 3 minutes.

Pour kirsch into a Turkish coffee server or small saucepan. Mix in cornstarch. Warm over medium heat.

When kirsch is almost boiling, pour over cherries and ignite.

Serve at once.

Chocolate Mousse

Serves 4

170 g	*(6 oz) semi-sweet chocolate*
90 g	*(3 oz) unsalted butter*
30 ml	*(2 tbs) Tia Maria*
4	*egg yolks*
5	*egg whites*
45 ml	*(3 tbs) icing sugar*

335

Baked Melon

Serves 4

2	*small cantaloups, cut in two*
500 ml	*(2 cups) fresh strawberries, washed and cut in two*
30 ml	*(2 tbs) brandy*
250 ml	*(1 cup) sugar*
3	*egg whites*
15 ml	*(1 tbs) vanilla*

Remove seeds from cantaloups and scoop out flesh with a melon-ball cutter. Place in a mixing bowl.

Add strawberries and brandy; marinate for 30 minutes.

Place sugar and egg whites on top of a double boiler. Beat ingredients with an electric beater until mixture forms peaks. Add vanilla and continue beating for 1 minute.

Place melon halves on a cookie sheet. Fill with fruits and cover with meringue. Broil in the oven at 260°C (500°F) for few minutes.

Serve.

Technique: Baked Melon

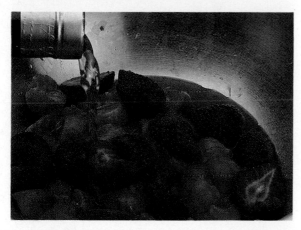

1 Remove seeds from cantaloup.

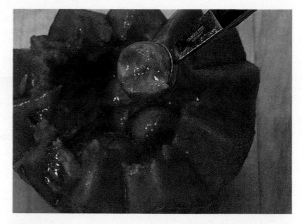

2 Scoop out flesh with a melon-ball cutter. Place in a mixing bowl.

3 Add strawberries and brandy.

4 Place sugar and egg whites on top of a double boiler.

5 Beat until mixture forms peaks.

6 Fill melon halves with fruits and cover with meringue.

Sweet Bananas

Serves 4

4	ripe bananas, peeled
50 ml	(1/4 cup) slivered almonds
50 ml	(1/4 cup) brown sugar
30 ml	(2 tbs) rum
45 ml	(3 tbs) maple syrup
	zest of 1 lemon
	juice of 1 lemon

Preheat oven to 180°C (350°F).
In a well buttered gratin dish, place bananas, brown sugar, rum, maple syrup and lemon juice; cook in the oven for 8 to 10 minutes.
Sprinkle with almonds and lemon zest; broil in the oven for 3 minutes. Serve.

Baked Pears

Serves 4

4	fresh pears, peeled
125 ml	(1/2 cup) sugar
125 g	(4 oz) candied fruit
250 ml	(1 cup) water
	juice of 1/2 lemon
15 ml	(1 tbs) cornstarch
15 ml	(1 tbs) kirsch
15 ml	(1 tbs) grenadine

Preheat oven to 190°C (375°F).
Cut pears in two and core. Place in a buttered baking dish.
Pour sugar, candied fruit, water, and lemon juice over pears.
Bake in the oven for about 15 minutes or until tender. Baste occasionally with cooking liquid.
Remove pears and set on a serving platter. Place baking dish over medium high heat. Mix cornstarch and kirsch together and stir into dish. Add grenadine and when sauce has thickened, pour over pears. Serve.

NOTE: If you wish, serve with scoops of ice cream.

Sweet Bananas

Red and Green Grape Pie

Red and Green Grape Pie

Serves 6

250 ml	*(1 cup) plain yogurt*
2	*egg whites, beaten stiff*
15 ml	*(1 tbs) Cointreau*
30 ml	*(2 tbs) sugar*
1	*graham craker pie crust, cooked*
	green and red grapes, washed and dried
	lemon juice

Combine yogurt, beaten eggs and Cointreau in a mixing bowl. Spread mixture over cooked pie crust.
Place grapes in a bowl. Add sugar and lemon juice; mix well.
Garnish pie with grapes. Refrigerate 15 minutes. Serve.

Carrot Cake

Serves 6

250 ml	*(1 cup) sugar*
125 ml	*(1/2 cup) vegetable oil*
250 ml	*(1 cup) all purpose flour, sifted*
5 ml	*(1 tsp) baking powder*
5 ml	*(1 tsp) cinnamon*
2 ml	*(1/2 tsp) baking soda*
2 ml	*(1/2 tsp) salt*
2	*eggs*
375 ml	*(1½ cup) grated carrots*
125 ml	*(1/2 cup) chopped nuts*

Preheat oven to 180°C (350°F)
Place sugar and oil in a mixing bowl and mix with an electric beater.
Add half of dry ingredients; mix well.

Chocolate Dream

Add eggs, one by one, mixing between each addition.

Add remaining dry ingredients, carrots and nuts; mix well.

Pour cake mixture into a buttered and floured 20 cm (8 in) cake mold. Cook in the oven for 1 hour 15 minutes.

Carrot cake icing:

125 ml	*(1/2 cup) sugar*
30 ml	*(2 tbs) cornstarch*
30 ml	*(2 tbs) orange juice*
15 ml	*(1 tbs) lemon zest*
5 ml	*(1 tsp) butter*

Place sugar and cornstarch in a small saucepan. Add orange juice and remaining ingredients; stir and cook 8 minutes over low heat.

Cool and pour over carrot cake.

Chocolate Dream

Serves 4

8	*chocolate wafers, crushed*
500 ml	*(2 cups) whipped cream*
4	*large vanilla ice cream scoops*
60 ml	*(4 tbs) commercial chocolate sauce for desserts*
4	*maraschino cherries*
4	*individual glass dessert dishes*

Place a small amount of chocolate wafers at the bottom of each dish. Add 45 ml (3 tbs) whipped cream. Refrigerate for 30 minutes.

Place one ice cream scoop over whipped cream and top with chocolate sauce.

Decorate with whipped cream. Garnish with maraschino cherries. Serve.

Hot Sabayon

Serves 4

Sabayon can be served on its own or to top fresh fruit dishes.

175 ml	*(3/4 cup) granulated sugar*
4	*egg yolks*
2	*whole eggs*
125 ml	*(1/2 cup) dry white wine*
45 ml	*(3 tbs) liqueur, to taste*

In a stainless steel mixing bowl, combine sugar, egg yolks, and whole eggs.
Place bowl over a saucepan three-quarters filled with barely boiling water. Beat mixture with a whisk for 3 to 4 minutes.
Add wine. Continue to whisk vigorously until very thick. Gradually add liqueur. Serve at once.

NOTE: If the white wine is replace by sweet Marsala wine, the dessert becomes a "Zabaglione".

Egg Nog

Serves 6 to 8

5	*egg whites*
5	*egg yolks*
250 ml	*(1 cup) 35% cream*
375 ml	*(1¹/₂ cups) milk*
125 ml	*(1/2 cup) whisky*
50 ml	*(1/4 cup) cognac*
45 ml	*(3 tbs) sugar*
	nutmeg

Place egg yolks into a mixing bowl. Add sugar and mix with an electric beater for 1 minute.
Pour in whisky and cognac while beating constantly. Incorporate milk; beat well.
Whip cream lightly and incorporate to mixture.
In a stainless steel bowl, beat egg whites with an electric beater until stiff. Incorporate to mixture with a whisk.
Refrigerate for 2 hours.
Pour egg nog into large glasses. Sprinkle with nutmeg. Serve.

Egg Nog

Pastry Cream

Yield: 625 ml (2-1/2 cups)

Use as a filling for pastry puffs, etc.

250 ml	*(1 cup) milk*
15 ml	*(1 tbs) water*
50 ml	*(1/4 cup) granulated sugar*
3	*egg yolks*
50 ml	*(1/4 cup) all purpose flour, sifted*
5 ml	*(1 tsp) vanilla*

Bring milk and water to a boil in a medium size saucepan over medium heat.

Beat sugar and egg yolks together using a spatula, in a mixing bowl. Mix for 3 to 4 minutes until eggs become foamy and almost white in color.

Mix flour into eggs with a spatula.

Gradually add vanilla to boiling milk. Pour half of mixture into eggs. Stir constantly with a wooden spoon.

Replace saucepan over medium low heat. Gradually incorporate mixing bowl contents into saucepan. Stir constantly with a wooden spoon.

Continue to stir, over medium heat, until mixture becomes very thick.

Transfer to a bowl. Cool and cover with buttered wax paper.

This cream will keep, covered and refrigerated, for 48 hours.

Frozen Almond Soufflé

5	*egg yolks*
5	*egg whites*
175 ml	*(3/4 cup) powdered sugar*
175 ml	*(3/4 cup) ground nuts (almonds, filberts, or walnuts)*
30 ml	*(2 tbs) dark rum*
500 ml	*(2 cups) 35% cream, whipped semi-sweet chocolate almonds (optional)*

Butter a springform mold and set aside.

Separate egg yolks from egg whites.

Mix yolks with powdered sugar and beat until light and fluffy. Add nuts and rum.

Whip cream into mixture.

Beat egg whites until they form stiff peaks. Fold into mixture.

Pour mixture into mold.

Freeze.

To serve, sprinkle soufflé with chocolate and decorate with almonds.

Banana Nut Cake

Serves 6

125 ml	*(1/2 cup) margarine*
250 ml	*(1 cup) sugar*
2	*eggs*
3	*bananas*
50 ml	*(1/4 cup) chopped nuts*
2 ml	*(1/2 tsp) baking soda*
500 ml	*(2 cups) flour*
15 ml	*(1 tbs) baking powder*
45 ml	*(3 tbs) rum*
50 ml	*(1/4 cup) buttermilk pinch of salt*
1	*22 cm (8½ in) springform cake mold, buttered and floured*

Preheat oven to 180°C (350°F).

Cream margarine and sugar; blend well.

Add eggs, one at a time, beating thoroughly after each addition.

Purée bananas in a blender. Incorporate purée to egg mixture. Stir in nuts.

Sift dry ingredients together. Add half of sifted ingredients to banana mixture.

Incorporate rum and buttermilk; mix thoroughly.

Add remaining dry ingredients; blend well.

Pour batter into mold. Cook in the oven for 1 hour.

When cake is done, remove from the oven and set aside for 5 minutes.

Unmold and cool.

Spread cake with your favourite frosting.

Banana Nut Cake

Technique: Banana Nut Cake

1 Cream margarine and sugar; blend well.

2 Add eggs, one at a time, beating thoroughly after each addition.

5 Incorporate purée to egg mixture.

6 Stir in nuts.

3 Blend well.

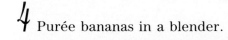

4 Purée bananas in a blender.

7 Add half of sifted ingredients to banana mixture.

8 Incorporate rum and butter milk.

Chocolate Cake

Serves 6

175 ml	(3/4 cup) margarine
375 ml	(1½ cups) sugar
3	eggs
425 ml	(1¾ cups) flour

2 ml	(1/2 tsp) baking powder
45 ml	(3 tbs) cacao
125 ml	(1/2 cup) milk
5 ml	(1 tsp) vanilla
	pinch of salt
1	22 cm (8½ in) springform cake mold, buttered and floured

Preheat oven to 170°C (325°F).

Cream margarine in a bowl. Add sugar and eggs; blend well with an electric beater. Sift dry ingredients together. Add half of sifted ingredients to egg mixture with a spatula.

Incorporate milk and vanilla.

Add remaining dry ingredients. Blend thoroughly.

Pour batter into mold. Cook in the oven for 1 hour and 10 minutes. When cake is done, remove from the oven and set aside for 5 minutes.

Unmold and cool.

Spread with lemon frosting or your favourite frosting.

Technique: Chocolate Cake

1 Cream margarine in a bowl.

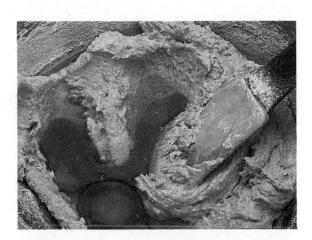

2 Add sugar and eggs. Blend well.

3 Sift dry ingredients together. Add half of sifted ingredients to egg mixture.

4 Incorporate milk and vanilla.

5 Add remaining dry ingredients.

Index

Chapter I

Batters, 6-11
Basic Crêpe Batter, 7
Dessert Crêpe Batter, 10
Basic Batter for
  Deep Frying, 10
Beer Batter for Fish, 7
Sweet Batter for Fruits, 7
Batter for Vegetables, 7
Batter for Vegetables or
  Fruit Fritters, 7

Butters, 12-17
Anchovy Butter, 14
Bercy Butter, 13
Bordelaise Butter, 16
Chive Butter, 14
Clarified Butter, 13
Garlic Butter, 16
Kneaded Butter, 14
Maître d'Hôtel Butter, 14
Salmon Butter, 13
Shrimp Butter, 13
Tarragon Butter, 14

Stuffings, 18-25
Stuffing 1, 20
Stuffing 2, 22
Stuffing for Capon, 25
Chestnut and
  Sausage Stuffing, 25
Stuffing for Duckling, 20
Stuffing for Fish, 25
Stuffing for Small Fowl, 19
Stuffing for Goose, 20
Meat Stuffing, 19
Stuffing for Suckling Pig, 20
Potato Stuffing, 19

Marinades, 26-31
Marinade 1, 27
Marinade 2, 28
Marinade 3, 30
Beer Marinade, 27
Marinade for Small Cuts, 30
Marinade for Fish, 27
Marinade for Game, 27
Oil and Lemon Marinade, 27

Chapter II

Stocks, 32-37
Basic Brown Beef Stock, 34
Basic Chicken Stock 1, 33
Basic Chicken Stock 2, 34
Basic Fish Stock
  (Court Bouillon), 33
Basic Fish Stock
  with Vinegar, 33
Stock Ménagère, 36
Turkey Stock, 36
Veal Stock, 36
Basic Vegetable Stock, 34

Sauces, 38-53
Béarnaise Sauce, 48
Bourguignon Sauce, 46
Basic Thin Brown Sauce, 42
Basic Medium-Thick
  Brown Sauce, 43
Curry Sauce, 52
Devilled Sauce, 39
Dill and Caper Sauce, 41
Basic Fish Sauce, 43
French Dressing
  or Vinaigrette, 50
Herb Sauce for Fish, 48
Hollandaise Sauce, 50
Horseradish with
  Walnut Sauce, 48
Lime Butter Sauce, 50
Madeira Sauce, 43
Mousseline Sauce, 47
Brown Mushroom Sauce, 44
Cold Mustard Sauce, 50
Portuguese Sauce, 47
Remoulade Sauce, 51
Roux, 39
Brown Roux, 39
White Roux, 39
Sauce Charcutière, 45
Sauce Parisienne, 45
Sauce Ravigote, 41
Tartare Sauce, 52
Spicy Tomato Sauce, 48
Clear Vegetable Sauce, 50
Basic White Sauce, 40
Basic White Sauce
  (Béchamel Sauce) Thin, 41
White Sauce
  (Béchamel Sauce) Thick, 41

Soups, 54-77
Celery and Chesnut
  Velouté Soup, 71
Chilled Avocado
  Soup, 63
Chilled Mexican
  Soup, 72
Clam Chowder, 60
Fish Chowder, 55
Manhattan Clam
  Chowder, 71
Country Beef Soup, 64
Cream of Asparagus Soup, 60
Cream of Carrot Soup, 75
Cream of Cucumber Soup, 63
Cream of Leek Soup, 72
Cream of Mushroom Soup, 69
Parmentier Cream Soup, 66
Cream of Yellow Pepper, 64
Cream of Pumpkin Soup, 76
Cream of Turnip Soup, 58
Gazpacho, 71
Herb Soup, 77
Lentil Soup, 75
Minestrone Soup, 62
Mushroom and Barley
  Soup, 55
Onion Soup au Gratin, 58
Potato Soup, 75
Potage Breton, 55
Potage aux Carottes, 58
Soupe Normande, 64
Vegetable Soup, 76
Vichyssoise, 69

Chapter III

Hors-d'Oeuvre and Small Entrées, 78-97
Ailloli on Toast
  (Garlic Dip), 80
Anchovy Canapés, 86
Asparagus Tartlets with
  Hollandaise Sauce, 90
Avocado à la Martin, 86
Stuffed Celery Stalks, 79
Cheese Dip, 82
Cocktail Mushroom Caps, 79
Mushroom Caps Stuffed with
  Crab Meat, 80
Curried Mushroom
  Canapés, 80
Roquefort Canapés, 84
Smoked Salmon Capanés, 87
Crêpes Stuffed with Salmon
  Roes, 94
Crêpes Stuffed with
  Shrimp, 94
Endives au Gratin, 92
Halibut Served on Lettuce
  Hearts, 84
Hearts of Palm Deep Fried
  in Batter, 82
Hearts of Palm Salad, 82
Curried Indian Meatballs, 90
Mushroom Barquettes, 82
Mushroom à la Crème
  on Toast, 92
Marinated Mushroom, 84
Mini Pizza, 97
Baked Oysters au Gratin, 92
Coquille of Scallops and
  Peppers, 96
Brochette of Scampi, 89
Butterfly Shrimp, 89
Shrimp on Toast, 89
Snails Bourguignon, 96
Snails au Gratin, 89
Snails Provençale, 92

Index

Pasta, 98-103
Gnocchi, Tomato Cream
  Sauce, 102
Macaroni à la Barbara, 99
Macaroni Casserole au
  Gratin, 101
Macaroni with Olives, 99
Penne with Tomato
  Sauce, 101
Spaghetti, Tomato and
  Mushroom Sauce, 99
Tortellini with Peppers, 103

**Fondues and Eggs,
104-117**
Egg Chasseur, 105
Eggs with Cream, 108
Poached Eggs Forestière, 110
Eggs Florentine, 106
Eggs à la Française, 106
Eggs Gascon, 112
Baked Eggs with Chicken
  Liver, 116
Eggs Orientale, 110
Scrambled Eggs, 109
Party Beef Fondue, 105
Cheese Fondue, 105
Quiche Maison, 112
The Art of Making
  Omelettes, 105
Omelette à la Mireille, 115
Omelette Mousseline with
  Cheese, 114
Mushroom Omelette, 116

Chapter IV

Salad Dressings, 118-123
French Dressing with
  Aillolo, 122
French Dressing with
  Garlic, 122
Vinaigrette Dressing for
  Potatoes, 119
Roquefort Dressing, 119
Mayonnaise, 119
Green Mayonnaise, 119
Plum Sauce, Chinese
  Style, 122
Chick-Pea Vinaigrette, 119

Salads, 124-139
Garlic Croutons, 134
Rice and Artichoke Heart
  Salad, 132
Boiled Beef Salad, 132
Caesar Salad, 126
The Everyday Salad, 128
Green Salad, 132
Macaroni Salad, 131
Mushroom Salad, 128

Chick-Pea Salad, 125
Pol's Potato Salad, 135
Roquefort Salad, 137
Salade St-Georges, 127
Tomato Salad, 130
Vegetable Julienne
  Salad, 136
Leeks Vinaigrette, 138

Vegetables, 140-163
Deep Fried Bananas, 141
Fresh Beans, 141
Steamed Broccoli, 141
Asparagus Crêpe, 150
Spinach Crêpe, 154
Eggplant Turkish Style, 142
Braised Endives, 148
Buttered Flageolets, 148
Marinated Hot
  Vegetables, 151
Mushroom Provençale, 146
Mushroom Tomatoes, 162
Stuffed Onions, 160
Deep Fried Onion Rings, 156
Stuffed Green Peppers, 160
Potato Chips, 144
Potato Gnocchi, 141
Potato Surprise, 144
Surprise Baked Potatoes, 146
Dutchess Potatoes, 160
Potatoes au Gratin, 153
Lyonnaise Potatoes, 163
Parisienne Potatoes, 161
Ratatouille, 155
Carrots with Hollandaise
  Sauce, 142
Spinach au Gratin, 142
Spinach Tomatoes, 148
Mexican Succotash, 158
Breaded Tomatoes, 159
Stuffed Tomatoes, 156
Fried Won Ton, 148
Zucchini Italian Style, 152
Sautéed Zucchini, 141

Rice, 164-169
Rice à l'Égyptienne, 165
Gruyère Rice, 168
Rice à l'Orientale, 165
Rice Pilaf, 165
Fluffy White Rice, 166
Rissoto à la Milanaise, 168
Rissoto à la Piémontaise, 168
Riz d'Athènes, 167
Riz à la Grecque, 166
Seafood Rice, 168

Chapter V

**Fish and Crustaceans,
170-211**
Cod à l'Espagnole, 184
Cod au Gratin, 174
Grilled Cod, 199
Coquille St-Jacques, 187
Alaska Crab Legs, 200
Deep-Fried Fish, 204
Fish Loaf the Easy Way, 208
Frog's Legs Provençale, 190
Poached Halibut with
  Mushroom Sauce, 178
Boiled Lobster, 189
Broiled Lobster au
  Persil, 200
Lobster à la Lincoln, 208
Lobster Newburg, 196
Brochette of Mussels, 178
Mussels à la Crème, 175
Fillet of Perch with
  Mushrooms, 177
Perch au Gratin, 185
Pickerel à la Coker, 171
Broiled Fillet of Porgy with
  Shallot Butter, 171
Barbecued Salmon, 172
Baked Salmon in Foil, 178
Salmon Loaf, 196
Poached Salmon with
  Mousseline Sauce, 172
Salmon Poached in Court
  Bouillon, 180
Poached Salmon with
  Vegetables, 202
Scallop Skewers, 198
Scampi au Gratin, 207
Scampi Provençale, 211
Scampi Served in Scallop
  Shell, 187
Seafood Brochette, 193
Seafood à la Nautilus, 192
Shrimp With Peas, 204
Shrimp Provençale, 211
Shrimp and Tomato
  Sauce, 203
Sole Bretonne, 194
Fillet of Sole with
  Mushrooms, 210
Fillet of Sole Nouvelle
  Cuisine Style, 182
Fillet of Sole with Nuts, 194
Lake Trout Amandine, 181
Lake Trout Baked in
  Foil, 176
Turbot au Gratin, 171

Index

Chapter VI

Fowl and Game, 212-239

Chicken Arlesienne, 232
Broiled Chicken Breast, 217
Chicken Casserole, 237
Cashew Chicken, 216
Chicken with Egglant and
  Cheese, 231
Everyday Chicken, 226
Chicken Kiev, 237
Fried Chicken Legs, 213
Chicken New Orleans, 231
Chicken Normande, 226
Chicken aux Olives, 213
Pineapple Chicken with
  Rum, 228
Chicken à la Point, 226
Roast Chicken, 213
Chicken Vol-au-Vent, 213
Coq au Vin, 223
Duck With Green
  Peppercorn, 238
Marinated Braised Duck, 223
Duck Marinated in
  Red Wine, 218
Duck with Stuffed Olives, 237
Duck à l'Orange, 214
Cornish Hen Casserole, 231
Stuffed Cornish Hen, 234
Pheasant Imperial, 232
Roast Rabbit, 221

Meat and Variety Meats, 240-319

Boeuf Bourguignon, 248
Beef Kidney Sautéed in
  Red Wine, 265
Beef Sautéed with
  Onions, 259
Beef and Vegetable Pie, 274
Brochettes of Beef, 241
Roast Beef, 246
Skipper's Brochettes, 263
Stuffed Cabbage Rolls, 259
Swiss Style Chuck Steak, 263
Club Steak Bordelaise, 266
Club Steak with Cognac, 242
Club Steak with Green
  Peppers, Mushrooms and
  Celery, 262
Club Steak Nouvelle
  Cuisine, 300
Club Steak au Poivre, 244
Filet Mignon with
  Hollandaise Sauce, 286
Rolled Flank Fit for a
  King, 250
Stuffed Beef Flank, 241
Goulash, 261
Ham Jardinière, 308
Hamburger à la Ritz, 284

Hamburger Victor, 256
Braised Lamb Stew, 290
Leg of Lamb Stuffed
  with apples, 276
Leg of Lamb Boulangère, 292
Stuffed Leg of Lamb
  à la Française, 304
Lamb Chops with
  Tomatoes, 302
Lamb Navarin, 304
Lamb Shish Kebabs, 270
Calf's Brain with Capers, 254
Calf's Liver on Skewers, 270
Calf's Liver Bergerac, 258
Préparation of Calf's
  Brain, 297
Chicken Livers Chinese
  Style, 263
Chicken Liver Party
  Paste, 255
Chicken Livers Soubise, 268
Chicken Livers on
  Skewers, 255
One For Three, 242
Pâté de Campagne, 312
Pork Brochette, 316
Breaded Pork Chops, 312
Pork Chops à la Diable, 275
Pork Chops, Mexican
  Style, 308
Deep-Fried Pork Fingers, 298
Roast Loin of Pork, 306
Cold Roast of Pork with
  Garlic, 297
Stuffed Pork Tenderloin, 315
Marinated Pork
  Spareribs, 318
Pot-au-Feu, 259
Braised Short Ribs à la
  Martin, 310
Rib Roast à la Française, 246
Rib Roast à l'Italienne, 305
Rib Steak à la
  Bordelaise, 278
Les Saucisses à
  l'Italienne, 276
Farmer's Sausage with
  Sautéed Vegetables, 286
Pork Sausage with
  Risotto, 298
Steak, Chinese Style, 243
Preparation of
  Sweetbreads, 283
Braised Sweetbreads, 283
Grilled Sweetbreads with
  Béarnaise Sauce and
  Watercress, 266
Top Round Strogonoff, 242
Blanquette of Veal, 281
Veal Chops with Artichoke
  Hearts, 284
Croquettes of Veal, 283
Veal Kidneys with Madeira
  Wine, 257

Veal Marsala, 272
Stuffed Paupiettes of
  Veal, 288
Veal Scaloppini
  Printanière, 294
Braised Shoulder of
  Veal, 278
Roast Veal with Cherry
  Sauce, 255

Chapter VII

Desserts, 320-349

Almond Cake, 332
Frozen Almons Soufflé, 344
Sweet Bananas, 338
Brownie Date Loaf, 324
Banana Nut Cake, 344
Chocolate Cake, 348
Lorna's Lemon Bread
  Cake, 330
Cantaloup surprise, 326
Carrot Cake, 340
Chantilly Cream, 328
Cherries Jubilee, 334
Chocolate Quatre Quart, 321
Crêpe Stuffed with
  Chestnut, 329
Caramel Custard, 321
Thick Custard Cream, 322
Peach Custard, 328
Chocolate Dream, 341
Basic Pie Dough, 322
Basic Sweet Dough, 322
Egg Nog, 342
Baked Melon, 336
Chocolate Mousse, 335
Pastry Cream, 344
Peach Melba Nouvelle
  Cuisine, 322
Flambéed Peaches in
  Orange Sauce, 330
Baked Pears, 338
Bread Pie, 330
Red And Green Grape
  Pie, 340
Strawberry Pie, 326
Apple Pudding, 328
Coconut Pudding, 326
Creamy Pudding, 328
Strawberries Romanoff, 334
Hot Sabayon, 342
Zambia Salad, 321
Strawberry Sundae, 330